Advance Praise for
*Challenges in Implementing Corporate Governance
Whose Business is it Anyway?*

A must-read for directors of companies in Asia who want to make sure their companies are following best practice corporate governance standards. The book provides guidance of where directors should start when beginning their directorships and also is a helpful tool for the review process of how effective the Board is (or how the Board can improve).

Angelina Kwan
*Director and Chief Operating Officer,
Asia Pacific Region Cantor Fitzgerald LP*

I think I have learned a lot more about corporate governance and its fundamental issues reading this book. It is a good, comprehensive, and readable guide for directors to understand the issues relating to corporate governance.

Dato Krishnan Tan
*CEO
IJM Corporation Berhad*

Challenges in Implementing Corporate Governance is the most definitive book on corporate governance to date. John Zinkin challenges the norms on what defines the Board of Directors. He not only redefines their responsibilities but also stresses that board performance makes a difference to long-term business sustainability. The author illustrates the challenges of implementing Western-style corporate governance and why and how there is a need to go local in getting strategy and risk management right, to managing change and talent. The book looks at how defective governance implementation can destroy capital. This is a must-read for future and existing board members who are serious about their "license to operate."

Tay Kay Luan
*Director, International Assignments
Association of Chartered Certified Accountants*

In this book, John Zinkin challenges us with questions like "Is business ethics an oxymoron?" and provides answers to how a company can be run both responsibly and successfully. It is the right message in these turbulent times after all the financial excesses of the past years. *Challenges in Implementing Corporate Governance* delivers valuable advice for board members on their roles and responsibilities in order to carry out their duties effectively, as well as how to avoid the most common pitfalls and manage risk successfully. A must-read book for any board representative.

Peter Vogt
*CEO
Nestlé Malaysia*

CHALLENGES IN IMPLEMENTING CORPORATE GOVERNANCE

WHOSE BUSINESS IS IT ANYWAY?

CHALLENGES IN IMPLEMENTING CORPORATE GOVERNANCE

WHOSE BUSINESS IS IT ANYWAY?

JOHN ZINKIN

WILEY

John Wiley & Sons (Asia) Pte. Ltd.

Other Wiley Editorial Offices
John Wiley & Sons, 111 River Street, Hoboken, NJ 07030, USA
John Wiley & Sons, The Atrium, Southern Gate, Chichester, West Sussex, P019 8SQ, United Kingdom
John Wiley & Sons (Canada) Ltd., 5353 Dundas Street West, Suite 400, Toronto, Ontario, M9B 6HB, Canada
John Wiley & Sons Australia Ltd., 42 McDougall Street, Milton, Queensland 4064, Australia
Wiley-VCH, Boschstrasse 12, D-69469 Weinheim, Germany

Library of Congress Cataloging-in-Publication Data
ISBN 978-0-470-82522-8

Typeset in 10.5/13 Sabon Roman by MPS Limited, A Macmillion Company, Chennai, India
Printed in Singapore by Saik Wah Press Pte. Ltd.
10 9 8 7 6 5 4 3 2 1

CONTENTS

FOREWORD

Good corporate governance ensures proper accountability, probity and openness in the conduct of a company's business, resulting in a business environment that is fair and transparent, and where companies can be held accountable for their actions. Only with good governance can companies create wealth and ensure the management of such wealth in a sustainable manner for its shareholders and other stakeholders. Good corporate governance therefore also holds the balance between economic and social growth.

The global financial crisis of 2007–08 demonstrated yet again the devastating impact of poor governance on financial markets and its participants. Regulatory measures to reduce systemic risk, protect investors and uphold fairness and efficiency of markets will come to naught if they are not accompanied by the practice of strong governance as reflected in the way business is conducted.

This book could not have come at a more appropriate time. Lessons need to be shared and learned. The range of corporate governance issues covered is comprehensive. The critical aspects of corporate governance in terms of the role of the board and its members, the delivery of sustainable good results, the management of risk, and performance measurement and reward among others, underscore the challenges that top management of companies must deal with and invest effort and resources into.

John has been active in the promotion of good corporate governance. He has spoken widely on the subject, published articles in the media and run numerous corporate governance seminars and workshops for directors of PLCs. His many years of experience in this regard have enabled him to gain many unique perspectives and insights into the challenges of putting into practice the principles of good corporate governance. This comes through very clearly, making his book compelling, instructive and practical.

I congratulate John on his outstanding effort.

Tan Sri Zarinah Anwar
Chairman
Securities Commission Malaysia

ACKNOWLEDGMENTS

The views expressed in this book are personal and are based on my experiences in running workshops on corporate governance in Malaysia and presenting arguments to regulatory conferences. They do not represent those of the Securities Commission, Malaysia, or of the Securities Industry Development Corporation. If I have failed to interpret the views of others correctly, or have ascribed to what they have written meanings they did not intend, then the fault is entirely mine, and I apologize to them and to my readers in advance.

I am deeply indebted to the following people who have given me great help, insight, and support in writing this book.

I would like first of all to thank Dr. Gary Dirks, Ian Pollard, Joan Sheridan, and Dato Krishnan Tan, who read the entire manuscript with the mindset of the prospective target audience. I have tried to incorporate their comments wherever possible to make sure that the book is easier to read and understand from a director's perspective. I would also like to thank Shireen Muhyiddin, who took the time to look at the first six chapters through the eyes of a socially responsible investor and pointed me in the direction of Joe Studwell's excellent and provocative book.[1] I am grateful to Attila Emam, whose discussions on risk management proved invaluable in ensuring that I approached this difficult subject appropriately without leaving anything out in Chapter 7. I would also like to thank Professor Didier Cossin, Angelina Kwan, Goh Ching Ying, Irene Dorner, and Julian Wynter for the unique insights they gave me into the nature of the financial crisis as it unfolded.

I owe a debt to Stephen Young of the Caux Round Table for his penetrating and thoughtful writing on business ethics and corporate governance; to Paul Krugman, Robert Shiller, and Joe Stiglitz for their fearless analysis of what happened in the financial crisis; and to John Bogle for showing how sophisticated financial services have subtracted value from the real economy.[2]

I originally intended to update *Corporate Governance*, a book I co-authored with Peter Wallace in 2005. When I raised this with Nick Wallwork of John Wiley, he suggested that perhaps the time had come instead for a new book on the subject as a result of the spectacular failures on Wall Street. I am grateful to him for that suggestion. I must also thank John Owen for his editing: he sharpened my writing and forced me to clarify points which I took for granted but the general reader might not have understood. This book is the better for his input.

Last, and most important, I would like to thank my wife Lisa for her loving understanding and full support while I was writing this book in my spare time. I dedicate it to her in loving gratitude.

Endnotes

1 Studwell, J. 2007, *Asian Godfathers: Money and Power in Hong Kong and Southeast Asia*, London: Profile Books.
2 Bogle, J. 2009, *Enough: True Measures of Money, Business, and Life*, Hoboken, NJ: John Wiley & Sons.

INTRODUCTION

I have been involved with the promotion of good corporate governance in Malaysia since 1999, when the Malaysian Code of Corporate Governance was written as a reaction to the 1998 Asian Financial Crisis. At the time it made sense for Malaysia to look at the UK's Combined Code as a basis for developing its own code for two reasons: first, the UK was the leader in the field; and, second, something needed to be done quickly if confidence in the stock market was to be restored.

In the ensuing years, as a result of countless workshops and seminars I have run for directors of Malaysian public-listed companies, it became clear to me that adopting a Western code of governance built on different assumptions about what matters in life and how capital markets are structured created as many problems as it sought to solve—most particularly for independent non-executive directors.

Given that other stock markets in Asia share many of the same characteristics as Malaysia's, it should not be a surprise that they too face many of the same problems in implementing good corporate governance (CG).

The problems of implementing good CG come in two distinct parts. The first is caused by the adoption of codes from jurisdictions that are culturally different and built on a different underlying stock-market structure and assumptions about how boards are supposed to work based on different ownership structures and levels of market sophistication. The second is created by the generic difficulties boards have in translating conformance or compliance (which is what regulators look at) into good performance (which is what concerns shareholders).

The problems of translating regulation-driven compliance into good performance have been put under the spotlight by the global financial crisis (GFC). Although the GFC has been concentrated in financial institutions mainly in the US and the UK, it has highlighted such serious failures of CG in those institutions and others in Switzerland and Germany that it has brought capitalism into discredit.

The critical aspects of the failure in CG relate to performance rather than conformance or compliance. Companies were destroyed by a combination of three elements that are essential to good performance which were found to be wanting: first, a lack of proper understanding by the board of the business and its strategy; second, a total lack of appreciation of both the strategic risk and, more important, the systemic risk created by new product-markets into which financial institutions entered because others were doing it too; third, a total failure by boards to ensure that reward and remuneration systems for top executives and CEOs reflected the long-term needs of the business, rather than encouraging irresponsible behavior that put the company's future at risk and, as it turned out, the entire global financial system in jeopardy.

This book discusses the problems posed by the differences in assumptions about how companies are supposed to run once they are listed and who the prime beneficiaries of the firm should be—whether it is shareholders (the regulatory perspective of good CG) or stakeholders, which raises a much wider set of issues, particularly in Asian countries where government-linked entities form a large part of stock market capitalization. The US and the UK governments are just beginning to find themselves in potentially similar positions as a result of their bailouts of financial institutions and, in the case of the US, of GM and Chrysler.

Chapter 1 introduces why CG matters and explains why adopting a Western-based view of CG may not be totally appropriate in markets that are structured differently and based on a different set of values.

Chapter 2 deals with the need for boards to take a wider view of their responsibilities than simply maximizing shareholder value. It discusses the role of the firm's primary stakeholders—customers, employees, community and shareholders—and their claims on the company. It makes the case that an excessive focus on maximizing shareholder value will ultimately put the company's "license to operate" at risk. It argues that boards should regard corporate responsibility not as an add-on but as an early-warning mechanism in setting strategy. It also makes the case that it is necessary to reject inappropriate theories taught at business schools which make the task of reconciling competing stakeholder claims harder and less natural than it should be.

The following chapters are about how to make good CG operational. Chapter 3, for example, explores the role of the board in defining the firm's business purpose, vision and values; and then examines the six primary roles set out by the revised Malaysian Code of Corporate Governance. It then discusses the levels to which boards should get involved with management, arguing that the approach the board takes to its role and the level to which it needs to be engaged in the business will depend on the particular circumstances of the company.

Chapter 4 looks at board composition and argues that the roles of Chair and CEO should not be combined, not only because that would represent an excessive concentration of power in the hands of one person, but because the two roles are quite distinct. This is in contrast to the majority of American boards, where the roles are still united in the person of the "imperial CEO." It then discusses the roles and responsibilities of executive and non-executive directors and explores some of the very real problems independent non-executive directors face in an Asian context, where dominant shareholders are often the norm, making it difficult for them to be truly independent in the Anglo-Saxon sense.

Chapter 5 argues that many of the major failures of corporate governance have been the result of boards making poorly informed decisions. These may be the result of problems of board culture; dysfunctional board dynamics where the company's vision and mission are misunderstood, where conflicts of interest exist and there is lack of trust within the board; of dysfunctional processes resulting from a lack of transparency and poor information, poor planning of meetings, and poor decision-making; and an inadequate understanding of risk and its dynamics; or all of them combined. It goes on to suggest ways to resolve these problems using the Carver Policy Governance® model, emphasizing the importance of good information, and making clear what the role of committees is.

Chapter 6 deals with the four factors for getting from good governance to good results: getting strategy right; making informed decisions; managing change; and converting strategy into action. Good governance, as defined by regulators and auditors, does not automatically guarantee good results, nor does bad governance automatically guarantee bad results.

Chapter 7 explores the different types of external risk that companies face: political, economic, financial, socio-cultural, technological, competitive, and systemic. It deals in some detail with the problem of systemic risk and how it arises as a result of what is known as "the tragedy of the commons." It then looks at the internal risks and explores the four characteristics of an effective risk management system. Finally, it explores the four stages of matching the company's risk profile to the risk appetite of shareholders by establishing what shareholders value about the company; identifying the risks around the key drivers of shareholder value; determining the preferred treatment for the risks; and communicating these to shareholders.

Chapter 8 makes the case that we often measure and reward the wrong things. The resulting measures and their associated rewards promote irresponsible behavior by CEOs and their top management team in particular, leading to a failure to assess long-term risk either to the company or to the system within which it operates. Existing measures also fail completely to take into account the social, environmental and human costs of courses of action that mean companies get away with damaging their social and environmental ecosystem. It also explores the fact that the time value of money can put future generations at a disadvantage in any investment evaluation by understating the cost or benefit of results in the future.

To round things off, we look at the current problems of capitalism as a result of the GFC and what needs to be done to save it from itself and rebuild public trust in the system.

Chapter 9 owes its title to an excellent book by Raghuram Rajan and Luigi Zingales.[1] It looks at the failure of modern Anglo-Saxon capitalism and concludes that there is a better way forward which can maintain the unrivalled success of capitalism in raising standards of living, but without its excesses. Such an approach requires boards to understand that they have a wider responsibility than simply that to their shareholders. They must find ways of reconciling the claims of customers, employees, and the community if they are to stay in business. This in turn means that they need to think ahead about how society perceives what their companies do, as this will change over time. Failure to understand this may lead to the company being put out of business altogether or being so heavily regulated that it becomes difficult to provide a fair return.

It is my hope that readers of this book will recognize that the fault does not lie in capitalism per se but in its defective implementation. I hope that the Anglo-Saxon model will find a way of healing itself and correcting its excesses, which are so socially disruptive and in violation of the principles of moderation adopted by all great cultures and religions. Should it fail to do so, there will no doubt be more crises and they will be more serious. As a result, the US and the UK will lose their moral authority when it comes to matters of governance and surrender their leadership to an Asia that is only too keen to step into their shoes.

Endnote

1 Rajan, R. G. and Zingales, L. 2003, *Saving Capitalism from the Capitalists*, Princeton, NJ: Princeton University Press.

1

DO WESTERN CODES OF CORPORATE GOVERNANCE APPLY IN ASIA?

This chapter makes the case that good corporate governance (CG) does matter, but that adopting Western codes of CG without understanding the underlying differences in market structures, types of ownership and culture may lead to unexpected problems in implementation within the board in many Asian markets.

Why CG Matters

As a general principle, CG matters because investors are vulnerable to conflicts of interest and managerial incompetence. They are not well protected by contract and so have to rely on the law to protect them from conflicts of interest and on good CG to protect them from managerial incompetence.[1] If good CG protects shareholders from managerial incompetence, it should lead to better performance, justifying any interest third parties have in how the company is run.

Although there is a fair amount of evidence to suggest that good CG does have a positive impact, there is also evidence to the contrary.[2] On balance, it seems that good CG does in fact lead to better results in terms of higher profits and better dividends. Also the cost of debt (using bond yield spreads as a proxy) would appear to be lower the more independent the board[3]—one of the indicators of good CG.

When investors think of the benefits created for them by good CG, they split into three groups:

- The first group believes that companies with good CG will perform better over time—that over the long term good CG will translate into higher stock prices, yielding higher upside potential. Studies in the US,[4] Germany[5] and, most recently, India[6] tend to support this point of view.
- The second group sees good CG as a means of limiting or reducing the risks to which a company is exposed. They believe the existence of good CG will reduce the chances of bad things happening to the company and, if they do materialize, the company will recover faster because it has good CG in place to deal with the problems as they arise.
- The third group recognizes the importance of self-fulfilling prophecies. They regard CG as a fad, but go along with it because so many investors increasingly think it matters, and therefore they expect share prices to reflect this fact.[7]

Perhaps the most convincing reason for believing that good CG leads to superior shareholder value comes from an American study which argues that companies can be thought of as republics.[8] Those companies that had boards that felt less accountable to the shareholders did less well than the companies where boards took their responsibilities to shareholders more seriously. Companies can choose to be like democracies—granting great powers to the voters; or they can choose to be like dictatorships—protecting the management from being accountable to the voters. Consequently, the study looked at the "democracies" and compared how they have performed in contrast to the "dictatorships." The "democracies"—the companies with the lowest management power and the highest shareholder rights—appear to have outperformed the "dictatorships" by a "statistically significant 8.5 percent per year" in firm valuations.[9]

In addition, firms with lower shareholder rights were less profitable and had lower sales growth than other firms in their industry. The study also shows that a dollar invested on September 1, 1990 would have grown to US$3.39 in the "dictatorship" portfolio by December 31, 1999, but would have grown to US$7.07 in the "democracy" portfolio—representing an annual growth rate in value of 14 percent and 23.3 percent, respectively, with the "democracies" outperforming "dictatorships" by 9.3 percent per annum.[10] Two possible factors contributing to these findings might be:

- *Bad investment decisions*: The more firmly entrenched the managers are, the more protected they are from hostile takeover and the more likely they are to invest unwisely from a shareholder's perspective.[11]
- *Agency costs*: One of the most important sets of agency costs arise as a result of acquisitions, where the acquiring firm is subjected to negative returns. So value-destroying capital expenditure for acquisitions may be one of the reasons for the poorer performance of "dictatorships," particularly when some of the other agency problems are found to be caused by low managerial ownership, high free cash flow and diversifications.[12] Indeed, the evidence suggests that during the 1990s the "dictatorship" firms did in fact indulge in inefficient acquisitions, not so much to create empires but, rather, in an apparent attempt to stave off imminent collapse.[13] Presumably, shareholders in the "democracies" would not have agreed.

German experience[14] supports this, as follows:

- Firms with higher governance ratings delivered higher market-to-book ratios, with an increase in the firm's corporate governance index of three points (out of a total of 30) leading to an increase in the firm's market capitalization of 2.8 percent. This translated into a 12.5 percent increase of market capitalization of the company's book asset value.
- Buying high corporate-governance rated (CGR) firms and shorting low CGR firms would have earned higher returns of around 12 percent per year during the period under review.
- Firm-specific CG affects asset pricing because it is treated as a risk premium for which investors require added returns to compensate for the risk they take. Firms with better CG and engaged investors can deliver lower ROE and still interest shareholders.[15]

The Indian study supported these findings with the following conclusions.[16] Provided companies exceeded a certain CG threshold score then:

- The better-governed firms command a higher market valuation and are less leveraged and have higher interest cover.
- They provide higher return on net worth and capital employed and their profit margins are more stable.
- Their P/E ratios and dividend yields were higher than those in firms whose CG scores are lower.

Portfolio Turnover Affects the Value Placed on CG . . .

However, there is an important caveat: good CG does not interest all shareholders equally. Investors with a low portfolio turnover—defined as selling between 0 and 40 percent of their portfolio in the space of a year—were willing to pay a 12 percent premium on average. The reason for this is that they were in the stock for longer, and good governance pays off over the longer term. Investors who regard the market as a casino are "punting" on a stock, and they are only interested in the very short term. In markets where there are no capital gains taxes, investors can quite literally buy and sell a stock several times in a day. Thus investors with a high turnover rate—defined as selling between 41 percent and 100 percent—were only willing to pay a 7 percent premium. As long as their profits exceed their commission costs, they are ahead.[17] "Stir-frying," as this activity is called in Hong Kong for example, is not about good governance; it is about gambling.

. . . as does the Asset-Management Philosophy

Value investors are interested in the long term and so are more likely to appreciate good CG than growth investors where the growth in the company can hide failures of CG. Although these errors might cause profits to be lower than they otherwise should be, this does not matter so much when there are high price-earnings multiples justified by prospective profit growth. In fact, the difference in the two attitudes is best illustrated by the two quotes below, cited in a McKinsey research paper:[18]

Value investor: "A good board may help lift an underperforming stock and capture hidden value."

Growth investor: "One major shareholder . . . said that he did not want to talk about governance or anything else and had bought our stock only because of a growth trend he foresaw in the industry as a whole."

It is perhaps no accident that the greatest CG failures have occurred either in markets that were growing rapidly—ASEAN before the 1997 Asian Financial Crisis, China in the period 1995–2003[19]—or in sectors where growth was taken for granted, as in IT, telecoms and energy in the US before the crunch time when failures in CG were discovered to have been systemic and occurring over a period of several years before the economy turned down.[20]

The 2007–08 financial crisis followed the same pattern, with unbelievable rates of growth in asset-backed securities and credit-default swaps hiding the basic flaws of CG in the system.[21]

We can conclude that CG does matter to investors for the following reasons:

- It provides them with some protection they otherwise would not have, other than through expensive legal recourse.
- There is some evidence to suggest that good CG delivers better shareholder value over the long term *within* given markets.
- There is also evidence to suggest that markets with a better reputation for CG require a lower risk premium than those that have a less good image.

However, other things being equal, the importance attached to good CG depends on the time horizons of investors—a function of their assets, portfolios and investment philosophies—and whether they are growth investors or value investors. Growth investors care less about CG than value investors, as growth can compensate for failures of CG.

Yet this does not deal with the more difficult question; namely, does a system of good CG developed in one jurisdiction work well in another or are there additional factors that must be taken into account for good CG to happen?

Anglo-Saxon CG may not Apply Everywhere

The Anglo-Saxon system of CG depends on three pillars being in place: self-discipline, market discipline, and regulatory discipline.

Self-discipline

Of these three pillars, self-discipline is the most important as it is the foundation of ethical business practices. At the heart of the Anglo-Saxon capitalist system were the concepts of deferred gratification (the basis of any investment decision), savings and reciprocity or mutual trust, best expressed in the phrase "My word is my bond." These foundations of the capitalist system were first developed in Calvin's Geneva and were written about by Max Weber when he developed the concept of the Protestant work ethic.[22]

Since the 1960s, with the advent of the credit card, followed by the instant news of the CNN world we live in today, the idea of deferred gratification has been under attack and we now live in a society that values instant gratification instead, best exemplified by the values of Gen Y.

This explains the importance of consumption in the Anglo-Saxon economies and it also helps explain the extraordinary packages that CEOs, traders and celebrities receive at the expense of those members of society who are engaged in building the social and economic foundations for the next generation.

More seriously, the focus on the present at the expense of the future has led to justifying the risky behaviors of the financial-services industry that put the entire economic and financial system at risk. The fact that many Americans no longer seem to believe in the Protestant virtues but, rather, in so-called Prosperity Christianity may explain why they cast common sense aside and borrowed to the hilt,[23] when encouraged to do so by unscrupulous mortgage brokers, aided and abetted by conflicted credit rating agencies and financial engineers who created the toxic financial assets that brought down Bear Stearns, Lehman Brothers, Merrill Lynch, and AIG.

My concern is that unless we rediscover the importance of deferred gratification we will continue to undermine the foundations of capitalism and that exhortations by the West to Asia to spend more and save less will only encourage a shift of bad behavior from one hemisphere to the other, leading to future failures of CG.

Market discipline

This is the idea that the market would punish egregious behavior, for which there was some evidence already discussed earlier in the chapter. Companies that are badly governed will attract fewer investors; have to pay a higher premium in terms of ROE for the investors they do attract; and could be subject to hostile takeovers by companies that are better managed. That, at least, was the theory. In practice this has not happened as often as theory predicted, and it certainly did not happen in markets that were not liquid and that had concentrated ownership structures, making it difficult for raiders to buy enough shares to change the management.

So the Anglo-Saxon model did not quite work the way it was supposed to in markets with dispersed ownership; and it certainly did not work the way it was supposed to in markets with concentrated ownership because the majority shareholders could do what they wanted at the expense of minorities.[24] While CG is a critical issue in markets where there is neither liquidity nor dispersed ownership, these very factors make it extremely difficult for independent directors on boards to fulfill their roles as expected in the Anglo-Saxon codes.

The structure of many Asian markets makes market discipline more problematic. Although Asian capital markets have changed from those of old, many of today's constituents still include closely held family firms, which in certain instances and under certain circumstances can be seen to act as though there are no conflicts of interest between their objectives as owners and their goals as managers. However, a more recent development is the emergence of state-owned or -influenced entities and public-listed companies where the managers and the owners may have differing priorities and objectives.

Each of these situations poses a different set of CG challenges to the owners, investors, regulators, and managers involved.

Family-owned public-listed companies affect market discipline . . .

Once owner-entrepreneurs or partners, for that matter, have decided to go to the market to access capital, divergence between the objectives of the dominant shareholder (the former owner or owner's family) and those of the other shareholders—minority shareholders—often arise.

In these circumstances, some former owner-entrepreneurs have at times continued operating as if nothing had changed. On occasion, owners have undertaken transactions of which the other investors had no knowledge; sometimes, those transactions were simply not what the new investors had put their money into the enterprise for. At other times, related party transactions moved money raised by public listings into private hands—and this was clearly not what the new investors had bought into.

. . . So does "National Service" in government-related entities

CG priorities become less clear-cut in countries where government-linked entities or enterprises in which the government has a serious stake are required to do "national service," investing in projects of perhaps weak financial viability, but of importance either politically or as part of a nation-building agenda.

In 2003, South Korean banks appear to have been "requested" by the government to assist with the restructuring of the banking industry without due regard for the best interests of their shareholders, on grounds that "national service" required them to do so. For example, when there was a credit-card liquidity crisis, Kookmin Bank "volunteered" to buy credit-card debt—a move believed to be the result of government pressure, and not the best solution for generating shareholder value.[25]

The prolonged saga of the Hynix restructuring in 2003 is another one that only makes sense when seen in terms of "national service" (see Appendix A). The difficulties faced in resolving the SK Global crisis, where creditors automatically assumed it was the duty of SK Corp and SK Telecom to provide financial assistance, shows how much there is a traditional expectation that the South Korean *chaebols* will come to the help of distressed sibling organizations—regardless of whether such an action is in the interests of their shareholders.

Among these conflicts of interest in the web of cross-holdings and non-transparency, there are signs that change is on the way. When the SK saga resurfaced in June 2003, this time Kookmin Bank began to make discounted sales of SK Global stock in order to write off debt and disentangle itself from the problems surrounding this particular *chaebol* (see Appendix B).

Regulatory discipline

This is the set of rules and laws that are designed to help the functioning of the capital market so that it can be vibrant, efficient, and fair. The CG regulatory landscape has changed quite dramatically in the last 20 years, as can be seen by comparing Figure 1.1 and Figure 1.2. It is also clear that Asia has caught up with the developed capital markets, at least in terms of laws and codes.

Malaysia's journey in CG began with the introduction of the Malaysian Code in 1999, followed by the establishment of the Minority Shareholder Watchdog Group (MSWG) in 2000. In 2001, Bursa Malaysia (the stock exchange) revamped the listing requirements to include a specific section in the annual report on CG, requiring companies to comply with the Code or explain why they did not do so. In 2004, the securities laws were amended to incorporate whistle-blowing provisions and redress mechanisms for breaches in securities laws. This was followed in 2005 by Bank Negara Malaysia (the central bank) publishing "Guidelines on Corporate Governance for Licensed Institutions" dealing with banks and insurance companies and the introduction of the so-called Green Book by the Putrajaya Committee on GLC High Performance to upgrade the effectiveness of GLC Boards (discussed further in Chapter 3). In 2007, the Malaysian Code was revised as was the Companies Act to tighten up further on CG (the impact of the revised code is discussed in Chapter 4).

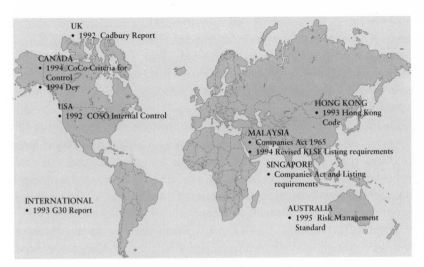

FIGURE 1.1 The evolving CG landscape
The global landscape less than 15 years ago
Source: SIDC-PWC Non-Executive Director Development Seminar: "Is it Worth the Risk?" (2009).

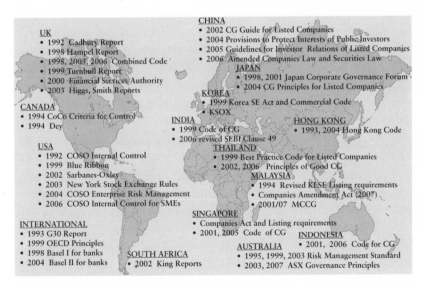

FIGURE 1.2 The evolving CG landscape
The global landscape in recent years
Source: SIDC-PWC Non-Executive Director Development Seminar: "Is it Worth the Risk?" (2009).

Enforcement in much of Asia is often another matter and that is because of a climate of ignorance or indifference regarding the seriousness of white-collar crimes. When the media lionize Nick Leeson or Jerome Kerviel it becomes difficult for junior magistrates and even circuit court judges to think that white-collar crime needs to be punished severely—after all, it appears to be a victimless crime. Added to that is the fact that white-collar crime is often very tricky to prove, and it becomes only too apparent that in many Asian jurisdictions, the penalties are not sufficient to deter; indeed, they are almost an invitation to commit the crime. This is a problem for the US and UK as well, though it must be said in the US's favor that people do go to jail, regardless of their social or political standing.

In Asia the predominance of partly listed family-owned businesses and government-linked entities creates a totally different context for a CG model to operate in. The quite different system of regulation and demands for transparency that apply in the Anglo-Saxon shareholder capitalist model would actually provide information to the competitors of the family firms, as well as reduce the family's or government's ability to run the company.[26] Figure 1.3 below shows the difference in the two contexts very clearly:

In Asia, Latin America, and much of Europe the model is about achieving and retaining control, rather than allowing the market to operate freely, through:

Control model of corporate governance found in Asia, Latin America, and much of Continental Europe

Market model of corporate governance prevalent in United States and United Kingdom

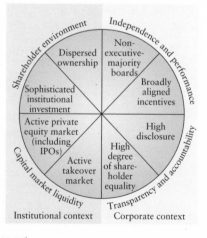

FIGURE 1.3 Two models, a world apart
Source: Coombes and Watson (2001) cited in Wallace and Zinkin (2005).

- Concentrated ownership and a reliance on family or bank finance (public or private), which determine the shareholder context.
- Boards with aligned incentives such that the board is dependent on the same outcomes as the controlling shareholders.
- Limited disclosure and inadequate minority protection.
- Illiquid capital markets with restricted takeover activities and an underdeveloped new-issue market.

This is different from the underlying assumptions operating in Anglo-Saxon stock markets where there are:

- Dispersed shareholdings and sophisticated institutional investors who look at the fundamentals rather than treating the market and its stocks as a way to make short-term profits (at least in theory, though some of the momentum trades by hedge funds are not that different from the syndicate manipulations of penny stocks in some Asian jurisdictions) to create a quite different shareholder environment—one where shareholders have equal rights and minority shareholders can expect to have some form of protection.
- A somewhat different role and structure for the board in order to do this—with non-executive, independent directors in the majority, and the incentives of board members not so closely aligned with those of the dominant or controlling shareholder (if there is one) but, rather, aligned with the interests of the absent owners represented by all holders of non-preferential shares—however few shares they actually hold.

As a result, in the Anglo-Saxon model, transparency and accountability are extremely important and shareholders are, in principle, expected to be treated equally and are also entitled to have access to a great deal of information, which could indeed aid competitors.

The Need to Localize CG to Meet Asian Conditions

In Asia, the fact that family firms or family interests are so important—more so than in the UK and the US—makes it difficult to argue that what is right in a highly liquid market with extremely dispersed ownership is correct for relatively illiquid markets with highly concentrated ownership structures and a greater dependence on family or bank finance rather than equity.

Even if family firms were not the only complicating factor, many Asian markets also have entities upon which the government can apply pressure in the interests of "national service" at the expense of individual shareholders. This is more serious because, in the case of many of these markets, the countries are young, and the governments believe they have a duty to build their nations through "pillar industries" and other forms of direction of capital to projects whose justification is not only economic. They are therefore unlikely to abandon the practice because they still see it as part of the nation-building agenda. In the past 30 years there was no such pressure in the UK or the US, though a developed country like France exhibits similar tendencies, and the US is now exhibiting many of the same behaviors as a result of the global financial crisis, with the bailouts of GM and Chrysler.

The importance attached to good CG depends on the time horizons of investors—which is, as mentioned earlier, a function of their assets, portfolios, and investment philosophies (whether they are growth or value investors). However, there are signs that things are changing for the better.[27] This message is reinforced by the recent research undertaken by CFO Research Services in collaboration with the ACCA in June 2006 on Corporate Governance, Business Ethics and the CFO. Their findings were as follows:

- CFOs acknowledge that a good ethical culture has become a requirement in business, as it affects the overall reputation and brand of the company. It improves relationships with banks, institutional investors, suppliers, and employees (p.5).
- However, implementing ethical codes is still a challenge in Asia, especially when they are dealing with smaller companies in less well-developed countries (p.6).[28] Part of this is the problem that so much of Asian business culture is "person-driven" rather than "process-driven" (p.16).[29] Relationships also matter more in Asia than in the West and this affects how business is done between companies, as is acknowledged by DuPont's CFO.[30] Whether we are talking about a large SME, Mulitex, or one of the leading multinationals, it would appear that global standards still need to be localized—with the attendant problems this can pose.
- Nevertheless, three-quarters of the 160 respondents say their companies have instituted written codes of ethics and 54 percent have systems in place for assessing adherence to their codes (p.17).
- The pressure for improvements does not come from institutional investors—only 6.8 percent of the respondents say they feel

pressure from investors above all else. Shareholders in Asia seem to be more interested in profit and dividends, or just simple growth prospects (p.23).[31]

- Surprisingly, Sarbanes–Oxley has made a difference, forcing companies to rethink their processes, and despite the high costs of compliance, 48 percent of the respondents thought it had a positive effect on the development of an ethical culture for all companies, regardless of whether they were listed in the US; 24 percent felt it only enabled those listed in the US to improve their ethical culture.

Finally there is the problem of the different expectations owners have of their independent non-executive directors (INEDs). Being an effective INED is hard, even in the UK, as has been recognized in the Higgs Report and now in the Walker Report.[32] It is that much harder in Asia, because the boardroom reality is different, as is shown in Table 1.1 below.

TABLE 1.1 Expectations Compared

Anglo-Saxon Expectations	Asian Expectations
1) To represent the interests of the owners (especially minority shareholders) the INED must be independent, for without independence the INED cannot be effective through the process of fearless, but constructive challenge.	1) In family-founded and -led companies, the families know better than minority shareholders where the best interests of the organization lie, so there is no need for INEDs who, in any case, do not understand the business, because they cannot give it the time and attention it requires.
a. Independence of thought guarantees effectiveness as it allows the INED to bring fresh insight to the Board, allowing the positions taken by the executives to be examined from a perspective that does not reflect vested interests.	a. INEDs do not have sufficient access to people to understand the determinants of decisions; and if they were to be granted the access, it would undermine the chain of command and mislead managers about lines of authority.
b. The process of challenge and scrutiny by the INED leads to better-informed decision-making and so raises the effectiveness of the organization.	b. Harmony is important and challenge may lead to conflict— something to be avoided in most Asian cultures—so, in practice, Asian INEDs will not challenge.

(*continued*)

TABLE 1.1 (*continued*)

Anglo-Saxon Expectations	Asian Expectations
c. Diversity of views and backgrounds serves to create a better debate of ideas and approaches put forward by the CEO.	c. Since the Asian crisis, organizations must react faster than before and do not have the luxury of time to debate ideas.
d. The INED's independence from the organization allows fundamental questioning of the organization's "ends" and the "executive limitations" placed on the CEO, because independence means that the INED has no stake in the shape of the organization or in choosing the beneficiaries it seeks to serve.	d. In "High Power Distance" cultures, people do not question their superiors, by virtue of their position rank and title. Thus even though the INED has the freedom to question, in practice this goes against cultural norms.
2) The presence of INEDs reminds the board that its fiduciary duty is to the shareholders as owners, hence the appointment of INEDs to chair the key committees of the board. Independence is essential if there is to be a system of checks and balances on executive power.	2) The best guarantors of the interests of the shareholders are the founding family, whose investment in the firm and commitment to the firm over the long term is greater than that of minority shareholders who are only interested in short-term performance.
3) To be effective, INEDs must	3) Effective INEDs are not independent.
a. Have access to information in a timely, accurate manner so that informed decisions can be made based on appropriate challenges of the assumptions made by the CEO.	a. The Higgs Report (2003) recognized that non-executive chairmen cannot be regarded as independent because they are so intimately linked to the organization—the same is true for INEDs.
b. Spend sufficient time on the organization's issues, so the number of boards they can sit on must be limited, and they must be involved in, and care about, the decisions taken by boards on which they sit.	b. For INEDs to spend the time and effort needed to be effective, they must be paid appropriately by the company. Once they are paid properly, and can only sit on a limited number of boards, they lose their independence.

Source: Non-Executive Director Development Series; directors training program run by SIDC and PWC for listed companies on the Malaysian stock exchange.

So can we really apply Anglo-Saxon codes of CG in Asia? Perhaps the best answer to this difficult question was given by Jaime Zobel de Ayala II, the seventh-generation president and CEO of Ayala Corporation in the Philippines, in an interview with McKinsey in 2002:

In the West, the pendulum seems to swing between the model of the tightly controlled family company and that of the widely held public company. I feel strongly that between these two extremes lies the most sustainable model. There is an ever-increasing tension between the institutional investors' focus on quarterly results and the need for long-term strategy and stability. Widely held public companies are seeing a dramatic rise in their CEO turnover, often because there is no single large institution willing to tell the CEO, "Look, hang in there. Let's agree on our long-term strategy. Even if it takes a short-term hit, you know we'll back you up." . . . What we try to do at Ayala is to structure partnerships that can agree on a long-term vision and to provide stability at the board level. By going public at the same time, we get the dynamic tension from the outside institutional-investor community to deliver financial returns over the short to medium term.[33]

Conclusion

Clearly there are grounds for some optimism. The regulatory infrastructure is becoming ever more supportive of good CG. Increasingly, countries have to worry about the "beauty parades" conducted by external consultancies and analysts on the state of CG in each market. CG and ESG[34] indices are being developed in country after country, and there is a steadily increasing demand by both boards and regulators for training in what makes for a high-performance board.

However, this does not mean that what works in the US and UK should be adopted in its entirety in Asia. The structural and cultural conditions of each market must be taken into account, as must the social and political context in which business operates. If countries have government-linked companies listed on the stock exchange, and if the reality is that families dominate that which is not government-linked, then the dynamics of the board are going to be different from what can be expected in New York or London. This makes implementing good CG more complicated, but not impossible.

Endnotes

1 "If the position of stockholders cannot be well protected by contract, then how is it made viable? There are two mechanisms in particular that serve this function. One is the law: rules that require managers

(agents) to act in the best interests of stockholders (principals). *The other is governance: a set of provisions that enable the stockholders by exercising voting power to compel those in operating control of the firm to respect their interests.* Legal rules can best address relatively clear conflicts of interests; *managerial competence, except in occasional cases such as Enron and Parmalat, falls in the domain of governance.*" [emphasis added] From Scott, K. 2002, "Agency Costs and Corporate Governance" in *The New Palgrave Dictionary of Economics and the Law*, London: Palgrave Macmillan: 26–7, cited in Wallace P. and Zinkin, J. 2005, *Corporate Governance*, John Wiley & Sons (Asia): Singapore: 2–3.

2 Hermalin, B. and Weisbach, M. 1991, "The Effects of Board Composition and Direct Incentives on Firm Performance," *Financial Management* 20: 101–12; Shleifer, A. and Vishny, R. W. 1997, "A Survey of Corporate Governance," *Journal of Finance* LII:2: 737–83; Mitton, T. 2001, "A Cross-Firm Analysis of Corporate Governance on East-Asian Crisis," *Journal of Financial Economics*, May: 5–50; Becht *et al.* 2003, "Corporate Governance and Control," in *Handbook of the Economics of Finance*, Constantinides *et al.* (eds), Elsevier: North Holland: 3–109; Denis, D. K. and McConnell, J. J. 2003, "International Corporate Governance," European Corporate Governance Institute Working Paper No 05/2003: 1–62; Holderness, C. G. 2003, "A Survey of Block Holders and Corporate Control," *FRBNY Economic Policy Review*: 51–64; Gugler, K. *et al.* 2004, "Corporate Governance and Globalization," *Oxford Review of Economic Policy* 20(1): 129–56.

3 Anderson, R. *et al.* 2004, "Board Characteristics, Accounting Report Integrity and the Cost of Debt," *Journal of Accounting and Economics* 37: 315–42.

4 Gompers, P., Ishii, J. and Metrick, A. 2003, "Corporate Governance and Equity Prices," *The Quarterly Journal of Economics* 118(1): 107–55; Brown, L. D. and Claylor, M. L. 2004, "Corporate Governance and Firm Performance," Working Paper, Georgia State University, USA.

5 Drobetz, W., Schillhofer, A. and Zimmermann, H. 2003, "Corporate Governance and Expected Stock Returns: Evidence from Germany," ECGI Working Papers Series in Finance, Number 11/2003, February 2003.

6 Banerjee, A. *et al.* 2009, "Corporate Governance and Market Value: Preliminary Evidence from Indian Companies," Standard and Poor's, September 2009, at: www.standardandpoors.com.

7 Felton, R., Hudnut. A. and Van Heeckeren, J. 1996, "Putting a Value on Board Governance," *McKinsey Quarterly* 4.

8 Gompers, Ishii and Metrick, op. cit.

9 Ibid.: 110.

10 Ibid.: 120.

11 Ibid.: 131.

12   Ibid.: 132.
13   Ibid.: 134.
14   Drobetz, Schillhofer and Zimmermann, op. cit.: 23–32.
15   Rather, with adequate disclosure and transparency standards in place, it is ultimately the capital market which rewards good governance practices (high CGRs) and punishes bad ones (low CGRs). To this end, corporate governance should be understood as an opportunity and not an obligation from a firm's perspective: "However, with governance being a more popular topic for the management and supervision of firms, we believe that professional investors will become more active in shareholder engagement programs in the future . . . this will ultimately lead to higher expected returns and lower valuations for those firms with governance deficits, since investors want to be compensated for their increased monitoring and second opinion activities. Similarly, by removing certain governance malfunctions, large investors are able to achieve a higher valuation for their assets, since the required return becomes lower."—Drobetz *et al.*: 32–3.
16   Banerjee, op. cit.
17   Felton, Hudnut and Van Heeckeren, op. cit.: 171.
18   Ibid.: 172.
19   This refers to the many cases in the Asia region such as the influence of the *chaebol* in South Korea but also the many complicated links that existed between the political and business spheres in Thailand, the Philippines, Indonesia and Malaysia. The GDP growth rate in the region in the five years leading up to the 1998 financial crisis was between 5 percent at the lowest, for the Philippines, and 9 percent at the highest, for Malaysia. In China, one of the main sources of CG scandals has been the banking industry. Although graft and bad lending were supposed to be a thing of the past, as recently as May 2003, Liu Jinbao, Chief Executive of Bank of China, was detained on charges of corruption and illegal lending.
20   Patsuris, P. 2002, "The Corporate Scandal Sheet," Forbes, at: http://www.forbes.com/2002/07/25/accountingtracker.html, August 26.
21   Turner, A., 2010, "Household and unincorporated business borrowing from the banking and building society sectors grew from about 14 percent of GDP to 76 percent of GDP, while deposits grew also, but less dramatically from 39 percent to 72 percent . . . Thus the total balance sheet of the UK banking system, defined to include all legal banking entities operating in London, had by 2007 reached around 500 percent of GDP, compared with 34 percent in 1964. What do banks do, what should they do and what public policies are needed to ensure best results for the real economy." Lecture given on March 17, 2010 at the Cass Business School.

22   Weber, M., 1905, *The Protestant Ethic and the Spirit of Capitalism* (New York: Charles Scribner and Sons, 1958).

23   "In his book *Something for Nothing*, Jackson Lears describes two starkly different manifestations of the American dream, each intertwined with religious faith. The traditional Protestant hero is a self-made man. He is disciplined and hardworking, and believes that his 'success comes through careful cultivation of (implicitly Protestant) virtues in cooperation with a Providential plan.' The hero of the second American narrative is a kind of gambling man—a 'speculative confidence man,' Lears calls him, who prefers 'risky ventures in real estate,' and a more 'fluid, mobile democracy.' The self-made man imagines a coherent universe where earthly rewards match merits. The confidence man lives in a culture of chance, with 'grace as a kind of spiritual luck, a free gift from God.' The Gilded Age launched the myth of the self-made man, as the Rockefellers and other powerful men in the pews connected their wealth to their own virtue. In these boom-and-crash years, the more reckless alter ego dominates. In his book, Lears quotes a reverend named Jeffrey Black: 'The whole hope of a human being is that somehow, in spite of the things I've done wrong, there will be an episode when grace and fate shower down on me and an unearned blessing will come to me—that I'll be the one.'" Hanna Rosin, "Did Christianity Cause the Crash," *The Atlantic*, December 2009, at: http://www.theatlantic.com/doc/200912/rosin-prosperity-gospel?pid=ynews.

24   "Obviously, corporate governance is not a problem for the 100 percent-owner-manager of a business. Nor is it much of a problem for the majority stockholder (or group) which controls the Board of Directors and can fire the managers at any time. (Protection for minority interests in such a firm will have to come primarily from legal rights, since their voting power is generally ineffectual.) So CG is an issue mainly for minority stockholders, in a firm controlled by the managers where there are no significant stockholders that can easily work together. In that situation, the stockholders potentially can still exert control to protect their interests, but face formidable difficulties (in terms of transaction costs and inadequate incentives) in actually acting together." (Scott, 2002: 26–27), cited in Wallace and Zinkin 2005, op. cit.: 2–3.

25   A better choice would have been to privatize its 75 percent subsidiary Kookmin Credit Card. This move would have allowed Kookmin Credit Card to cut the costs of funding as a result of leveraging the parent's bigger balance sheet and better credit rating—to the benefit of the minority shareholders of both Kookmin Credit Card and the bank itself. Source: Credit Lyonnais Securities, 2003 Emerging Markets Corporate Governance Watch.

26   Coombes, P. and Watson, M. 2001, "Corporate Reform in the Developing World," *McKinsey Quarterly* 4, "Emerging Markets": 90.

27 "Perhaps most encouraging is the fact that a number of companies in Thailand are already following best practices in many areas of CG and have been rewarded by the market with higher valuations. Market incentives of this kind provide local benchmarks and encourage more companies to improve their CG practices once they come to the realization that good governance actually pays." Hoschka, T. C., Nast, G. R. and Villinger, R. 2002, "Better Boards in Thailand," *McKinsey Quarterly* 3: 23–6.

28 "Perhaps we need a two-tier system, with global standards in key ethical areas underscored by room for flexibility at the local level. Each country has its cultural values, its upbringing, and so it's very difficult to bring in a motherhood ethical governance system. A customized system could enable companies to project themselves internationally but keep customers and suppliers happy closer to home." Sriram, K., Group Manager of Internal Audit for Hong Kong Garment Trader Mulitex ("Corporate Governance, Business Ethics and the CFO": 6).

29 "Internal relationships matter even more. Sriram describes the culture at Mulitex as 'person-driven,' with an emphasis on one-to-one interaction. This he notes is at odds with the global push for process-driven governance. 'In a process-driven environment, what you learn on courses or from textbooks can really be put into practice,' he says. 'In a person-driven environment it's difficult to get into formal structures and compartmentalization.' The company's directors value loyalty of their staff, and are reluctant to make changes that smack of heavy-handedness."—Ibid.: 16.

30 "But if much has changed since 1863 [when DuPont began trading in gunpowder in China] some things remain the same. 'A lot of business is still done through relationships,' observes Daniel Leung, DuPont's regional finance director for Greater China. 'The giving and receiving of token gifts is an important part of the culture and generally seen as part of the relationship-building process.' . . . [T]o help staff negotiate tricky cross-cultural mores, policies on so-called 'business courtesies' are laid out in a 20-page Business Conduct Guide that is distributed in all 70 countries where the company operates . . . As Leung points out: 'A black and white approach is just not practical in China. While standards are global, you have to ensure that the local organization understand the standards in the context of the local environment.'"—Ibid.: 24.

31 "At least one CFO wasn't surprised. 'I just look at the recent IPO of the Bank of China in Hong Kong, a world record subscription,' he said. 'Many of the subscribers were institutional investors—Western mutual finds—even though the Western media have been vocal in their criticism of past wrongdoings at the BOC. How come people forgot all that?' But he also regards this as a form of myopia that may apply to

investors worldwide. 'To me this suggests that whether they are Asian or European or American, investors are really only interested in growth prospects.'"—Ibid.: 23.

32 Walker, D. 2009, "A review of corporate governance in UK banks and other financial industry entities," July 16, 2009.

33 Gibson, K. 2002, "A Case for the Family-Owned Conglomerate," *McKinsey Quarterly* 4: 133–4.

34 ESG = Environment, Sustainability, and Governance.

2

WHAT IS THE BUSINESS
OF BUSINESS?

This chapter deals with the need for boards to take a wider view of their responsibilities than simply maximizing shareholder value. It deals with the firm's primary stakeholders—customers, employees, community, and shareholders, in that order—and their claims on the company, and it makes the case that an excessive focus on maximizing shareholder value will ultimately put the company's license to operate at risk. It argues that boards need to regard protecting their license to operate as the most important responsibility directors have and this requires them to regard corporate responsibility not as an add-on but as an early-warning mechanism in setting strategy. It also argues that rejecting inappropriate economic theories makes reconciling competing stakeholder claims easier and more natural.

In making the case that there is more to business than maximizing shareholder value, I would like to begin by asking the question posed by Milton Friedman in 1970: "What is the business of business?"

The answer to this question may seem obvious. Business schools everywhere teach Friedman's answer and analysts repeat it: the purpose of business is to maximize shareholder value.

But what exactly does this apparently simple statement mean? Are companies supposed to maximize shareholder value at the expense of customers, employees, and the community? Are we talking about the short term or the long term, and what exactly do we mean by short and long term? Is it OK for companies to break the law, pay fines, and get away with doing this again and again as long as the fines they pay are less than the profits they make by breaking the law? Are we talking about maximizing profits or some cash-based measure instead?

As directors and senior managers think through the implications of these questions, it is clear that maximizing shareholder value is not as unambiguous an objective as might appear at first sight.

The famous Johnson & Johnson Credo, written in 1935 by General Robert Wood Johnson, puts satisfying customers first, respecting employees second, being a good citizen third, and giving the shareholders a fair return last:

> We believe our first responsibility is to the doctors, nurses and patients, to mothers and fathers and all others who use our products and services. In meeting their needs everything we do must be of high quality. We must constantly strive to reduce our costs in order to maintain reasonable prices. Customers' orders must be serviced promptly and accurately. Our suppliers and distributors must have an opportunity to make a fair profit.
>
> We are responsible to our employees, the men and women who work with us throughout the world. Everyone must be considered as an individual. We must respect their dignity and recognize their merit. They must have a sense of security in their jobs. Compensation must be fair and adequate, and working conditions clean, orderly, and safe. We must be mindful of ways to help our employees fulfill their family responsibilities. Employees must feel free to make suggestions and complaints. There must be equal opportunity for employment, development, and advancement for those qualified. We must provide competent management, and their actions must be just and ethical.
>
> We are responsible to the communities in which we live and work and to the world community as well. We must be good citizens—support good works and charities and bear our fair share of taxes. We must encourage civic improvements and better health and education. We must maintain in good order the property we are privileged to use, protecting the environment and natural resources.
>
> Our final responsibility is to our stockholders. Business must make a sound profit. We must experiment with new ideas. Research must be carried on, innovative programs developed and mistakes paid for. New equipment must be purchased,

new facilities provided and new products launched. Reserves must be created to provide for adverse times. When we operate according to these principles, the stockholders should realize a fair return.[1]

I find it revealing that the Credo puts satisfying its stakeholders in this order and argues that by following this order the shareholder will obtain a fair return. In my view the justification for making a profit given in the Credo is one of the best. The Credo also poses an interesting question: Why a "fair" return and not a "maximum" return? Surely all that is needed is to recover the cost of capital? If that is done, then resources have not been misallocated and the economy will prosper.

The problem with fair return is that unlike bankers, who are satisfied if principal and interest are repaid, investors are looking for more than simply recovering their costs of capital. Investors, who can get into and out of shares during the course of a day, are looking for maximum returns and one of the problems we now face is that so many investors have little loyalty to or interest in the companies in which they invest. They have become speculators, punters or "stir-fry" shareholders as they are called in Hong Kong: their only interest is in making their money work 24 hours a day to yield maximum short-term returns because they can, and do, move on to greener pastures.

Creating and Maintaining Satisfied Customers

To appreciate why the Credo put customers first, let's go back to the beginning, when entrepreneurs start their companies. Why do they do it? Time and again, they do not talk about shareholders or about maximizing profits. Rather, they talk about their ideas; how they believe they will change the world; and how they want to make a difference.

Akio Morita, the founder of Sony and the father of the Walkman, wanted his engineers to make a product that would allow his daughter to listen to music as she walked to school. His focus was on making a difference to his daughter's life. Steve Jobs had a vision of a computer in every home when he and Steve Wozniak set up Apple. Sergei Brin, one of the founders of Google, believes that knowledge is a good thing and wants to do good by making information available to everybody.[2] Datuk Tony Fernandes talked about the revolution in travel he wanted to bring to Malaysians who had never been in a plane when he founded Air Asia. Henry Ford wrote this when he changed all of our lives by creating the mass-produced motor car:

I will build a motor car for the great multitude . . . it will be so low in price that no man making a good salary will be unable to own one—and enjoy with his family the blessing of hours of pleasure in God's great open spaces . . . When I'm through everybody will be able to afford one, and everyone will have one. The horse will have disappeared from our highways, the automobile will be taken for granted . . . and we will give a large number of men employment at good wages.[3]

What is interesting in Henry Ford's vision is that he did not just look at the impact he would have on customers. He also made the point that he would give a large number of men employment at good wages, recognizing the importance of employees. He even considered the effect on the environment and thought it would be beneficial because the most serious pollution problem in London in 1894, for example, was horse manure from all the horses on the roads.[4] The automobile solved that problem, unfortunately only to replace it later with others. Nevertheless, his primary focus was on the way he would change the world for the better for his customers.

So the late Peter Drucker was right when he wrote:

It is the customer who determines what a business is. For it is the customer, and he alone, who through being willing to pay for a good or a service, converts economic resources into wealth, things into goods. What the business thinks it produces is not of the first importance—especially not to the future of the business and to its success. What the customer thinks he is buying, what he considers "value" is decisive—it determines what a business is, what it produces, and whether it will prosper.

The customer is the foundation of a business and keeps it in existence. He alone gives employment. And it is to supply the consumer that society entrusts wealth-producing resources to the business enterprise.[5] [emphasis added]

All great and enduring companies understand this. But do all board members? If customers are the primary stakeholder, then understanding what is important to customers is essential.

In a competitive world, customers have choices. If they do not like one company's products or services, they can go to its competitors. This battle for customers forces businesses to innovate, for it is only by creating new and better products and processes that offer superior value that a new business can gain share at the expense of existing ones. This means that even market leaders cannot rest on their laurels. What was good enough for customers yesterday may not be so today, and certainly will not be tomorrow.

Often boards boast an impressive array of retired civil servants, ambassadors, and generals. They undoubtedly provide value through their connections and understanding of governments and of the political process, domestically and internationally. But do they really understand customers, with their endless need for innovation and their ability to go elsewhere if not satisfied? Perhaps not. After all, civil servants value order and stability and tend to dislike innovation. There are rarely competitors to government departments or to the armed forces. Citizens have to use government services whether they like them or not, and countries cannot choose who their armed forces will be.

That is not to say that all that matters is satisfying the customer. To do that would be at the expense of the other three key stakeholders: employees, community, and shareholders.

Work is Worship

I am always struck by the fact that the Arabic word for work and worship is the same: *Ibadah*. This reminds me that work was never supposed to be drudgery, but an uplifting activity, giving meaning to life and dignity to workers. Indeed Islam recognizes that every person must strive to do their best and in these circumstances work will truly be an act of worship. Islam also recognizes that doing business is a blessing because it allows us to meet other people and create value in so doing. Effort is essential, however. One of the reasons why gambling is *haram* (forbidden) in Islam is that the reward does not reflect effort and so it undermines character.

For employees to realize their potential at work, two things are needed: a favorable environment, and the will to work, which I take for granted.

We need three things to create a favorable working environment: first, we should respect our employees for their skills and the diversity of their ideas; second, we should reward and recognize people for the work they do rather than compensating them; third, we should imbue their work with meaning by providing a "line of sight" to the purpose of the organization as a whole.

Treat people with respect and dignity

Frederick Taylor's principles of scientific management and Henry Ford's development of mass production brought undreamed-of advances in productivity, lowering costs of production dramatically and thus making products affordable for the masses. However, these advances came at a terrible price: the deskilling of work and the treatment of workers as costs to be minimized rather than as assets to be invested in.

Wherever possible in the Anglo-Saxon world, capital was used to deskill work, to reduce the company's dependence on people and their workers' implicit knowledge. The Germans, and to a greater extent the Japanese, have resisted this Anglo-Saxon approach to workers.[6] They have valued the skills and judgment of their workers, looking to them to provide ideas and take responsibility for achieving levels of quality that Anglo-Saxon firms have found hard to emulate.[7]

The success of Toyota was, in large part, the result of the company empowering its employees to take personal accountability for the quality of every car they make.* But it is more than that; it is also the fact that Japanese managers do not differentiate themselves from workers. When Japanese companies first went to Britain, they did away with separate dining rooms and executive washrooms; they wore the same clothes as the workers; they knew how the job was done; they spent time with the workers on the factory floor. Even today the top managers of Toyota do not drive luxury limousines; they do not pay themselves obscene salaries, unlike their counterparts at GM or Ford.[9] The result of this different approach, of a willingness to share the same conditions as the workers, was quite startling. The same British workers who were regarded as the bane of their British managers, producing low-quality output at high cost because of appalling productivity, suddenly became star workers in the new Japanese companies. Nissan in Sunderland and Sony at Bridgend found that some of the best quality and highest productivity globally came from their British workers. Why? They were

---

*Its recent severe quality problems appear to have come from pushing too hard for growth at the expense of these core values.[8]

treated with dignity and respect, valued for their contributions and ideas, regardless of their level in the organization. In short, people were treated fairly.

There are two other aspects to fairness and these involve boards directly. The first is the pay that they grant to CEOs. The second is that mistakes made by boards affect workers much more severely than the top management team.

How much should CEOs be paid? This question has become a political issue as a result of the bailouts in the US, where CEOs have been paid astronomical sums of money regardless of their performance. This clearly is a matter for boards to decide, but perhaps some parameters can be advanced as guidelines.

Alfred Sloan, the founder of General Motors, was reputed to have said that 26 times the average worker's pay was appropriate. By the late 1970s this had risen to around 50 times. In 2004, it was 531 times, as against 25 times in the UK, 16 times in France and 11 times in Germany.[10] It is not obvious that American CEOs perform better than their British, French or German counterparts. Nor is it obvious that the job of a CEO has become more than 10 times more demanding since the 1970s. What does seem clear is that the pay of US CEOs and the way it has been structured has become a major threat to capitalism as we know it.[11]

Strategic mistakes made by the board always hurt workers more than top management. When companies go bust or get taken over, there are layoffs. The workers suffer disproportionately. There are two simple reasons for this: workers tend not be as re-deployable as top management, particularly once they are over 40. They tend to have sector-specific skills, whereas top management are more likely to have an array of generalist skills, as well as their original specialties, which makes them more employable elsewhere and easier for them to move into another industry if necessary. While workers can seek work elsewhere, their choices are more limited. Unskilled workers are likely to have to downgrade their expectations considerably to get rehired.

What is more, top managers normally have ample financial cushions to fall back on, even in times of crisis. The likes of Hank Greenberg, Dick Fuld, Chuck Prince, and Stan O'Neal may have lost millions of dollars on paper and a great deal of "face" but they still have more than enough left for their daily needs. Employees whose 401Ks[12] were wiped out when Enron, WorldCom, and Lehman Brothers collapsed have lost their pensions.

Don't compensate; reward and recognize

We spend most of our waking lives working. If we do this without enjoying what we do, we have to be compensated for this misuse of our time and creative energies, which is why I dislike the word "compensation." Compensation means "money that is paid to someone in exchange for something that has been lost or damaged or for some inconvenience."[13] Compensation assumes that we do not enjoy what we do when we are at work. This is not to say that work cannot be boring at times or that working for a terrible boss is not hell or that gossiping colleagues are not a pain.

What I find distressing about the use of the word "compensation" is the underlying assumption that people do not want to work and derive no pleasure from a job well done—the result of the philosophies of Taylor and Ford discussed earlier. It totally ignores the idea of *Ibadah* and runs counter to Aristotle's dictum that "Pleasure in the job puts perfection in the work."

Aristotle recognized that doing a job well can be a reward in itself, a point emphasized in the writings of Kouzes and Posner who stress the fact that intrinsic motivators are more crucial than extrinsic ones, such as pay. Indeed, they argue that if employers come to see work as something people do merely for pay, ignoring the meaning and self-fulfillment to be found in doing a job well, they will structure work in a strictly utilitarian fashion, with disastrous results. Writing about New Economy companies they say: "Have big stock option plans or huge signing bonuses really done much to make them successful? There's very convincing evidence that reliance on extrinsic motivators can actually lower performance and create a culture of divisiveness and selfishness, precisely because it diminishes our inner sense of purpose."[14]

If this is true of New Economy companies, how much truer is it of Wall Street, where selfishness seems to be the justification for every immoral, but strictly legal, pay deal?

I therefore much prefer the terms "reward" and "recognition," as these allow us to celebrate the successes of our colleagues because they have gone the extra mile. They are also positive, energizing ideas, whereas compensation is a negative one, encouraging minimalist thinking.

Every job matters when there is a "line of sight"

There is an old story about a visitor to a quarry who watched two men at work cutting blocks of stone. Although they were doing exactly the same work, one man was sour-faced and slow; the other was happy and productive. The visitor asked the sour-faced man what he was doing. He answered: "I am cutting blocks of stone." When the second man was asked the same question, he answered: "I am building a palace." The first man had no idea of the broader purpose or how he fitted into the scheme of things. As a result he felt lost, disenfranchised and purposeless. The second man was energized by his sense of purpose; he understood where he fitted into the scheme of things and his work was worthwhile.

As long as people know where they fit and how they contribute to the mission of their company, they will feel their job matters; they make a difference and they will enjoy coming to work, regardless of how small their job.[15]

It is critically important for the board to define clearly what the organization's purpose is, what its vision and values are, and we will look at this in detail in Chapter 3. For the moment, suffice it to say that the purpose of the organization must be understood by all who come to work, because it allows them to explain to their family and friends what they do and why it matters—and therefore why they matter. The company's values define how they are expected to behave toward each other and toward customers and therefore how they can contribute toward creating and maintaining satisfied customers and a good work environment.

Employees who enjoy their work create satisfied customers; they are unpaid ambassadors promoting the company to their families and friends. Employees who do not enjoy their work create dissatisfied customers; they are paid saboteurs, complaining about the company to anybody who will listen. An environment where work really is worship creates value for all.

The Rights of the Community and the License to Operate

Companies, like people, do not exist in a vacuum. They are surrounded by members of the community, each with their own often overlapping, conflicting agendas and demands, acting as customers, employees, investors, taxpayers, and citizens. In return for allowing the company to go about its business, the community expects the company, through its board decisions, to behave responsibly, though the definition of responsible behavior varies by group and over time. This is what is meant by the "license to operate."

Recognizing externalities

To maintain its license to operate the board must reconcile these different agendas and recognize that what was acceptable in the past might not be in the future. Doing this is made more difficult by the fact that companies do not measure the costs they create that affect society as a whole. Such "externalities" are not recorded in the P&L statement. If society finds itself bearing too many of these external costs, it will redefine the company's license to operate. The failure to preserve the license to operate may put the firm out of business. It is therefore a key responsibility of any board to understand what gives it its current license to operate and how this could be threatened in the future.

When a company grows very rapidly, its activities may increase congestion, pollution, emissions or waste, all of which add costs to the community and damage the environment. Yet the company is not responsible for the costs it has imposed on others or, increasingly, on Mother Nature. As many people have been born in my lifetime as in the history of the planet before I was born and demographers say that the human population will rise by another 40 percent before it starts to decline. This has happened simultaneously with rapid industrialization, so that the industrial footprint of mankind—with all the attendant waste, depletion, pollution, and global warming— has increased exponentially.

As a result natural capital is increasingly scarce, while human and financial capital are in plentiful supply. Good economics requires that the factors of production are brought to bear on the scarcest resources to achieve the best returns. Yet we are still imprisoned in a mindset more appropriate to a time in our history when human resources and financial capital were scarce and nature's bounty was limitless. Gradually, this truth is dawning on us because of impending water crises as a result of retreating glaciers. The disappearance of flora and fauna and the threat posed to the oceans reinforce this realization. We are now beginning to understand that climate change is a real issue that has to be faced. However, we have still to find adequate mechanisms to set prices on the damage caused.

Equally, when companies cut back on employment to save costs, they do not pay for the social costs of people losing their jobs or the emotional costs of being thrown onto the scrapheap. What about companies whose products, while legal, have harmful economic, social or physical side effects? Who pays for these costs? Should Wall Street's investment banks pay for the damage they have created through irresponsible lending and selling of subprime mortgages; or credit card companies for replacing a culture of savings with one of excessive indebtedness? Should casinos pay for the damage they do to families when gamblers lose all they have on one throw? Should alcohol and tobacco companies pay for the medical costs caused by their products? Should companies that bribe and corrupt pay for the long-term social costs they create by bringing the law into disrepute?

Companies that continue to create externalities regardless of the costs risk having their license to operate removed; boards that do not realize this are failing in their fundamental duty. The problem is that we are not measuring the cost of these externalities and so many companies are, in fact, unsustainably profitable and boards are tempted to ignore the issue.

Does this mean that all companies must be made to pay for the externalities they create and account for them in the P&L? Maybe they should, but then who is going to decide what the price is, when it is so difficult to measure the cost impact of such activities? We will revisit the problems of externalities in Chapter 8.

Early-warning radar

The idea of the license to operate acting as the board's early-warning system has great value. At least once a year, boards should look at the environment in which they operate and think about the social and legal changes that are brewing, reflecting the different prices society is willing to pay for the externalities they create.

In nineteenth-century Britain it was accepted that eight-year-olds could work a mile underground in coal mines. Today this is immoral everywhere. Hong Kong was built on the opium trade. Today we spend huge amounts of money trying to destroy the drug cartels. In my lifetime tobacco was cool, symbolizing poise and sexual success. Today it is dangerous to health. Fast food symbolized the dynamism of America. Today it is contentious, accused of contributing to the obesity epidemic spreading around the world. Food-and-beverage companies used to be focused on taste alone; now they need to worry about the impact they have on health.

Consequently it is essential that boards do not take their company's license to operate for granted and that they understand that what defines a responsible relationship with the community in which they operate and with society at large changes over time as understanding increases and standards rise.

Are Shareholders the Most Important Stakeholders?

Company law is clear: boards are answerable to shareholders, which suggests that they are the most important stakeholders. The law defines the firm as an entity subject to private ownership through shares—thus removing it from the social arena and placing it in the economic arena:[16]

> As with all private property, the owner had absolute rights over his/her property as long as the law was obeyed and public order maintained. As a result society was transformed from a society of community to a society of contracts. *Consequently it was argued that it is in the interest of the private owner, as the residual claimant of firm profits, to optimize firm management so as to maximize profits as this enhances overall efficiency.*[17][emphasis added]

Yet, as must be obvious by now, it is possible to imagine a company without shareholders, with finance being provided by banks or trade credit. Many companies choose precisely this way of funding; in particular, SMEs use trade credit and money from family and friends.[18] However, it is not possible to imagine a company without customers—no customers; no business. It is equally difficult to imagine a company without employees, for it is they who create and deliver value for customers and for shareholders.

So why do shareholders feature so prominently in the law? It is because they are uniquely at the mercy of the company, facing total loss when things go wrong; which is why boards have a fiduciary duty to look after shareholder interests. However, this is not the same as arguing that boards must maximize shareholder returns, even though that is precisely the claim being made.[19]

When investors care about company strategy and long-term value creation, they behave more like proprietors, leaving less room for conflict between their objectives and those of the board and management. They understand the need to balance long-term value creation—which requires investment in R&D in new products and processes to create sustainable future income streams and thus makes demands on present cash flows—with the need to deliver short-term profits and dividends. They are willing to defer present shareholder returns for future gain because they will still be shareholders when the long-term benefits materialize. On this basis, the claim for investor primacy makes sense, which is what the International Corporate Governance Network (ICGN)[20] stipulates.[21]

Yet, with notable exceptions such as Warren Buffett, most investors in Anglo-Saxon markets are no longer long-term, loyal holders of stocks. They are more interested in what will happen in the next 90 days than with where the company is going in the next five to 10 years. Net present value (NPV), where the concept of the time value of money gives greater weight to what is happening now than in the future, reinforces this short-term focus, often at the expense of the other key stakeholders. Day-traders do not even care about the next 90 days! Arbitrageurs on the Chicago Board of Exchange make decisions based on the emotions of the moment and their trades affect the prices of shares in the NYSE as short-sellers fail to find buyers (because the buyers as investors need more time to decide than the computer-generated trades allow, this creates conditions such as those that led to the crash in market value of October 1987's Black Monday).[22]

Unfortunately, regulatory requirements to declare quarterly earnings legitimize short-term thinking. Another unintended consequence of "good governance" was the effect of the use of stock options to align management and shareholder objectives. The focus on 90-day earnings combined with stock options caused many CEOs to consider the short-term share price as the critical measure of their effectiveness. As a result, some did whatever was necessary to keep the share price high in the short term, ranging from relatively benign buybacks, using up cash that might have been better invested in sustaining the long-term future of the company, to straightforward fraud. In some part, US failures of governance may be the result of this unintentionally toxic combination of the need to satisfy analysts every 90 days with huge executive bonuses in the form of options, reflecting often artificially boosted share prices.

Maximizing shareholder returns assumes shareholders have the long-term interests of the company at heart. Yet too many shareholders have little interest in, or understanding of, the business purpose of the companies in which they invest. They want maximum returns in a 90-day time horizon, pressurizing boards to sacrifice long-term considerations for short-term demands; to sacrifice employees and harm communities in the interests of shareholder return; and to do whatever it takes to keep the share price high. Because they have no moral compass to tell them that how money is made matters as much as how much money is made, too often top management bow to these pressures. The resulting failures of governance should not really surprise us.

Is Business Ethics an Oxymoron

This lack of ethical foundation is unfortunately reinforced by what is taught at many business schools. Just before he died, Professor Sumatra Ghoshal wrote that business schools had much to answer for because they had taught theories which were mathematically elegant but wrong.[23]

Particularly harmful mental models result from these theories, which, when combined with Taylor and Ford's view of work, go a long way to explaining why being at work is not uplifting for many people and why managers behave unethically. Into this category fall Coase's theory of the firm;[24] Jensen's Agency theory;[25] Williamson's Transaction theory;[26] and Porter's "Five Forces."[27]

Coase's theory

According to Coase, the existence of the firm—what it does, its boundaries—is determined by whether it costs more to do something inside the firm or outside it. This idea recognizes the importance of externalities and argues correctly that firms will do all they can to externalize their costs. At the heart of this idea is a view that all that holds the elements of the firm together are cost-related contracts, as opposed to relationships.

This thinking underpins the view that a firm is a temporary alliance of resources, brought together to get a task done. In other words, the firm is a purely economic instrument. Once the task is completed, the organization is reconfigured to meet the next challenging task. Hence outsourcing, "offshoring" and downsizing come easily to Anglo-Saxon managers.

The problem with this idea is that it totally ignores the social aspect of work: that people value and enjoy the relationships they have with each other. That is where this idea goes wrong, at least for most people in most countries outside the English-speaking world. That is why Malaysians and other Asian communitarian groups find downsizing even more difficult—they respect and value the relationships that make work a social activity as well as an economic and legal one.

Jensen's, Williamson's and Porter's theories

Jensen argued that there is a conflict between the manager acting as agent and the shareholder acting as principal. Managers can be expected to look out for their own interests; and in the 1970s and early 1980s, it was argued that they did so at the expense of shareholders, culminating in the infamous leveraged buyout of RJR-Nabisco in 1989.[28]

This view of the basic conflict between managers and shareholders was reinforced by Williamson's arguments about "bounded rationality" affecting the minimization of transaction costs in the firm.[29] Essentially Williamson made two important points about the nature of the firm. The first was that companies seek to minimize the costs of their transactions and the second was that this is not done as rationally as we might believe. He argued that we need to adjust traditional economic theory as proposed by Coase, for example, to take human nature into account. "Bounded rationality" includes forms of deceit which can be active and passive; ex-ante and ex-post. It covers lying, stealing, and cheating. It recognizes the existence of deliberately incomplete or distorted disclosure of information, the breaking of contracts and renegotiating their terms. In Coase's world, contractual agents accurately disclose information and execute contracts to the letter. Williamson rules out obedience to contracting agents by others, since self-interest is the basis for bargaining.

Williamson's world is a nasty one where people cannot be trusted to do the right thing, whether it is honoring a contract or looking after employees' and shareholders' interests, because they have no real moral sense or moral compass. Combine this with Jensen's view of how managers behave, and it is hardly surprising that business schools began to teach that managers cannot be trusted to do the right thing. The resulting bad joke is that the initials MBA stand for "Morally Bankrupt Agent"—hence the idea that we must do whatever it takes to achieve the desired results.

Porter's contribution to this pernicious mindset comes from his famous "Five Forces" framework, which sees everybody in the value/supply chain in competition with everybody else for market margin. This is a zero-sum, dog-eat-dog mindset, which reinforces the idea that we can expect everybody to work along the lines postulated by Williamson. It ignores the Japanese idea of collaboration across the entire value and supply chain so that one supply chain competes with another, as opposed to competing internally among its members for available market margin. Collaborative supply chains appear to have done better than those that work on the basis of the Five Forces. We only have to compare the fortunes of the Japanese car makers with those of the Americans![30]

Is it possible that Toyota's current problems with quality are the result of them having moved into a more adversarial mode a la Michael Porter with their supply chain as they sought to drive down costs even further with companies they did not treat as partners because they were not part of the original supplier group?

Sadly, as Ghoshal argued, teaching these four frameworks reinforces the mental model that business is a nasty world where nice guys finish last. We need to set the record straight and make the case that business should be based on commonly accepted ethical principles where people are treated with respect.

The Importance of Reconciling Different Agendas

Every dollar of the company's cash flow has competing claims on it. Customers want the lowest prices and best products; employees want the best terms and conditions; investors want maximum returns and banks have to be repaid; and then the taxman wants increased contributions to pay for the government's activities. These demands cannot all be met simultaneously; and yet failure to satisfy them will lead to customers defecting; employees going elsewhere; investors selling shares; banks foreclosing.

It is the job of the board to find the optimum balance between these competing claims so that customers remain loyal, employees stay motivated, investors invest in the stock, banks continue lending and the government is satisfied. Hard though this is, it is still the easiest part of the board's job in protecting its LTO.

Boards must understand that their companies do not exist in a vacuum and that their LTO depends on their ability to reconcile conflicting demands while recognizing the external costs they impose on society. How society prices these externalities changes over time, and a failure to understand this and foresee what could happen will put them out of business.

In these conditions it becomes obvious that boards must do more than just maximize shareholder returns, particularly if the time horizon in question is only 90 days. Yet, in the US at least, CEOs who presided over falling share prices for more than 180 days were often terminated by their boards in the name of the shareholder, and simultaneously rewarded handsomely for their failures, sending very mixed signals to other CEOs and to the community as a whole.

So what should boards do instead?

They must, at a minimum, ensure that they follow the logic of the Johnson & Johnson Credo. They must ensure the company has:

- loyal customers by providing fit-for-purpose products and services, recognizing that customers' needs change over time and that they have choices;
- motivated employees, who believe that "work is worship" so that they create real value through their dedication to their customers and colleagues;
- a long-term LTO so that society does not decide that it no longer wants the products and services provided;
- loyal shareholders who agree with the company's strategic objectives and priorities.

Endnotes

1   See http://www.jnj.com/connect/about-jnj/jnj-credo
2   "Enlightenment Man," *The Economist Technology Quarterly*, December 6, 2008: 27.
3   Collins, J. C. and Porras, J. L. 1991, "Organizational Vision and Visionary Organizations," *California Management Review*, Fall 1991: 47.
4   "In 1898, the first international urban-planning conference convened in New York. It was abandoned after three days, instead of the scheduled 10, because none of the delegates could see any solution to the growing crisis posed by urban horses and their output. The problem did indeed seem intractable. The larger and richer that cities became, the more horses they needed to function. The more horses, the more manure. Writing in the *Times* of London in 1894, one writer estimated that in 50 years every street in London would be buried under nine feet of manure. Moreover, all these horses had to be stabled, which used up ever-larger areas of increasingly valuable land. As the number of horses

grew, ever-more land had to be devoted to producing hay to feed them (rather than producing food for people), and this had to be brought into cities and distributed—by horse-drawn vehicles. It seemed that urban civilization was doomed.

Of course, urban civilization was not buried in manure. The great crisis vanished when millions of horses were replaced by motor vehicles. This was possible because of the ingenuity of inventors and entrepreneurs such as Gottlieb Daimler and Henry Ford, and a system that gave them the freedom to put their ideas into practice. Even more important, however, was the existence of the price mechanism. The problems described earlier meant that the price of horse-drawn transport rose steadily as the cost of feeding and housing horses increased. This created strong incentives for people to find alternatives." See: http://www.thefreemanonline.org/columns/our-economic-past-the-great-horse-manure-crisis-of-1894/#

5 Drucker, P. 1955, *The Practice of Management*, Oxford: Butterworth Heinemann: 35.

6 Berger, S. 2005, *How We Compete: What Companies around the World are Doing to Make it in Today's Economy*, New York: Doubleday.

7 Fukuyama, F. 1995, *Trust: The Social Virtues and the Creation of Prosperity*, New York: Free Press.

8 "Toyota CEO Akio Toyoda's Apology: 'I Take Full Responsibility'; Toyota CEO Responds to Allegations Toyota Was 'Safety Deaf'; Apologizes for Safety Defects Linked to Deaths" by B. Ross, ABC News, February 24, 2010.

9 Liker, J. 2004, *The Toyota Way: 14 Management Principles from the World's Greatest Manufacturer*, New York: McGraw-Hill.

10 Steger, U., and Amann, W. 2008, *Corporate Governance: How to Add Value*, John Wiley and Sons: Chichester: 13.

11 "In 1992 . . . CEOs held 2 percent of the equity of US corporations, today [2003] they own 12 percent, which is one of the most spectacular acts of appropriation in the history of capitalism." Brenner, R. 2003, "Towards the Precipice," *London Review of Books* 25(3), cited in Doogan, K. 2009, *New Capitalism: The Transformation of Work*, Cambridge: Polity Press.

12 "A section 401(k) plan is a type of tax-qualified deferred compensation plan in which an employee can elect to have the employer contribute a portion of his or her cash wages to the plan on a pretax basis." See http://www.irs.gov/taxtopics/tc424.html.

13 http://dictionary.cambridge.org/define.asp?key=15595&dict=CALD

14 Kouzes, J. M., and Posner, B. Z. 2007, *The Leadership Challenge*, 4th Edition, San Francisco: Jossey-Bass: 174.

15 Knowing where they fit in the greater scheme of things makes a big difference to people's sense of purpose and therefore enjoyment in what they do. It is, however, a necessary but not a sufficient condition, as there

are many for whom personal ambition and a personal circumstances matter as well.

16 North, D. C. 1973, *The Rise of the Western World*, Cambridge: Cambridge University Press; Braudel, F. 1985, *La Dynamique du Capitalisme*, Paris: Arthaud.

17 Alchian, A. 1961, *Some Economics of Property*, Santa Monica: Rand Corporation.

18 It should be recognized that the creation of the limited-liability company created a much larger pool of capital, which has allowed us to develop the modern economy much faster, and has also helped finance the growth of global businesses, which in turn have led to "capitalism with Chinese characteristics" taking more than 200 million people out of poverty in China.

19 "*Unlike shareholders, non-shareholding stakeholders may readily compare what they receive from the firm with what they were contractually promised by the firm.* Even where communities lack contracts with the firm, they may readily compare the conduct of the firm with the requirements of the law. Whatever their informational disadvantages with respect to managers, non-shareholding stakeholders may relatively easily identify discrepancies that, in turn, give rise to legally cognizable claims against the firm. In short, *unlike shareholders, non-shareholding stakeholders have complete or near-complete contracts with the firm and it is the completeness of their contracts that obviates the need for fiduciary obligations.*" [emphasis added] Marcoux, A. 2003, "A Fiduciary Argument Against Stakeholder Theory," *Business Ethics Quarterly* 13(1): 18.

20 The ICGN's website (http://www.icgn.org/about/) tells us the following about the organization: "The International Corporate Governance Network (ICGN) is a not-for-profit body founded in 1995 which has evolved into a global membership organization of 450 leaders in corporate governance in 45 countries, with institutional investors representing assets under management of around US$9.5 trillion.

The ICGN's mission is to **raise standards of corporate governance worldwide**. In doing so, the ICGN encourages cross-border dialogue at conferences and influences corporate governance public policy through ICGN Committees. We promote best practice guidance, encourage leadership development and keep our members informed on emerging issues in corporate governance through publications and the ICGN website.

ICGN members include institutional investors, business leaders, policy makers and professional advisors. Our members join from across the world and have a mutual interest in promoting good corporate governance. This enables the ICGN to draw on three unique strengths:

Breadth and expertise which extends across the global capital markets to include senior decision makers and opinion leaders in the practice of corporate governance;

Magnitude of institutional investors who collectively represent funds under management in excess of US$15 trillion, giving a focus on the role of shareholders responsible for the long-term savings of the wider community; and

Geographic diversity with members drawn from every region including Africa, Europe, Latin America, the Middle East, North America, and South and East Asia.

The ICGN incorporated as a company limited by guarantee under the law of England and Wales in January 2008."

21 *"The overriding objective of the corporation should be to optimize over time the returns to its shareholders.* Where other considerations affect this objective, they should be clearly stated and disclosed. To achieve this objective, the corporation should endeavor to ensure the long-term viability of its business and to manage effectively its relationships with stakeholders." [emphasis added] Monks, R. and Minow, N. 2001, *Corporate Governance*, 2nd edition, Oxford: Blackwell Publishers: 255.

22 Bookstaber, R. 2007, *A Demon of Our Design*, John Wiley & Sons: 31.

23 Ghoshal, S. 2005, "Bad Management Theories Are Destroying Good Management Practices," *Academy of Management Learning & Education* 4(1): 75–91.

24 Coase, R. 1937, "The Nature of the Firm," *Economica*.

25 Jensen, M. C. and Meckling, W. H. 1976, "Theory of the Firm: Managerial Behavior, Agency Costs, and Capital Structure," *Journal of Financial Economics*.

26 Williamson, O. 1975, *Markets and Hierarchies: Analysis and Antitrust Implications*, New York: The Free Press: 29–30, 35–7; Williamson, O. 1985, *The Economic Institutions Of Capitalism: Firms, Markets, Relational Contracting*, New York: The Free Press: 44.

27 Porter, M. E. 1980, *Competitive Strategy: Techniques for Analyzing Industries and Competitors*, New York: The Free Press.

28 Burroughs, B. and Helyar, J. 1990, *Barbarians at the Gate*, New York: HarperCollins.

29 Williamson, 1985, op. cit.

30 A respectable defense can be made for US auto manufacturers along the lines that they continued to produce the kinds of cars many Americans wanted to buy and that they stuck by the unions in the rust-belt states, honoring the pension and medical benefits contracts costing an extra US$1,400 per car (see "Detroitosaurus Wrecks," *The Economist*, June 6, 2009: 9). At the same time, it can be argued that the Japanese held their suppliers captive, leaving them with the less-profitable parts of the value chain and the more difficult job of managing the inventory holding costs, all while earning lower wages.

3

THE ROLE OF THE BOARD

This chapter looks at the role of boards in defining the business purpose, its vision and values; and then at the board's six principal functions. It goes on to discuss the levels to which boards should get involved with management, arguing that its approach will depend on the particular circumstances of the company.

We begin by revisiting why we have boards at all. The source of the board's authority comes from the owners of the company. Normally these are the shareholders, but not always, as in the case of cooperatives or other forms of mutual where the employees may be the owners. Ownership structures can be even more complex where there are dominant majority shareholders sitting uncomfortably alongside minority shareholders, as is so often the case in Asia with its plethora of public-listed family firms or enterprises in which the government has a dominant interest.

Investors range from those who have little or no power to those who have a controlling interest in the operations of the company. Moreover, boards have the right to create different classes of ownership with different rights and powers within a given structure. This range of conditions is at its most extreme in Asia, making it that much more difficult for Asian boards to know how best to deliver good CG. Nevertheless, the simple fact is that boards of all types are given their authority to act by the owners, however they are defined.

Boards exist because companies are a legal entity distinct from the people who own and operate them. The reason for this separation is to protect owners from unlimited liability while giving the managers freedom to act. Boards exist when ownership is too dispersed for the owners to manage and direct the company on their own. Boards also exist because family firms go to the market for funding. Sometimes they also go to the market not just for the funds, but for the additional challenge they receive from their boards as a result of having to answer to the market, thus forcing them to the next level of professionalism. This means that the agency problem (discussed in the previous chapter) is a natural symptom of a gap between ownership and stewardship of the assets.

Boards have the authority needed to direct and govern, but with this authority comes accountability to shareholders. The board sits at the top of the chain of command. As a result the board:

- Cannot abdicate its prerogatives and "hand them over" to the Chair or CEO since they are either employees of the board or one of its component parts.
- Must be able to control what it does before it attempts to control anybody else.
- Has authority; it does not merely advise or supervise. It has a specific and definable job with six core responsibilities.
- Is the sole source of company authority so that no group or person, other than the owners, has any authority unless the board has granted it to them.
- Must be more than a reactive final authority lest it allows catastrophic failures of CG to happen on its watch. It should instead be recognized as the highest source of initial authority. The board should initiate rather than respond to the demands and agendas of the CEO and line management.[1]

This means that the board cannot blame the Chair or the CEO or any committee for a breach of CG:

It alone is accountable and so a failure to perform by the Chair, by the CEO, by any committee, or by the company itself, is a failure of the Board. Boards cannot escape from this responsibility, though whenever there have been major failures of CG, the Boards have initially tried to blame the CEO or the CFO rather than admitting that they have failed. Equally it is crucial to remember that boards only have authority as a group; nobody on the board has any authority unless the board has specifically granted it.[2]

This accountability poses a serious operational problem. How should a board empower line management to do its job of running the company and at the same time retain the ability to challenge effectively, without second-guessing management? This is an important question given that the role of boards is to govern and direct, not to manage. If the board over-delegates to the point of abdication it lets the owners down; if it under-delegates in order to control the business, it usurps the rightful role of the managers and still fails the owners as a result. So knowing what to do and getting the balance right between being "hands-off" and "hands-on" is becoming increasingly difficult as more CG codes of increasing complexity are introduced around the world.

This can be translated into board roles in four ways: first, determining and agreeing the purpose of the organization; second, defining the CEO's choices and room to maneuver; third, defining the way the board itself operates; and fourth, how executive power is delegated from the board to the organization through the CEO–board relationship. The last three of these, which are operating issues, will be dealt with in Chapter 5. Here, I will cover the core strategic role of the board: defining why the organization exists by agreeing its purpose.

Agreeing the Organization's Purpose

Regardless of whether an organization is a not-for-profit or driven by the profit motive, the board needs to define and agree on the impact the organization will have on the external environment. These are the effects that explain why they should exist and continue to do so, justifying their existence. They are the criteria by which their effectiveness in making the agreed difference can be measured. Arriving at agreement has three parts:

- Defining who the recipients or beneficiaries of the organization are;
- Determining the impact, difference, change, benefit or outcome to be observed in the lives of the organization's beneficiaries; and
- Agreeing the costs of delivering such desired outcomes to customers, and, as a result, the rates of return that are implied by such activity—such rates of return acting as performance standards by which the effectiveness of the organization is judged.

Another way of discussing the purpose of the organization is to look at what John Carver calls the "Ends" of the organization.

When Carver talks about Ends he does not just mean results. In his view:

> The board must begin from the broadest, most inclusive, and general levels first, and then gradually refine the process as the definition gets narrower. However, beginning with a wide definition of the organization's purpose does not mean that the Ends statement is generic; quite the reverse—the Ends statement must frame what it is that makes the organization unique, through the results the organization seeks to deliver to its specifically defined unique set of customers, and then the value and priorities assigned to the achieved results and the consequent satisfaction of those customers. Ends policies take a great deal of thought and time to develop, as they justify the very existence of the organization. . .
>
> . . . In setting out to define the Ends [it is important to remember] the following points of caution:

1. Do not assume that the existing mission statement serves to define the Ends policies of the firm, because mission statements rarely define precisely who will benefit from the activities of the organization, in what way and at what cost.
2. Defining the Ends will be difficult, because it is not necessarily obvious what benefits should arise from the activities of the organization, or at what cost.
3. Attributes of Ends need to be rigorous. Here the temptation needs to be resisted to confuse activities and intentions with the prescribed results—they are not the same.
4. Do not assume the existing strategic plan is or contains Ends. Plans usually contain goals and objectives and means to achieve them, and that is the point: they are means to achieving the Ends, not the Ends themselves.
5. When developing Ends, do this with a long-term perspective. The board should seek to define what it is the organization is trying to achieve over several years, not just months—and in so doing the board should think carefully about future developments in the needs and profiles of the organization's beneficiaries.[3]
6. Ensure the Ends can in fact be attained. Ends capture the achievements for which the CEO will be held responsible—so the board must find the right and delicate balance between what is easily doable and what is a realistic stretch.

7. Do not let current organizational structures constrain the thinking. Do not allow staffing structures to drive the thinking of the board about the impact the organization should have in the future to justify its existence—organizations must be capable of change if they are to survive in a changing world.

8. Do not let measurement problems get in the way of deciding what should be the Ends of the organization. The problem here is to avoid going for what is measurable, rather than what is meaningful.

9. Expect to find there is information that is needed but not available. [This] approach demands spending a great deal of time understanding what is being asked of the organization: what is doable; who are the prospective beneficiaries, and how should the organization decide between different groups and their priorities; what do the owners really want, and how does the board deal with disagreement between different groups of owners; what are acceptable costs to achieve the Ends envisaged; what are external stakeholders' interests and how do they change over time; and how should the organization respond to these different pressures without losing its sense of purpose?[4]

Setting a broadly defined purpose for the organization is important for a simple reason that I call the "NASA problem." When President Kennedy established NASA, it was given one specific purpose: to put an American on the moon within 10 years. This was very effective, and by focusing the organization on one single-minded objective, the US was able to overtake the USSR in space and indeed put an American on the moon in the designated time. NASA's problem came afterward. What was it supposed to do next? It lost its sense of purpose and direction. So it is important to frame the purpose of the organization sufficiently widely that it does not lose its sense of purpose and direction after achieving a critical milestone on its journey into the future.

The same applies in business. What does Honda do after it has crushed Yamaha—the focus of much of its past purpose? What does Komatsu do after it has stopped Caterpillar? That is why long-term statements of purpose are more generic.

We can say that the key role of any public-listed company is that it must serve an economic purpose, though that is not the same as arguing that the objective of business is to maximize shareholder value. Yet for most public-listed companies, monetary shareholder value is a key reason for existence and, as Peter Drucker argued, this can be best achieved by creating and maintaining loyal customers.[5] In determining how satisfying the Ends are for a business is best measured, we can include other ideas: its return on capital must exceed its risk-adjusted cost of capital; its performance must be ranked against that of its peers; the risks it runs must reflect the risk appetites of its owners; and the board should not change its risk profile without first obtaining the agreement of the shareholders.

A problem arises when there is a conflict between the desires of different groups of shareholders. This happens often in Asia, where many companies are really family firms that have been listed or else are companies where the government has a controlling interest. In these cases, there is a real issue about what the board is trying to achieve, as illustrated in Table 3.1.

On the left-hand side of the table is a generic statement of the aim of a public-listed company that has a truly diversified ownership base, where no single investor dominates the direction and purpose of the firm. This is what John Carver calls a Level 1 statement. Below it are Level 2 statements—qualifying statements—whose role is to define more precisely what Level 1 means and how it is measured.

On the right are equivalent statements for a family firm. As can be seen, the objectives and the ways in which these objectives are

TABLE 3.1 Potential Conflicts in the Firm's Ends

Publicly Traded Company	Family Firm
Level 1: "The ultimate aim of the company is return on shareholder equity better than the return for firms of similar risk characteristics."	**Level 1:** "The overall aim of our company is shared family wealth and work."
Level 2: "Risk characteristics for comparison will include similar size, industry, and maturity of market. Better return will mean above the median for such firms, rather than above the average."	**Level 2:** "Our first priority is that the family stays together, with appropriate, satisfying and rewarding work for every adult member who chooses to be in the company. Our second priority is that the worth of the company, and therefore the worth of each family member's shares, grows at a rate reasonably comparable to indexed funds."

Source: Wallace and Zinkin (2005): 57.

measured are different, leading to divergent expectations and definitions of success. So it is hardly surprising to see that family firms tend to have longer-term time horizons and are never under the 90-day scrutiny that public-listed firms face every quarter. Being listed has its advantages, but it also has drawbacks which many family firms find unacceptable, which is why they do not list.

So when family firms go public they may find themselves facing unexpected internal contradictions as to what their purpose is, illustrated by the divergence between the objectives on the left and the right in Table 3.1. It is these contradictions that lead to so many failures of CG in Asia. Essentially, they are caused by the founding family still behaving as if it owns the whole of the company and feeling that the minority shareholders can be ignored. Too often, the founder CEO forgets that once the company is listed, other people— the minority shareholders—have a right to intervene and affect decisions regarding strategic direction, time horizons, investment, and dividend policy in ways which may not reflect the priorities and preferences of the family. Too often, the lure of cash created by listing, or the added status of being the CEO of a public-listed company, clouds the need to think through the very real constraints the family will have to face in its long-range decision-making.

Not so long ago I was doing a workshop with a successful public-listed company where every variant of these problems was manifested in our discussions. The founders were at loggerheads because each wanted their son to become the next CEO. The nominee directors from two major shareholders had different long-term visions of the company, but agreed on not wanting either son to become the next CEO. The independent non-executive directors (INEDs) were caught in the crossfire.

These internal contradictions and the tensions they create in the board often make the role of the INEDs almost impossible in an Asian context, and we will deal with the resulting behavioral issues in Chapter 4.

Even though a family founder's resentment may poison board dynamics, it is perhaps understandable, particularly if the minority shareholders are day-traders or people who, in the picturesque Hong Kong phrase, "stir fry" shares. After all, the family has the long-term view and, as the majority or controlling shareholders, they have more "skin in the game." Why should they pay attention to shareholders who have no long-term interest in the direction and success of the firm? There is only one answer to this question: once they list the company, they are obliged by regulation to adhere to the principle of "One share, one vote." While we might sympathize with them, they should perhaps have thought of these issues before listing their company.

Companies in which governments have a controlling interest, known in China as state-owned enterprises (SOEs) or in Malaysia and Singapore as government-linked companies (GLCs), pose similar problems for boards. What is the purpose of a company that is controlled by government? Where does the national agenda end? Where do the firm's activities begin? What are the rights of shareholders when the nation has other priorities which are translated into strategies or actions that do not necessarily take into account what minority shareholders want? The government as controlling shareholder has wider objectives than those of a privately held public listed company. It may be interested in national well-being; the creation of an industry and industrial base. It may also be interested in fair prices for its products rather than maximizing profits, because they form an essential part of the nation's industrial development process. Table 3.2 illustrates the potential conflict.

The same concern applies, only more so, in banking; hence the anguish Americans went through as they saw the prospect of large parts of Wall Street being nationalized. Public-listed banks will not lend to firms unless there is a good commercial case for doing so. Government-controlled banks in Asia have sometimes allocated funds to pet projects without due regard for the expected returns, or, worse

TABLE 3.2 Potential Conflicts in the Firm's Ends

Publicly Traded Company	GLC or SOE
Level 1: "The ultimate aim of the company is return on shareholder equity better than the return for firms of similar risk characteristics."	Level 1: "Our objective is to contribute to the well-being of the people and the nation."
Level 2: "Risk characteristics for comparison will include similar size, industry, and maturity of market. Better return will mean above the median for such firms, rather than above the average."	Level 2: "Our first priority is to promote and create business and job opportunities in our industry and provide quality products and services at a fair price. Our second priority is to enlarge the country's industrial base and ensure a clean and safe environment."

Based on Wallace and Zinkin (2005): 57.

still, have propped up "friends" at the taxpayers' expense. Some in Asia might argue that the Wall Street bailouts were not that different.[6]

In these circumstances it is tricky for boards to decide where to draw the line in cases when the government wants a program or project to be started on grounds of the wider public good, even though it hurts profitability. Responsibility for protecting the interests of minority shareholders in an SOE or GLC could put directors into conflict with the objectives of the controlling shareholder.

This potential conflict of purpose makes it all the more important for Asian companies to make explicit what they exist to do and where their priorities lie. Such transparency makes it possible for the company to attract those shareholders whose objectives and risk appetite match those of SOEs or GLCs and family firms. If the objectives are clearly articulated, then buyers of equity will know where they stand and can make informed decisions as a result. The problems of CG only really happen when there is a lack of clarity about the Ends of GLCs and family firms.

Recognizing the importance of this issue, in 2005, the Malaysian government, in the shape of the Putrajaya Committee on GLC High Performance (PCG), published the so-called Green Book to help GLC boards adhere to the standards prescribed by the Malaysian Code. Specifically the Green Book required the composition of the boards to follow what was prescribed by the Code and defined expected board behavior, operations and interactions. More important still, it articulated what the board's responsibilities were as follows:

> . . . Strategy setting, corporate performance management, development of future leaders and human capital, and risk management. Boards need to co-own the corporate strategy with management by being active in the development of the strategy and by setting performance targets. Once the company's goals and target KPIs have been jointly agreed, Boards need to intensify the corporate performance management to ensure that these are achieved. Increasingly, and particularly so for GLCs, Boards need to be more engaged in the development of the company's leadership pool and in the succession, termination and hiring of CEOs. As companies grow in size and complexity, the Board has a bigger task to understand and manage the company's risks. In fulfilling these roles and responsibilities, *the Board should adopt a shareholders' perspective, while balancing all valid stakeholder interests.* (Emphasis added, p. iii.)

Agreeing the Organization's Vision and Values

Once boards have decided on the company's business purpose, they then need to define its vision and values. These are critically important in that they explain how the company sees itself and wishes to be seen when it achieves its business purpose (the role of vision) and how it expects to behave as it does so (the role of values). Both of these should translate into goals that are SMART: specific, measurable, attainable, realistic, and time-bound.

The importance of vision

All companies embark on a journey of some kind, with a destination somewhere in the future. Just as ships need a defined destination to allow navigation, companies also need to identify a destination, recognizing that the route might change as a result of external technological, social or competitive pressures that affect the company along the way. Just as when ships are occasionally buffeted by the waves or blown off track by storm-force winds sailors need to know how to make corrections to get them back on course, so too do boards need the same sense of destination and the ability to get the company back on track should they go off course. This is the role of vision.

The difference between physical navigation and directing a company is that typically the destination for a ship or aircraft has little emotional value. It is a physical place. In the case of companies, it is an emotional place. The company's vision is an emotionally charged call to action: visualizing what success will feel and look like for all members of the organization so that they can go the extra mile to achieve it. It also needs to spell out what failure to achieve that vision will be and feel like.

The other difference between physical navigation and directing a company is that the physical destination is fixed by its geographical coordinates. It does not move. In the case of a company, the destination is often comparative—such as "Being recognized as the best in . . ." In such circumstances, a company's vision is both a destination and a never-ending journey, reflecting the innovations and improvements of competitors who are also trying to improve their standing with key stakeholders. The race still needs to be won, but there is no clear finishing line. Each year, the finishing line moves further from the start as the standards of suppliers and competitors rise and the expectations of customers become more demanding. The role of vision in helping the organization achieve good results, however they are defined, is dealt with in more detail in Chapter 6.

The importance of values

The recent scandals of CG and the financial crisis that started in 2007 are the result of failed values, often referred to as the wrong "Tone at the Top." Wall Street has been found wanting in part because of a culture where top managers were incentivized to take ever bigger risks, putting not just their companies at risk in the medium- to long-term, but the very financial system itself. The other contributing factor was the fact that the models used by the "quants"[7] were too simple, giving inadequate weight to "fat tails"[8] and rare events known as "Black Swans,"[9] whose frequency was underestimated, making it difficult to predict a time when risk in all asset classes became correlated, rather than being entirely uncorrelated, as was originally assumed.[10]

This was not just the result of following the four pernicious mental models discussed earlier in Chapter 2, but also of a culture where there was an excessive emphasis on achieving results, regardless of how this was done. In the US, the creation of financial products that nobody understood and their packaging and distribution to third parties, which lay at the heart of the collapse of confidence in financial institutions around the world, could only happen in an environment where the values of the originators of these products were sorely lacking. They could not care less what happened to the people who bought them without understanding the exposure they faced from doing so.

Such people worked on the "Greater Fool" theory of finance—a type of musical chairs, which is fine as long as the music plays and there is someone else who will pay an increasingly inflated price for products whose value has become disconnected from the underlying reality.[11] This approach was articulated most clearly by Citigroup's Chuck Prince who, in an interview with the *Financial Times*, said: "When the music stops, in terms of liquidity, things will be complicated. But as long as the music is playing, you've got to get up and dance. We're still dancing."[12]

Even if we can argue in his defense that some people knew what they were doing (Goldman Sachs, for example), others did not. Their excuse for their immoral behavior, if they even thought about it, lay in the convenient opt-out of *caveat emptor* or "buyer beware!" A different value system would not have condoned such behavior.

Organizations and managers who focus only on "ends values" without considering "means values" are asking for trouble. If all that matters is getting the job done, people under pressure will cut corners. They will indeed do whatever it takes, without paying attention to the long-term consequences for employees, customers and the community as a whole.

It is, therefore, one of the board's most important roles to determine and define what the values of the organization are, for these set the tone that determines how employees behave toward customers, suppliers and each other. Values will also frame how the organization does business as a whole: what type of business it gets into and whether it behaves responsibly.

The role of values is discussed in further detail in Chapters 6 and 8.

The Six Principal Responsibilities of the Board

All boards have six principal responsibilities to allow them to discharge their stewardship roles, as follows:

1. Reviewing and adopting a strategic plan for the company;
2. Overseeing the conduct of the company's business to evaluate whether the business is being properly managed;
3. Identifying principal risks and ensuring the implementation of appropriate systems to manage these risks;
4. Succession planning, including appointing, training, fixing the compensation of and, where appropriate, replacing senior management;
5. Developing and implementing an investor-relations program or shareholder-communications policy for the company; and
6. Reviewing the adequacy and integrity of the company's internal control systems and management-information systems, including systems for compliance with applicable laws, regulations, rules, directives, and guidelines.[13]

The first two responsibilities are discussed in depth in Chapter 6. The remaining four are the subject of Chapter 7.

How Should Boards Behave?

The answer to this question is that it depends on the type of board and on the state of the company.

Four types of board

Research by IMD,[14] a leading business school, suggests boards fall into four types: "VIP" boards, where the monitoring and controlling function and the advising and coaching functions are low; "Scout" boards, where monitoring and control are still low, but advice and coaching are high; "Watchdog" boards, typical of the US, where trust is low and therefore monitoring and control are high, with little emphasis on advice and coaching; and "Challenger" boards, where great emphasis is placed on both monitoring and control as well as the advice and coaching responsibilities.

The "VIP" board: Perhaps the most common type around the world, here INEDs are chosen from the "great and good" because of their connections and their experience in other fields.

There are two major obvious advantages in this approach: the good connections it creates may help the company get business and preserve its license to operate; and it avoids the perils of "group-think" by bringing together diverse viewpoints based on different experiences to solve problems.

There are also two serious and less-obvious drawbacks. First, in a rapidly changing and hyper-competitive world, variety of experience is no guarantee of its appropriateness. For example, civil servants the world over have little experience of competition. So despite their very real understanding of government, if the company does not deal with government, they may not be the most appropriate people to have on the board.

Second, as the earlier CG failures of Enron, and Swissair, and now Bear Stearns, UBS, Lehman Brothers, and Citigroup, remind us, sometimes it really is critical to understand in detail the technology or the products that the company is offering. In these circumstances being an expert in another field may not be enough to prevent the board being "snowed" by a CEO determined to get his or her way.

The "Scout" board: In some privately held companies, the founder-owner uses board members to help spot trends and challenge the management, while key decisions regarding the allocation of resources and direction are taken by the founder without board involvement. Such boards give advice and act as coaches, but do not monitor or control. As such, this type of board does not really operate according to the principles of the Malaysian Code—but then it does not need to, since it is not publicly listed. The difficulty comes when such companies are listed and founder-owners suddenly find the board is expected to get involved in many more elements of strategy than they are comfortable discussing. This change in circumstances may explain why some SMEs find public listing highlights problems of CG that were not obvious before.

The "Watchdog" board: Arising from the Enron scandal and the US Sarbanes–Oxley Act, this type reflects strongly the view that there is a deep-seated principal–agent conflict and that management cannot be expected to do the right thing by shareholders. It is increasingly common as a result of the recurring failures of CG and will no doubt become even more widespread following the recent failures in Wall Street.

It is low on trust and puts great emphasis on the role of the audit committee and controls. The audit committee is expected to be independent and expert. Where the chairman and the CEO roles are combined, typically such boards will have a senior independent or lead director whose job it is to act as a check on the power of the "imperial CEO" and sack him/her if need be. The lead director is expected to meet on a regular basis with the other independent directors without the CEO present.

The advantages of this type of board are that CEOs cannot become over-powerful, and there are effective mechanisms to terminate a rogue CEO. In theory, cases like Enron cannot recur. Yet in practice none of the recent failures of CG would have been prevented by this type of approach as the board as a whole failed, not just the CEO.

The disadvantages are that it makes speedy decision-making difficult, makes the CEO feel vulnerable, and adds greatly to the cost of doing business.

The "Challenger" board: Combining the best features of both the "Watchdog" and "Scout" boards, they are still very rare. Their dynamics are complicated, even in cultures where constructive challenge is welcomed and conflict is an essential part of progress based on the notion of thesis and antithesis followed by synthesis. They are much more difficult in cultures where conflict is to be avoided and harmony is to be preserved at all costs.

How Involved Should Boards Get?

Just as the type of board which suits a company best is dependent on the company's particular circumstances, so too is the degree to which the board should get involved in running the business. Most codes of governance make it clear that boards govern and direct and do not manage; managing is for the CEO, executive directors, and their line managers to do. They also make it clear that boards are totally accountable for what happens on their watch. So what are boards supposed to do?

When is it Difficult for Boards to Get Involved?

As illustrated in Figure 3.1, IMD's research identified four different situations that affect the board's level of involvement: two focusing on the CEO as the center of decision-making, and two involving a set of checks and balances, either formally or through the need to achieve consensus.

The research suggests small, market-driven firms in fast-moving industries worldwide tend to have dominant CEOs with dependent directors. Equally, family firms and state industries in China, India, ASEAN, Southern Europe, and Latin America are owner-dominated, making it difficult for truly independent directors to get involved in the decision-making process.

In these conditions, typically any early-warning assessment by board members of any changes in the climate of opinion toward the company's activities is done socially, and on an *ad hoc* basis. The board's strategic decision-making tends to occur only after management has already framed the issues, limiting the options to be evaluated by the board. The assessment process tends to be restricted to comparing and contrasting these options and testing them for robustness.

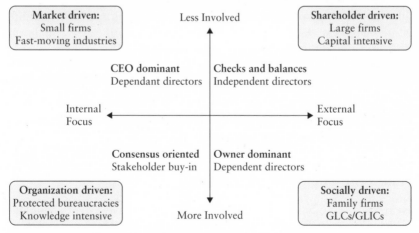

FIGURE 3.1 Effective board governance: Choosing the appropriate model
Source: Steger and Amann (2008): 19.

This may lead to the wrong issues being addressed or to hidden risks in the planning assumptions not being uncovered—as has been the case in the UBS and Swissair failures of CG and perhaps also in Citigroup's recent crisis. Plans typically are presented by management for reactive board approval; very rarely do boards initiate the process. Supervision is via key performance indicators (KPIs) and directors have little hands-on understanding of what is going on. In extreme cases, going to the board is regarded as no more than getting rubber-stamp approval for what line management wanted to do anyway. Certainly such boards will not see it as part of their remit to think the unthinkable and stress test the management's assumptions to see where the company could be at risk of catastrophic failure.

When is it Easy for Boards to Get Involved?

When boards are used as part of a checks-and-balances model, or if the culture requires a consensual approach, boards will get involved in the environmental scanning processes so critical to preserving the company's license to operate.

Such boards are expected to undertake a thorough evaluation of the assumptions underlying any forward planning; to check for fit with the company business model; and to get a fundamental understanding of the risks and consequences of each option. As part of this exercise, some boards may stress test the value chain to see where or how the company could experience failures that could damage its reputation or, in the worst case, lead to total collapse. Such a review must include whether the company has the resources to carry out its ambitions and, if not, where to find them either through acquisitions or collaboration, and the ability to leverage other people's skills—something that Malaysia's Air Asia, for example, has done rather well.

Such boards will supervise using agreed KPIs, but will also ensure that non-executive directors have firsthand experience of the business through personal discussion with line managers during visits to company subsidiaries and branches.

Hands-off, Hands-on or Hands-in?

Nearly every code of governance insists that boards govern, managers manage and boards should not second-guess line management. This implies a "hands-off, eyes-open" style of involvement and most of the time this is the right way for boards to behave.

However, there are conditions when a "hands-on" approach is better. Entrepreneurial start-ups require more involvement from their boards; especially if they are looking to the directors to give them guidance about how to run a company well. They may also be looking to their directors to provide them with the essential connections to win business in the early stages before they have established their reputations.

Companies facing a crisis of confidence, like Citigroup, or else a serious deterioration in their circumstances, like GM before it went bankrupt, cannot afford for their boards to be anything other than "hands-in." In such conditions the board must get involved in all aspects of the business, preferably before it is too late for the company to recover. That includes the hardest task of all, replacing the line management and finding people who can take their place and steer the company out of its troubles.

Conclusion

Boards act on behalf of the owners of the organization. As such, they must remember they are stewards whose prime purpose is to leave the organization in better shape than they found it. Whenever boards have forgotten this cardinal principle, failures of CG have resulted. However, boards can do more than just act as stewards (which suggests that they must follow a preordained direction for the organization)—they can determine a new direction, purpose, and mission as circumstances change.

Endnotes

1 Wallace, P. and Zinkin, J. 2005, *Corporate Governance*, Singapore: John Wiley & Sons: 43–4.
2 Ibid.: 44.
3 Combining points 1–3 with point 5 makes for precise mastery of CG as the first three points drive the board toward detailed specifications which will evolve and, at times, over short periods; while point 5 drives the board toward a longer perspective. There is a risk, however, that the board and the executive management will be whipsawed during volatile periods—such as now.
4 Carver, J. and Carver, M. M. 1997, *Reinventing Your Board*, San Francisco: Jossey-Bass: 139–41, cited in Wallace and Zinkin, op. cit.:48–9.
5 Drucker, P. 1955, *The Practice of Management*, Oxford: Butterworth Heinemann: 35.

6 Sheng, A. 2009, *From Asian Crisis to Global Crisis*, Cambridge: Cambridge University Press.

7 The term given to the mathematicians who were responsible for the financially engineered products that were supposed to be flawless.

8 So called because they show as bigger tails to bell-shaped distribution curves, undermining the assumption that the curve is normally distributed and therefore changing the probabilities of expected outcomes.

9 So called because Europeans originally assumed that all swans were, by definition, white. Of course, they were wrong; Black Swans exist, but outside the limits of their assumptions.

10 Taleb, N. N. 2008, "The Fourth Quadrant: A Map of the Limits of Statistics," an *Edge* Original Essay, 15 September.

11 Lewis, M. 2008, "The End of Wall Street's Boom," Conde Nast Portfolio.com, December.

12 "Citigroup Chief Stays Bullish on Buy-outs," by Michiyo Nakamoto in Tokyo and David Wighton in New York, *Financial Times*, July 9, 2007.

13 Malaysian Code on Corporate Governance 2007: 10.

14 Steger, U. and Amann, W. 2008, *Corporate Governance: How to Add Value*, Chichester: John Wiley and Sons: 19–22.

4

THE ROLE OF BOARD MEMBERS

This chapter looks at board composition and argues that the roles of the Chair and CEO should not be combined, not only because that would represent an excessive concentration of power in the hands of one person, but because the two roles are quite distinct. It then discusses the roles and responsibilities of executive and non-executive directors and explores some of the very real problems independent non-executive directors face in an Asian context, making it difficult for them to be truly independent in the Anglo-Saxon sense.

Board Composition

Most codes of CG stipulate that the Chair and CEO should be separate people. In countries that followed the UK's Revised Combined Code on CG in 2003,[1] nearly all boards of public companies have separated these roles. This applies in Malaysia, Singapore, and Hong Kong.

The UK's Revised Combined Code called for:

1. Separation of the roles of the Chair and CEO. The Chair should satisfy the criteria of independence when being appointed, but, once appointed should no longer be regarded as independent when determining the board's balance between independent and dependent directors.
2. At least half of the board's members to be independent, using the Higgs Report's definition of independence.

3. Candidates for board selection to be drawn from a wider pool of talent.
4. The board, its committees and directors to undergo an annual performance review.
5. At least one member of the audit committee to have recent, relevant financial experience.
6. The Chair to be allowed to also chair the nominations committee, except when it is considering appointing the Chair's successor.

The Revised Malaysian Code of 2007[2] defines how the board should be constructed. Like the UK Combined Code, it stipulates that the roles of Chair and CEO be separated.[3] However, instead of requiring that half of the board consist of independent non-executive directors, it argues for one-third.[4] It also recommends that there should be a lead independent director, whether or not the roles of Chair and CEO are combined.[5] The nominations committee should consist exclusively of non-executives, the majority of whom should be independent.[6] The remunerations committee should be made up mainly or entirely of non-executives.[7] When it comes to the audit committee the Revised Malaysian Code is quite specific, arguing that the committee should consist of at least three people, the majority being independent, and it goes further than the UK's Revised Combined Code by specifying not just that all members must be financially literate, but that one member be a qualified accountant.[8]

Why Separate the Roles of Chair and CEO?

A respectable case can be made for keeping the roles of Chair and CEO in one pair of hands, if all we consider is the question of concentration of power. In France, the roles are combined into one position, that of the President Directeur General. Most companies in the US have a single position. The strongest argument for integrating the roles is probably something along the following lines: "The CEO and the chairman need to be intimately involved in the business, so I believe they should be the same person. If they are not, the chairman would be a figurehead or would usurp the role of the CEO."[9]

Some have argued that combining the two roles leads to speedier decision-making because people have to report to only one person. Yet combining the roles has often led to the creation of an over-powerful individual who dominates the board, makes independent directors ineffective and does not represent shareholder interests. The combined role may mean that the board only looks at an agenda driven by line management's interests, rather than those of the shareholders. As a result the principal–agency conflict discussed in Chapter 1 can become acute. Harold Geneen, a former CEO and Chair of ITT, put it best: "If the board of directors is really there to represent the interests of the stockholders, what is the Chief Executive doing on the Board? Doesn't he have a conflict of interest? He's the professional manager. He cannot represent shareholders and impartially sit in judgment of himself."[10]

Moreover, there are three key tasks that must be undertaken at the top of every public-listed company:

1. Someone must be accountable for running the company—the job of the CEO.[11]
2. Someone must run the board—the job of the Chair.
3. If we follow the thinking in the Revised Malaysian Code, there is a third job—that of Chief Governance Officer (CGO)—and this is done by the senior independent non-executive director, who is equivalent to the US's Lead Director.

In the previous chapter, I argued that the primary responsibility of the board is to determine the organization's purpose. Once this has been decided, it is the responsibility of the CEO to deliver this purpose. The CEO is not empowered by the board to deviate from these Ends. At the same time, it is the responsibility of the board as a whole to set boundaries around what the CEO can do in attaining the Ends.

The Role of the CEO[12]

We'll begin by looking at the role of the CEO, who has the most immediate impact on the organization's operations, if only because the CEO, unlike the board, has complete access to all the facts.

The CEO is answerable to the board and in carrying out his/her responsibilities will sometimes work with the board and sometimes without the board.

CEO: Answerable to the board

The board's authority granted to executive management is delegated through the CEO, who alone has the authority to implement agreed policies and is solely accountable to the board for achieving the organization's agreed Ends, while staying within the boundaries or executive limitations placed on him/her in fulfilling this role. Typically, this means that the CEO is tasked by the board **not to do anything**:

- Without taking into account the effect on long-term shareholder value of the consequences of health, safety, and environmental actions, political actions, and financing strategies.
- That is likely to cause the company to become financially distressed when adopting a financing strategy.[13]
- That could substitute personal risk preferences for those of shareholders as a whole when managing the company's risks.[14]
- To allow the company's assets to be inadequately maintained, unnecessarily put at risk, or to remain unprotected.[15]
- That subjects employees or subcontracted parties to undignified, inequitable, unfair, unsafe treatment or conditions.
- That is illegal, unfair, unjust, dishonest, or involves coercion or physical violence.
- That permits payments or rewards to be given unless they are in return for contributions toward achieving agreed board goals and are, at the same time, proportionate to their role in achieving such goals.

In addition, the CEO must report to the board at each board meeting and advise the board in a timely manner on issues that affect the organization's purpose, including:

- Any matters that materially affect company performance, in particular any potential strategic or political development that could affect the firm's license to operate.
- Recommending appropriate actions to deal with underperforming businesses or activities of the company.
- Any material issues that affect or could affect shareholders and the markets in which shareholders' interests are traded.
- Succession planning and talent-management programs to ensure continuity of purpose and appropriate organizational design to deliver what has been agreed.
- The effectiveness of the organization and management in implementing agreed strategy and tactics against suitable KPIs and benchmarks.

CEO: Working with the board

Working with the board, the CEO is responsible for setting the direction of the company; articulating the values of the organization; allocating resources appropriately, including succession planning; making informed decisions; and ensuring effective risk management.

Setting direction

This requires the CEO to define the company's mission and vision in a compelling way to the employees, making clear what success and failure will feel like. This call to action must appeal not just to reason but to emotions as well and must take into account the differing perspectives the internal stakeholders of the organization may have about the direction being set. As well as ensuring that there is emotional commitment to achieving the organization's goals, the CEO must align these goals with the company's values. Only where there is coherence, convergence, and alignment will the organization be able to achieve the goals set by the board.

When companies decide what business they will be in and which businesses they will avoid, these decisions are often made on purely financial grounds. Yet the most important strategic decisions are, in the end, ones of morality and integrity. Companies consist of people; and so one of the most important responsibilities of any CEO is to ensure that the people in the company are proud of what they do every day. Employees who are secretly ashamed of what their company does will demand higher pay for the same results; they will need to be compensated for what they do, because in their heart of hearts they will not want to do it.[16] They will be embarrassed when they have to explain to family and friends what the company does. Nobody wants to work for a company that regularly breaks the law, or damages the environment or makes unsafe products. On the other hand, when they are proud of what the company does, they will be great ambassadors for everything the company stands for. They will not look to be compensated, but to be rewarded and recognized for the great things they do for the company and society at large—and such rewards and recognition are not necessarily financial.

Articulating the values

The CEO is responsible for articulating the organization's values, the moral compass by which the employees determine how they should behave toward each other and to external stakeholders. Properly articulated, values translate into measurable performance and desired observable behavior that is reflected in the organization's KPIs. This allows employees and others to judge whether they are being true to the value of the organizational brand and what it stands for. As a result, they will know whether they are behaving in accordance with customer expectations.

CEOs must be able not just to articulate the values by which the company is to be judged, but to live by them. Such values define whether there is honesty in dealings, respect for other people's point of view, and a sense of responsibility and accountability to both the company and the community within which it operates. Often these are enshrined in corporate codes of conduct; but to bring them to life, it is essential that the right tone is set by those at the top. There is little sense in having codes of conduct if top management flout those codes and by their behavior prove themselves to be hypocrites and liars. Where there are no proper values, people will focus on the ends and ignore the means by which they are achieved. They will cut corners and put the safety of both employees and customers at risk. They will justify unacceptable working conditions on grounds that the bottom line demands them.

Allocating resources

The CEO is responsible for allocating resources appropriately to ensure that the strategy agreed by the board can be implemented. This means deploying people, cash and technology as required. Perhaps the most important of these is ensuring that there is a proper talent pipeline and that a systematic succession plan is in place. With the right people and mix of skills, anything can be achieved; with the wrong people and skills, it hardly matters whether the organization has enough of the other resources.

Effective succession planning and talent management are designed to prevent discontinuities in strategic direction, lapses in adherence to values and failures in implementation of the company's plans. In a rapidly changing and increasingly competitive world, the assumptions about how employees should think and what they need to know cannot be taken for granted. Succession planning recognizes that the skills and resources of today may not be suitable for the needs of tomorrow.

There are two other roles of the CEO working with the board—*making informed decisions* and *ensuring effective risk management*—that are so crucial that they are dealt with separately and in detail in Chapters 5 and 6, respectively.

CEO: *Working without the board, once authority has been delegated*

Working alone with the authority delegated by the board, the CEO must define performance, ensure the company's reputation is protected, represent the organizational brand to all employees, and create an integrated communication for all stakeholders.

Defining performance

It is the job of the CEO to agree with line management on the KPIs of the business. Many of these will be financial: margins, returns on assets, levels of working capital, debt-to-equity ratios, and so on. However, financials are lagging indicators, measuring the past. What is also needed are leading indicators that can provide useful early warning of potential trouble to come.

This need for both leading and lagging indicators is what underlies the idea of Balanced Scorecards. Moreover, with the rise of NGOs and the corporate responsibility agenda, CEOs now also have to worry about "triple bottom line" reporting.

In addition, as we learn more about what builds great, differentiated brands, CEOs must understand the critical moments of truth that enable organizations to deliver their brand promise and what to do should things go wrong. Standards of expected performance, reflecting the values of the company, must be agreed and measured for such moments so employees know what is expected when they try to deliver value to customers.[17] Chapter 7 deals with these issues in greater detail.

Protecting the company's reputation

This is about ensuring that the key elements of the brand promise made by the company to its internal and external stakeholders are coherent and consistent:

Internal stakeholders: Employees are the people who make everything happen; they deliver the brand promise to external stakeholders. Therefore the CEO must be able to represent what the organizational brand and its values stand for and how this translates into everyday behavior. In doing this, the CEO must be a clear role model. As a leader, the CEO must be able to communicate to employees what makes the organization special, and explain to them where they fit in delivering the vision. To do this effectively requires clear communication of what the organizational brand stands for, reinforcing coherence and internal consistency in objectives and between the different strategies it adopts to prevent employees becoming confused and embittered as a result.

External stakeholders: The policies adopted by the company, the products it offers, the people it uses to sell and deliver them to its customers, the promotion, the pricing, and the distribution methods used must all reinforce the positioning designated for the company and its products. Only the CEO has the authority to ensure this happens.

Representing the brand to employees

The task of the CEO is to give employees reasons to do what the organization expects of them. This requires an ability to create consensus regarding the big picture: the context in which the organization finds itself; the externally driven need for change; its urgency; what will happen if change is not implemented; and the likely success if change is undertaken effectively. In articulating these points, the CEO must also make clear where employees fit in; how the proposed changes are likely to affect their responsibilities, reporting relationships and new skills; what they are expected to do and how they will be measured in the future, given the new performance standards brought about by such change. In doing this, the CEO must not simply convince employees of the inevitability and desirability of such change, but must also generate sufficient passion and enthusiasm to get them to believe in a successful outcome, enabling them to be their best.

Creating integrated communication

Companies have multiple audiences: employees, customers, investors, analysts, media, suppliers, unions, regulators, legislators, civil society (principally NGOs), and the community at large.

Each of these groups is only interested in subjects that affect them. Yet all the messages the company broadcasts must somehow reflect an integrated approach so that there is no dissonance, no confusion about what the company is doing and stands for. The CEO is responsible for ensuring that there is an integrated communication architecture that reinforces the integrity and unity of the messages. This is all the more important if the company is changing its strategy, or if its license to operate is under threat as a result of social, legislative or regulatory changes.

The Role of the Chair[18]

It is the role of the Chair to manage the board's own governance process issues and the way in which it interacts with the CEO. This is a different set of responsibilities, which can only be carried out really effectively if there is no conflict of interest—hence the need for a separation of roles.

The Chair is responsible for representing the board to the shareholders and is also in charge of ensuring the integrity and effectiveness of the board governance processes, as well as the quality of the board–CEO relationship. These are three distinct roles.

Ensuring board effectiveness

The Chair is responsible for leading the board and ensuring it has effective governance policies. To do this, the Chair:

Leads the board in defining the values and standards the company will adhere to. An effective Chair creates a climate of trust between executive and non-executive directors, allowing the non-executives to contribute in board meetings in a professional atmosphere of constructive challenge.

Promotes the highest standards of CG, requiring, at a minimum, compliance with the provisions of the relevant code(s), upholding the highest standards of probity and integrity.

Is open to ideas and able to explain the company's actions and intentions. There is also a need for a balanced approach, where the consequences of decisions on all those who are affected have been carefully weighed up, as has the need for balance between present and future company needs.

Sets the board agenda, after consulting with the CEO and company secretary, taking into account the issues and concerns of all board members. To be effective, the Chair must propose forward-looking agendas, concentrating on strategic issues rather than going over proposals that are the province of line management and, in the worst cases, second-guessing the CEO. (Too many boards spend too much time discussing the numbers, which are inward-looking and focus attention on the past, instead of thinking about the future and the external environmental changes that pose threats to existing ways of doing business and provide opportunities for new ways of doing business).

Manages the business of the board by allowing sufficient time for discussion of difficult and sometimes contentious issues. If necessary, the Chair may arrange informal meetings beforehand so that non-executive directors can be thoroughly prepared without being pressured by unrealistic deadlines into making poor decisions.

Ensures the provision of accurate, timely, and clear information to help directors make informed decisions.

Acts as a facilitator by setting the style and tone of the meetings to ensure that no member dominates the discussion; that full discussion takes place and divergent opinions are drawn out to promote constructive debate. In this way the Chair can make sure that the outcome of discussions provides the CEO with logical and coherent policy that has been tested in discussion for the robustness of its assumptions. Consensus is essential and so the Chair may, when necessary, call for a vote.

Is able to see the big picture and have the ability to integrate, "to pull together the different threads of a complex issue, so that it acquires coherence. The skills of management are becoming increasingly specialized and so the fields of experience of directors are tending to become narrower. As a result, their approach to issues is likely to be determined in fair measure by their particular expertise. Chairmen, however, have to see the business as a whole, in the context of its environment, and be able to integrate the skills and perceptions of those seated around the board table."[19]

Has the authority to make decisions, establish policies, take action, or enter obligations within board governance policies as they affect the board governance process.

Takes the lead in identifying and helping with the development needs of individual directors and of the board as a whole to make sure that they work well as a team.

Builds an effective board with complementary skills, initiating change and succession plans in board appointments—subject to the approval of the board and the shareholders.

Arranges annual performance evaluation of the board, its committees, and the directors.

Ensures effective implementation of board decisions by providing appropriate documentation of what was agreed and ensuring that it is followed up at regular intervals.

Perhaps Sir Adrian Cadbury's words summarize best what makes for an effective Chair:

> The Chairman's place in all this does perhaps come nearest to that of the conductor of an orchestra; thus it is appropriate to close with Sir Ralph Vaughan Williams' words: "All their art and skill are valueless without that corporate imagination which distinguishes the orchestra from a fortuitous collection of players . . . it is for chairmen to capture that corporate imagination."[20]

Communicating with shareholders

The Chair is responsible for effective communication with shareholders and must act as a two-way bridge, representing the shareholders' interests back to the board so they understand the views of major investors, in particular the institutions. The Chair does this by:

Representing the company to its many publics and understanding their views and priorities. It helps greatly if the Chair and the CEO are open and even-handed in their dealings with the outside world. Companies should provide the maximum information possible and make it equally available to all who have a right to have it. If there are several spokespersons, they should ensure that they speak with one voice, following the same line, demonstrating to investors that they are confident and in control.[21]

Ensuring systematic contact with shareholders. Chairmen report to shareholders twice yearly in writing. At the AGM, they meet those who choose to attend face-to-face. They should use this occasion to encourage shareholders to ask questions, rather than priding themselves on the speed with which the meeting is concluded, because "... such questions give chairmen a feel for the issues which are on the mind of shareholders and in answering them they have the chance to put forward the company's point of view, persuasively and in a public forum."[22]

Ensuring board–CEO linkage. First of all, the Chair must create a close relationship of trust with the CEO, providing support and advice when needed. This must be done without usurping the executive responsibility that lies with the CEO. Then the Chair is responsible on a continuous basis for ensuring that the board is monitoring the performance of the CEO, and for advising and coaching the CEO regarding any performance shortfalls. Should these prove to be serious and insoluble, the Chair then has the duty to find a replacement, ensuring that the CEO leaves either voluntarily through resignation or involuntarily through termination. The Chair does this in conjunction with the Nomination Committee, if there is one.

At the same time, it is the Chair's job to ensure that the CEO is fulfilling the obligation to the board with regard to succession planning so that there is a deep enough bench of talented and experienced candidates waiting to replace him/her should there be an emergency, as well as a long-term succession plan. If the company is faced with a succession crisis because of the sudden departure of the CEO, for whatever reason, it is the Chair's job to find a good replacement in conjunction with the Nomination Committee.

The Role of the Chair: An Important Caveat

In Asia there are a couple of difficulties with the role of the Chair. In many instances the Chair and the CEO are members of the same family—the founders of the business. In such circumstances, even in the most egalitarian and independent of cultures, it is difficult to argue that the Chair will be truly independent or that the CEO, as the offspring of the Chair, will find it easy to exercise effective authority without being undermined in the presence of the patriarch on the board. Directors on the board are faced with a real dilemma if there is disagreement on the direction and priorities and how to reconcile these with the family's interests and those of the shareholders. This is made even more acute if the family still has a controlling bloc of shares and patriarch and offspring cannot agree on what should happen.

Often the justification for keeping the founder as the Chair, or indeed having a retiring CEO stay on as the Chair, is the wealth of experience and understanding they have of the business, which could be used in helping the new CEO learn the ropes and avoid costly errors. Yet, all too often, this undermines the effectiveness of the new CEO, as directors may experience divided loyalties. This is a real problem in the case of founders but, as Rick Thoman experienced when he succeeded Paul Allaire as CEO of Xerox, with the latter staying on as Chair it is a potential issue in any company.[23]

Both Sir Adrian Cadbury and Walter Wriston, former CEO of Citicorp, argue against keeping the previous CEO on the board as follows:

Sir Adrian Cadbury: "I personally favor CEOs making a clean break with their companies on retirement. I would like to see this become the accepted practice with the possibility of a consultancy as an exception . . . I am skeptical of the real value to a company of past experience, however vast."

Walter Wriston: "One reason for mandatory retirement is to assure the corporation of fresh leadership to meet changing conditions. If the new leadership wants to consult the old, no corporate structure is necessary: if consultation is not desired, no corporate arrangement will assure it. On the other hand, if the new CEO wants to get moving with his or her agenda, a board seat occupied by the retired CEO may be seen as an impediment to getting on with the job, particularly if new management feel that radical measures are called for."[24]

If the incoming CEO needs advice from the outgoing CEO, he/she can always ask for it. The key point is that the incoming CEO should be the one to seek advice rather than the outgoing CEO being the one to offer it.[25]

Having a former CEO on the board, let alone in the Chair, imposes too serious a constraint on the new CEO, particularly in much of Asia, where there is a tradition of deference to elders. The problem becomes even more acute—especially in Confucian societies—when the elder is in fact the father of the CEO.

The Role of the Lead Director

The Lead Director is not responsible for managing the board and the board agenda—those remain the province of the Chair. The Lead Director is expected to attend meetings with shareholders and to report back on their concerns and priorities to the non-executive directors. In cases of failure of the CEO, and in particular the Chair-CEO, to perform, it is the job of the Lead Director to act on behalf of the shareholders by obtaining the agreement of the non-executive directors that there is a problem and persuading the Chair-CEO to resign. When the resignation has been received, it is the Lead Director's job to find a replacement.

In short, the Lead Director's role is to act as an independent Chair would in dealing with a problem CEO. In addition the Lead Director is expected to chair meetings of independent non-executive directors in the absence of the independent Chair, if there is one. The Lead Director can also act as a back channel for shareholders if they are worried that their channel of communications through the Chair or CEO is not working well.

The Role of Independent Non-Executive Directors (INEDs)

INEDs have four primary roles: they challenge constructively and thus contribute to the development of strategy;[26] they scrutinize the performance of management in meeting the company's agreed goals and objectives and monitor the reporting of such performance; they must satisfy themselves that the financial information is accurate and the system of controls in place to manage risk is robust; and they are responsible for ensuring that executive directors are appropriately rewarded and, as part of this exercise, they are also key players in the appointment and removal of senior management, including the CEO.

It is widely acknowledged that perhaps the hardest thing for INEDs to do is to get the balance right between helping develop strategy and reviewing performance: "An overemphasis on monitoring and control risks non-executive directors seeing themselves, and being seen, as an alien policing influence detached from the rest of the board. An overemphasis on strategy risks non-executive directors becoming too close to executive management, undermining shareholder confidence in the effectiveness of board governance."[27]

Getting the balance right depends also on the type of board on which they serve (see Chapter 2). Their choice will affect the level of trust and collaboration in board meetings.

To succeed, INEDs must try to create a spirit of partnership and mutual respect with the executive directors, which will then allow them to focus on behavior and relationships as much as on structure, process and content.

INEDs are expected to support and challenge the top management team, showing in the process that they have sound judgment, high integrity and sufficient independence of spirit to question and probe, and sufficient maturity and tact to do this in a constructive and unthreatening manner. They also must demonstrate willingness to persevere in probing when they are not satisfied with, or do not understand, the answers they are being given. Too many of the recent failures of CG have been the result of boards allowing their companies to enter into activities whose risks were incompletely understood. This need to understand exactly the implications of decisions brought to the board is greater than ever, as business becomes more specialized and sophisticated. The failures of Bear Stearns, Lehman Brothers, Fannie Mae, and Freddie Mac and the problems experienced by UBS, Merrill Lynch, Citigroup, and AIG are not just failures of their CEOs alone, but also of the INEDs who did not challenge effectively and so allowed the companies to be placed in mortal danger.

Challenging the received wisdom of so-called expert line managers requires "sufficient strength of character to seek and obtain full and satisfactory answers within the collegiate environment of the board. The objectivity and fresh perspective acquired through their relative distance from day-to-day matters, combined with experience acquired elsewhere, is the basis for questioning and challenging the accepted thinking of the executive."[28]

There are few INEDs who are willing to appear ignorant or, worse, party-poopers when all seems to be going so well. Yet, that is exactly what they are expected to do, while maintaining their personal credibility and their ability to get on with the other members of the board. It is truly a difficult job.

Perhaps it is even harder for those INEDs who sit on the remuneration committee. They may be conflicted. On the one hand, shareholders expect them to ensure that the company pays the CEO the minimum to do the job well; on the other hand, they know that if they are generous, their backs will be scratched in return, either directly by the CEO who may also be an INED on a board of which they are CEO, or indirectly through the general inflation of CEO salaries that has taken place under the guidance of compensation and benefit consultants and headhunters, who have every interest in seeing the levels of CEO remuneration rise, at the expense of the shareholder.

In the past in the US, "imperial" CEOs gave short shrift to INEDs who showed true independence of spirit. This problem continues in much of Asia where such CEOs still exist, either as the founders of the firm or members of the founding family. It is made worse still in cultures that are deferential, where challenges are seen as an attack on established authority and are therefore regarded as illegitimate attempts to undermine the CEO, rather than as legitimate attempts to achieve greater clarity through genuine enquiry and discussion. How are INEDs who have grown up to respect elders or seniors to probe and challenge when they are acculturated to believe such behavior is wrong?[29] How are they to ferret out the information they need to make independent, informed judgments when the culture in many Asian countries is that information is power to be hoarded by the person who has it? How are they to argue their case forcefully when such behavior is regarded as the height of bad manners in a society that abhors confrontation and conflict, regarding harmony as a condition to be preserved above all? How do they maintain the true independence of spirit required by the Anglo-Saxon approach to CG when they feel that they are beholden to the CEO who has invited them on to the board?[30]

There are seven circumstances that could undermine the real or perceived independence of an INED—where he/she:

- has been an employee within a defined number of years (this depends on the jurisdiction);
- has a material business relationship with the company directly, or indirectly as a partner, shareholder, director or senior employee of an organization that has a material relationship with the company;
- receives remuneration in addition to a fee from the company, or participates in company-based options or performance-related schemes, or is a member of the company pension scheme;
- has close family ties with members of the company (advisors, directors or senior managers) that could cloud independence of judgment;
- holds cross-directorships or has significant links with other directors through involvement in other companies or bodies;
- represents a significant shareholder—either family or government entities, including state pension funds;
- has been on the board for more than 10 years.

Important as these tests might be, what really matters is independence of mind and action. If these are missing, the existence of directors on the board who are technically independent achieves nothing.

Even if codes are not very effective at guaranteeing independence of thought and action, they are good at spelling out the duties of a director, which can be divided into primary and secondary duties, as shown in Table 4.1.

TABLE 4.1 Duties of a Director

Primary Duties	Secondary Duties
Look after the company's best interests as a whole, that is to:	Ensure the quality of company information where a director must:
Act in good faith in the best interest of the company as a whole.	Take all reasonable steps to ensure that the board is doing what is necessary to prevent the falsification of accounting records.
Exercise the level of care, skill and diligence that can reasonably be expected from people of that level of ability and experience.	Provide proper explanations to the external auditor to help them interpret the information correctly.
Exercise the powers granted by the company's constitution for a "proper purpose."	Make sure that any overseas documentation is properly recorded.

Primary Duties	Secondary Duties
Refrain from or preventing any act that would adversely affect decision-making concerning the company.	Check the accuracy and completeness of any statements that are made by the company or in respect of the documents that are required by the relevant companies legislation.
Avoid conflicts of interest.	
Keep records where the director must:	Ensure that the financial statements comply with the appropriate financial reporting standards.
Ensure that proper accounting records are maintained to explain the transactions and financial position of the company.	
	Ensure that these financial statements are audited whenever audits are required.
Ensure that adequate measures are in place to prevent and detect false accounting records.	Provide documentation where a director must ensure that:
Prepare and issue the annual report, including audited financial statements presented at the AGM held within six months after the financial year-end.	Shareholders receive a copy of the annual report or the financial statements at least a set number of working days before the AGM.
Ensure that the financial statements comply with applicable approved accounting standards.	The annual return is filed with the Registrar within the time required.
Avoid conflicts of interest where a director must:	The following documents are available for inspection by the public: certificate of incorporation, constitution of the company, share register, register of directors, and address for servicing documents.
Declare fully to the board all dealings in shares of the company.	
Record material-relevant interests in any transaction in the interests register.	Ensure that shareholders can inspect shareholders' minutes, written communications to shareholders, and directors' certificates, and the interests register.
Avoid improper use of position, or use of any information obtained through that position, for personal gain or to harm the company.	
Ensure that his/her remuneration is fair to the company.	Deal with the Registrar to ensure that the board:
Deal with shareholders where a director must:	Notifies the Registrar of any changes to the constitution, issue of shares, acquisition of own shares or changes in the directors.
Determine and certify what is fair and reasonable consideration for the issue of shares or repurchase of shares on issue.	Delivers a copy of the share certificate to the Registrar, having certified that the consideration for a share, option, or convertible securities or financial assistance is fair and reasonable.

(*continued*)

TABLE 4.1 (*continued*)

Primary Duties	Secondary Duties
Respond appropriately to a written shareholder request for information held by the company.	Signs a certificate stating that the solvency test has been met when voting in favor of a distribution or provision of financial assistance to buy the company's shares.
Ensure the company does not carry out business in a manner that harms the creditors and shareholders.	Records in the interest register any relevant interest in the shares issued by the company or any interest in any transaction or proposed transaction involving the company, having previously notified the board.
Maintain the company's solvency and reputation by ensuring that the company does not incur an obligation unless there are reasonable grounds to believe it can meet it.	
Fulfill specific duties in the event of takeovers.	

Source: Wallace and Zinkin (2005): 263–5.

When people are approached to become directors, it makes sense for them to check what the obligations and liabilities of a director are, as shown in Table 4.2.

TABLE 4.2 Director's Obligations and Liabilities

Obligations	Liabilities
Directors are obliged to:	Directors may be liable if they:
Act honestly and in good faith in the best interest of the company.	Fraudulently take, apply, conceal or destroy any property of the company.
Act in accordance with their fiduciary duties. They must comply with the spirit as well as the letter of the law and remember that being a director requires high ethical and moral standards of behavior.	Falsify, destroy, alter or mutilate any company record with the intent to defraud or deceive.
	Knowingly are parties to the carrying on of any business of the company in a reckless manner.
Carry out their duties in a lawful manner and use reasonable endeavors to ensure that the company conducts its business in accordance with the law and a high standard of commercial morality.	Induce a person to give credit to the company through fraud or false pretences.
	Knowingly are parties to the carrying on of any business of the company with the intent to defraud creditors of the company.
	Are involved in "insider trading."
	Fail to ensure that the financial statements are:

Obligations	Liabilities
Be diligent, attend Board meetings and devote enough time to remain familiar with the nature of the company's business and context, including the political, legal, and social framework within which it operates. Directors should be aware of the statutory and regulatory requirements that affect the company.	Audited when an audit is required. In compliance with applicable financial reporting standards. Lodged with the relevant Registrar within the statutorily established timeframe in the company's country of incorporation.
Avoid all conflicts of interest wherever possible. Where a conflict arises, they must adhere scrupulously to the procedures provided by the law and the constitution of the company for dealing with conflicts. If there is a continuing or material conflict of interest, the director should consider resigning and should take into account the effects of resignation on remaining members of the board and on shareholders.	As members of the Board: Do not allow the auditor to attend shareholders' meetings or to address the shareholders on any part of the meeting business that concerns the role of the auditor. Fail to notify each shareholder that financial assistance has been given to another person to acquire shares in the company.
Observe the confidentiality of non-public information they possess as directors and not disclose it without prior agreement from the board.	Directors are also liable when the company does not: Provide shareholders on request with a statement of rights with regard to their holding and how these rights relate to other classes of shares.
Disclose confidential information only with the authority of the board (this concerns a nominee director, or any other director who has a special relationship to a particular shareholder or group of shareholders).	Register a shareholder unless the Board has resolved otherwise.
Ensure that listed companies have in place an approved procedure for buying and selling shares or securities in the company by directors, their relatives, and associates. Directors should not indulge in "insider trading" and should notify the board in advance of any intended transaction by them, their relatives, and associates.	Directors may be criminally liable if the company: Pollutes, unlawfully disposes of trade waste, or leaks, spills, or releases harmful substances. Fails to provide a safe working environment with adequate emergency procedures. Does not maintain an accurate record of accidents and fails to notify the relevant authorities.

(*continued*)

TABLE 4.2 (*continued*)

Obligations	Liabilities
Ensure that all shareholders or classes of shareholder are treated fairly according to their different rights.	Manufactures, stores, supplies, transfers, sells, or uses dangerous goods without a license or other than in accordance with specified conditions.
	Delays in reporting or fails to report an accident involving dangerous goods.
	Engages in misleading, deceptive, or unconscionable conduct, or makes false representation regarding its products.
	Supplies goods which do not comply with product safety and information standards.
	Accepts payment for goods when there are reasonable grounds to believe it will not be able to supply the goods in question.

Source: Wallace and Zinkin (2005): 267–70.

It also makes sense to have a checklist of questions to ask (see Appendix C) and, depending on the quality of the answers, only then decide whether it makes sense to join or remain on the board.

Endnotes

1 The Revised Combined Code on Corporate Governance (at: http://www.fsa.gov.uk/pubs/ukla/lr) incorporates the thinking of the 1992 Cadbury "Report of the Committee on the Financial Aspects of Corporate Governance" and the previous 1998 "Combined Code on Corporate Governance" (http://www.fsa.gov.uk/pubs/ukla/lr). The 1998 Combined Code included the recommendations of the 1995 "Directors Remuneration: Report of a Study Group Chaired by Sir Richard Greenbury" (London: Gee); the 1998 Hampel Report "Committee on Corporate Governance: Final Report" (London: Gee); and the 2003 Higgs Report "Review of the Role and Effectiveness of Non-executive Directors" (London: The Department of Trade and Industry).

2 Revised Malaysian Code on Corporate Governance, www.sc.com.my/eng/html/cg/cg2007.pdf, visited on February 1, 2009.

3 Ibid.: 10: "There should be a clearly accepted division of responsibilities at the head of the company which will ensure a balance of power and

authority, such that no one individual has unfettered powers of decision. Where the roles are combined there should be a strong independent element on the board. A decision to combine the roles of chairman and chief executive officer should be publicly explained."

4 Ibid.: "Non-executive directors should be persons of caliber, credibility and have the necessary skill and experience to bring an independent judgment to bear on the issues of strategy, performance and resources, including key appointments and standards of conduct. To be effective, independent non-executive directors should make up at least one-third of the board membership."

5 Ibid.: 11: "Whether or not the role of chairman and chief executive officer are combined, the board should identify a senior independent non-executive director in the annual report to whom concerns may be conveyed."

6 Ibid.: "The board of every company should appoint a committee of directors composed exclusively of non-executive directors, a majority of whom are independent, with the responsibility for proposing new nominees to the board and for assessing directors on an ongoing basis."

7 Ibid.: 14: "Boards should appoint remuneration committees, consisting wholly or mainly of non-executive directors, to recommend to the board the remuneration of the executive directors in all its forms, drawing from outside advice as necessary."

8 Ibid.: "The board should establish an audit committee comprising at least three members, a majority of whom are independent. All members of the audit committee should be non-executive directors . . . All members of the audit committee should be financially literate and at least one should be a member of an accounting association or body."

9 Monks, R. and Minow, N. 2001, *Corporate Governance,* 2nd edition, Oxford: Blackwell Business: 175, cited in Wallace, P. and Zinkin, J. 2005, *Corporate Governance,* Singapore: John Wiley & Sons: 98.

10 Ibid.: 99.

11 Ibid.: 98.

12 This section is based on Wallace and Zinkin 2005, op. cit.: 107–14.

13 Royal Bank of Scotland's difficulties in 2008 arose from taking on excessive debt for its part of the ABN-Amro acquisition at a time when credit markets ceased to function effectively; Northern Rock's demise was the result of an over-reliance on wholesale credit markets, as was the demise of Bear Stearns, Merrill Lynch and Lehman Brothers.

14 According to an IMD case study, the failure of CG at UBS, which nearly destroyed the bank and required Swiss government intervention in 2008, was caused by Marcel Ospel, the CEO, persuading the board to change the bank's risk profile when he took it into structured products whose risk implications were imperfectly understood, and which did not reflect the risk appetites of either its shareholders or key wealth-management clients.

15 In a world where many listed companies' tangible assets are a fraction of their market capitalization, the CEO must also recognize the need to enhance the value of the company's intangible assets: brands, processes, and intellectual property. This is less of an issue in many Asian markets where companies have still to build brands and intangible assets and market capitalization reflects net tangible assets more closely than in developed countries.

16 As pointed out in Chapter 1, compensation means "money that is paid to someone in exchange for something that has been lost or damaged or for some inconvenience." See http://dictionary.cambridge.org/define. asp?key=15595&dict=CALD.

17 For a full discussion of "moments of truth" and their effect on the brand promise, see Zinkin, J. 2003, *What CEOs Must Do To Succeed*, Kuala Lumpur: Prentice Hall: 256–61.

18 This section is based on Wallace and Zinkin 2005, op. cit.: 100–05.

19 Cadbury, A. 2002, *Corporate Governance and Chairmanship—A Personal View*, Oxford: Oxford University Press: 242.

20 Ibid.

21 Ibid.: 154.

22 Ibid.: 141.

23 "Thoman says now that he erred in not insisting that Allaire also step down as chairman when he transferred the CEO title. It wasn't that Allaire bossed Thoman around. The two worked out an arrangement by which Allaire would be permitted to attend top management meetings, but only if he promised not to speak. Although Allaire was as good as his word, he undermined his successor by his mere presence. Says one former top executive: "I knew it was doomed to fail when Rick and Paul would be in the same meeting and the line of eyes around the table would keep focusing on Paul even though Rick was doing all the talking": *BusinessWeek Online*, March 5, 2001.

24 Monks and Minow, op. cit.: 177.

25 Ibid.

26 Higgs, D. 2003, *Review of the Role and Effectiveness of Non-executive Directors*, London: The Department of Trade and Industry: 27.

27 Ibid.

28 Ibid.: 29.

29 "Knowing our culture, seniority plays a big role where one respects the seniors and founders as well . . . you don't question your elder and founder. In that sense, this is a downside in our Asian governance . . . if there is a distinction between Asian and Western governance." Lam Kee Soon, CPA Australia, Malaysian division president, quoted in "Company Fraud Linked to Strong Personalities," *The Edge Financial Daily*, February 23, 2009: 6.

30 Wallace and Zinkin 2005, op. cit.: 261.

5

WHY BOARDS FAIL AND HOW TO AVOID FAILURE

This chapter argues that many of the major failures of corporate governance have been the result of boards making poorly informed decisions. This may be the result of problems of board culture, with a weak Chair and a dominant CEO who does not listen to divergent opinions; dysfunctional board dynamics where the Vision and Mission are misunderstood, conflicts of interest exist and there is lack of trust within the board; dysfunctional processes resulting from a lack of transparency and poor information, poor planning of meetings, and poor decision-making; and an inadequate understanding of risk and its dynamics; or all of them combined. It goes on to suggest ways to resolve these problems using the Carver Policy Governance® model, emphasizing the importance of good information and clarifying the role of committees.

People get very emotional about CG failures that are the result of fraud; and rightly so. They seem to get less angry, however, about failures of CG that are the result of poor decisions and bad judgment. Yet often the frauds are the result of poor decisions taken earlier and it is the attempts of senior managers to cover up previous errors of judgment that lead them down the slippery slope into fraud and major scandal.[1] It is rare for a CEO to set out to defraud the company.

Warren Buffett did not mince his words when writing to the shareholders of Berkshire Hathaway about precisely this issue:

Many corporations still play things straight, but a significant and growing number of otherwise high grade managers—CEOs you would be happy to have as spouse for your children or as trustees under your will—have come to the view that it's okay to manipulate earnings to satisfy what they believe are Wall Street's desires. Indeed, many CEOS think this kind of manipulation is not only okay, but actually their *duty*.

These managers start with the assumption, all too common, that their job at all times is to encourage the highest stock price possible (a premise with which we adamantly disagree). To pump the price, they strive admirably for operational excellence. But when operations don't produce the result hoped for, these CEOs resort to unadmirable accounting stratagems. These either manufacture the desired "earnings" or set the stage for them in the future.

Rationalizing this behavior, these managers often say their shareholders will be hurt if their currency for doing deals—that is, their stock—is not fully-priced, and they also argue that in using accounting shenanigans in getting the figures they want, they are only doing what everybody else does. Once such an everybody's-doing-it attitude takes hold, ethical misgivings vanish . . . Bad accounting drives out good.[2]

What Buffett fails to mention, however, is that it is not just CEOs who are at fault, but boards as a whole, for letting them get away with it. There is also the unwillingness of supervisors lower down the organization to call a halt to risky behavior that seems to be paying off, as the following recent high-profile case clearly illustrates:

Kerviel said he was driven by a desire to make money for the bank, not himself, and his superiors had always congratulated him on his profitable trades. "They opened the car door, dangled the keys, and said go for a drive," Kerviel said. "At no point did they say: 'Stop this silliness.' If they had said 'stop,' I would have stopped. Instead, they kept saying: 'Well done.'"

He said that while he officially had a trading limit of $250 million, it was common at the bank for traders to be well over their limits. "I was frequently on the phone about placing up to €10 billion, and on a trading desk everyone can hear what everyone else is doing," he said. "I never hid anything."[3]

This failure of Société Générale SA to signal disapproval of Jerome Kerviel's actions led it to declare a trading loss of €4.9 billion in January 2008—the biggest trading loss ever declared by a bank at that time—three days after it discovered his unhedged positions.

Fraud is likely to be a symptom of other failures of governance: bad strategy; poor decision-making; hubris; and the lack of internal controls and systems that make the fraud possible because it is difficult to detect and easy to carry out. Yet people do not get so emotional about these underlying causes. Perhaps it is much harder to get excited about incompetence than criminal behavior.

Boards are equally accountable if the failure of CG can be shown to lie at their door, no matter what its origin. Failures of strategy; pay plans that reward only the upside and protect CEOs from the downside; allowing recklessness born of arrogance and past success; the absence of internal controls and inaccurate financial information— all are their responsibility.

Given that most directors are honorable men and women, why do boards fail to prevent the recurring scandals of CG?

Increasingly, in their attempt to carry out the six principal responsibilities, directors are flooded with too much information of all types by line management. Some argue that this is an attempt by management to make sure that they, the managers, will not be held liable for negligence, and the information overload is actually making it more difficult for directors to understand what they are looking at.

In addition to the problem of overload is the related issue that management gets to control the board agenda through the provision of the information they want the board to see rather than the information the board should have to do its job properly. This tends to lead to an excessive focus on looking at the past rather than into the future. This explains the following comment of Arthur Levitt, former Chairman of the US SEC, in a speech to the Directors' College at Stanford Law School: "There are too many boards that overlook more than they oversee; too many boards that substitute CEO directive for board initiative; too many boards that are reactive instead of proactive; and too many boards who never rejected an easy answer and never pursued a tough question."[4]

Five Reasons for Board Failure

There are five main reasons why boards do not perform as they should:

1. A dominant CEO who intimidates the directors.
2. A weak Chair who is unable to fulfill the role properly.
3. Dysfunctional board dynamics (usually a consequence of the first two).
4. Dysfunctional processes.
5. Inadequate understanding of risk dynamics.

In Chapter 4, we discussed the issues raised by the dominant CEO and the ineffective Chair and they are reflected typically in both dysfunctional dynamics and processes.

Dysfunctional board dynamics

Dysfunctional board dynamics normally are created by the following three contributory causes, individually or jointly:

Mission, vision and values are misunderstood

This can only happen when there is disagreement in the board as to the strategic direction of the company. Whenever there is discord between the CEO and the Chair on issues of this importance, companies get into serious difficulties, and as soon as the market gets to know of such disagreements, the effect on the share price is unfortunate, a point clearly illustrated by the Xerox case mentioned earlier.[5] Typically such problems are symptoms of a serious breakdown in the strategic direction of the company, resulting either from incompetent execution or else from a dramatic change in the company's circumstances that the board has not been able to foresee (perhaps because line management has kept the board in the dark, or else has kept the focus on the past rather than the changing future). Again, the case of Xerox and Rick Thoman exemplifies this. As the newcomer to the organization, Thoman had a view of the need to change the direction of the company, a view that was resisted by key incumbent members of the board with the silent endorsement of Paul Allaire—his predecessor.[6]

Lack of trust between board and management and within the board

The example of Xerox serves to highlight this dysfunctional dynamic as well. Rick Thoman and his new team were trying hard to change Xerox from the traditional box-selling organization it had always been to a vendor of document-management solutions. They quickly found themselves being undermined by the old guard, who were represented by Buehler and Romeril on the Xerox board, who in turn had the ear of Paul Allaire. When it became clear that faster change was needed than the old guard was able to stomach, they worked against Thoman, making his position impossible.[7]

Conflicts of interest and personal agendas

These happen when people on the board have personal issues that are hidden regarding direction, policies or procedures, and rather than recuse themselves or discuss the implications of their points of view openly, they go through the form of discussing and agreeing, only to sabotage agreed outcomes later.

Dysfunctional processes

These come in a number of forms:

Lack of transparency and information

Often this is the result of information overload, so that INEDs are "snowed" by the amount of paperwork they receive, with no clear documentation and no executive summary to help them focus on what is essential. Sometimes the company does not have the quality of information needed or, in worse cases, is not even gathering the information that INEDs need to make informed decisions.[8]

Perhaps more worrying is the information asymmetry that often exists in boards. CEOs have the best information in every field, with Chairs close behind, at least for the financials and risk management. When it comes to technical, manufacturing, and R&D strategy, the asymmetry is greater still.

Perhaps the most serious problem with information provided to boards is that 80 percent of board members feel it is not really helpful in framing the "bigger picture;" 63 percent of the directors felt the information was too general; more than 60 percent would like to receive information external to the company; 67 percent would like fewer financials; and nearly 80 percent felt the information provided was not sufficiently forward-looking.[9]

There is also an issue of where the information comes from. More than 90 percent of directors receive two-thirds of the information they need for board meetings from the company. The overwhelming majority of the information so provided came from the CEO and the top management team, and sometimes from middle managers. Boards therefore cannot assume that the information they receive is neutral and has not been massaged in some way to put the best gloss on events.[10]

Poor planning of meetings

Two factors often contribute to poorly planned meetings, which in turn cause problems of CG. The first of these is that many companies do not have a formal calendar, relying instead on an *ad hoc* timetable. This may lead to situations where key INEDs may not be able to attend because they are booked elsewhere. More importantly, there may be inadequate preparation for the board meeting, with too many items covered in insufficient depth. Leading practice is for each major topic to be fixed in the annual calendar so that line managers know when to prepare for the necessary information, and the INEDs can clear their minds to focus on the subject at hand, in addition to the financials. For example, succession planning and talent management could be done in the first quarter; technology in the second quarter; strategy in the third quarter, and so on.

The second factor contributing to poorly planned meetings is the fact that there are still too many companies that do not have proper agendas—which make clear what is to be discussed, whether this is for information or decision-making, and with specific time allocations for each item—or, equally important, accurate minutes which clearly reflect the tenor of the meeting; and flag exactly what actions are needed.[11]

Poor meeting management

It is the responsibility of the Chair to ensure that meetings are not dominated by a single individual and that every board member is actively involved in discussions without being browbeaten in any way by, say, the CEO. It is then up to the company secretary to confirm that the Chair's summary of what the directors have said is an accurate reflection of what they did say or meant to say.

Poor decision-making

This subject warrants an entire section on its own (see Chapter 6). However, insofar as it affects board processes there are three contributory factors which can lead to poor decision-making. These entail having:

- *No clear rules:* It is important that the rules by which decisions will be evaluated are spelled out so that all directors know where they stand in the process, and what is coming next.
- *No dissenting voices:* It is said that one of the first things Alfred Sloan, the creator of General Motors, did at his first board meeting was to ask his directors whether any disagreed with him over a particular point. When nobody did, he is supposed to have told them to go away and return at the next meeting with reasons why he was wrong. The point he was making was that he did not want a board of "yes men," because better decisions are made when they have been subjected to the process of challenge. For this to work, it is important that there is no culture of shooting the messenger, because without good messengers a board has no early-warning mechanism to alert them to possible bad news so that they can either pre-empt it or take action to lessen its impact.
- *No time to reflect:* Decisions taken in a hurry will give the board cause to repent at leisure. Quick decisions are well and good, but time for reflection is essential if the board is to assess possible alternatives. This is all the more critical when the decisions being taken are truly big ones. Decisions taken at speed are likely to be victims of group-think because there is not enough time to listen carefully to dissenting voices.

No follow-through, monitoring and control

While some companies know what needs to be done and have interminable board meetings debating and deciding what should be done, nothing actually gets done. Part of the reason for this is the disconnect between the board, which sets policy and direction, and middle managers, who actually get things done. All too often boards believe that by discussing an issue and analyzing it, they have achieved something, when it is all still to do.[12] The other problem occurs when a decision is taken but poorly implemented; the failure in this case is one of inadequate monitoring and control. Sometimes this is the result of inappropriate delegation to a specific board committee, which serves to disenfranchise board members who are not on it. Often this is the result of a failure of the Audit Committee to ensure that the proper internal controls are in place. Where it is a failure of the Remuneration Committee to control CEO compensation, it appears that sometimes this has been the result of committee members not fully understanding the implications of the package they are being asked to approve.

Avoiding Failure

Having established why boards fail, the rest of this chapter looks at how to avoid failure and deals with this in three parts: adopting John Carver's Policy Governance® approach; having the appropriate information; and using the Audit, Remuneration and Nomination Committees correctly.

The Policy Governance® Approach

To deal with the kinds of concerns outlined in Arthur Levitt's Stanford speech, John Carver set out to simplify board decisions by defining the role of the board as consisting of four separate but related responsibilities (as discussed in Chapter 4). These are to:

- Define the "Ends" of the organization: what it exists to do; how it will make a difference to its beneficiaries; and the returns it will achieve as a result.
- Set the boundaries or "Executive limitations" on the CEO's freedom to maneuver.
- Determine how the board itself would be governed through agreed "Governance Process issues."
- Delegate the authority of the board to the CEO through the "Board–CEO linkage."

Part of the problem is that what directors are expected to do by regulators does not translate readily into what they should do on a day-to-day basis, which in my view is better captured by John Carver's Policy Governance® framework.

At the risk of repetition, I think it is worth comparing and contrasting what regulators expect directors to do, and what John Carver *believes* directors actually need to do. This is shown in Table 5.1.

So how should boards go about doing what is required of them by regulators? Information presented to the board is normally in the form of a management report distributed to directors for them to read and digest before the meeting. Often directors complain that they are overloaded with information, making it more difficult for them to do their job properly.

John Carver argues that there are only two questions a director needs to ask: "Will what is being proposed deliver the agreed Ends

**TABLE 5.1 Regulatory Framework and Policy Governance®
Compared**[13]

Regulatory Framework	Policy Governance® Framework
The Board has six principal responsibilities:	**Role of the Board**
Reviewing and adopting a strategic plan.	It governs on behalf of the owners, translating their expectations into organizational performance.
Overseeing the conduct of the company's business to evaluate whether it is being properly managed.	It is the highest authority in the company, answerable to the owners for everything that happens.
Identifying principal risks and ensuring the implementation of appropriate systems to manage them.	It is the initial authority as well as the final authority. It should delegate its authority as much as possible, but without jeopardizing its accountability.
Succession planning, including appointing, training, fixing the compensation of and, where appropriate, replacing senior management.	It should recognize that governance and management are not the same; the **Board governs, management manages.**
Developing and implementing an investor-relations program or shareholder-communications policy.	**Tasks of the Board** Agreeing the purpose of the corporation—*"Ends issues."*
Reviewing the adequacy and the integrity of the company's internal control systems and management-information systems, including systems for compliance with applicable laws, regulations, rules, directives, and guidelines.	Restricting the choices open to the CEO—*"Executive limitations."* Defining the job of the Board—*"Governance process issues."* Delegating to the CEO—*"Board–CEO linkage issues."*

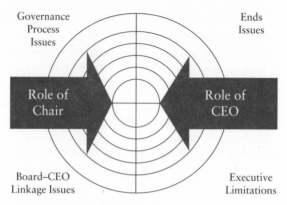

FIGURE 5.1 Different roles of Chair & CEO
Based on the Policy Circle by John Carver.

of the organization?" and "Is the CEO staying within the Executive Limitations that have also been agreed?" If the answer to both questions is "Yes," then the proposal can be approved, provided it does not also cut out other preferable options. Figure 5.1 shows the division of responsibility between the Chair and CEO in getting board members to this point.

Assessing CEO Effectiveness

The CEO's task is to deliver the agreed Ends of the organization (as discussed in Chapter 4) and to do this by remaining within the boundaries set by the agreed Executive Limitations.

In deciding whether or not the CEO is performing, it is important to have agreement on what is expected. This agreement regarding Executive Limitations can be expressed first of all in very general terms ("Level 1"), which become increasingly specific and precise ("Level 2" . . .) so that all in the boardroom understand precisely what is meant by achieving the Ends in question while staying within pre-agreed boundaries.

Thus for Level 1, a general statement of the Executive Limitations or operational boundary for a CEO could be as follows: "The CEO shall not cause or allow any practice, activity, decision, or organizational circumstance that is either unlawful, imprudent, or in violation of commonly accepted business and professional ethics."[14]

The problem with this statement as it stands is that it is still too general. For example, it is not inconceivable that Jeffrey Skilling, the now-imprisoned former CEO of Enron, could have argued that nothing that he did was unlawful (he took legal advice), imprudent (he had the best advice from investment bankers and Bank of America), or in violation of commonly accepted business and professional ethics (none of his advisors told him what he was doing was unethical or unprofessional).[15] So we need to be more specific about the boundaries of CEO behavior to rule out the kind of malfeasance that Skilling was guilty of. These are likely to be found at Level 2, as follows:[16]

a. *Treatment of consumers/customers:* "With respect to interactions with consumers or those applying to be consumers, the CEO shall not cause or allow conditions, procedures, or decisions that are unsafe, undignified, unnecessarily intrusive, or that fail to provide appropriate confidentiality or privacy."

b. *Treatment of staff:* "With respect to the treatment of paid and volunteer staff, the CEO may not cause or allow conditions that are unfair or undignified."

c. *Financial planning and budgeting:* "Financial planning for any fiscal year or the remaining part of any fiscal year shall not deviate materially from the Board's Ends priorities, risk fiscal jeopardy, or fail to be derived from a multiyear plan."

d. *Financial condition and activities:* "With respect to the actual, ongoing financial conditions and activities, the CEO shall not cause or allow the development of fiscal jeopardy or a material deviation of actual expenditures from Board priorities established in the Ends policies."

e. *Emergency CEO succession:* "In order to protect the Board from sudden loss of CEO services, the CEO may have no fewer than two other executives familiar with Board and CEO issues and processes."

f. *Asset protection:* "The CEO shall not allow the assets to be unprotected, inadequately maintained, or unnecessarily risked."

g. *Compensation and benefits:* "With respect to employment, compensation, and benefits to employees, consultants, contract workers, and volunteers, the CEO shall not cause or allow jeopardy to fiscal integrity or public image."

h. *Ends focus of grants or contracts:* "The CEO may not enter into any grant or contract arrangements that fail to emphasize primarily the production of Ends and, secondarily, the avoidance of unacceptable means."

i. *Communications and support to the Board:* "The CEO shall not permit the Board to be uninformed or unsupported in its work."[17]

Jeffrey Skilling failed to stay within the financial constraints set by the Level 2 limitations under items c, d and h above.

Assessing chair effectiveness

Figure 5.1 shows two areas of responsibility that belong to the Chair according to the Carver model: delivering good board governance and board–CEO linkages.

Delivering good board governance[18]

"The purpose of the Board, on behalf of the shareholders, is to see to it that [name of organization] (1) achieves appropriate results for appropriate persons at an appropriate cost and (2) avoids unacceptable actions and situations."

Once again, this Level 1 statement of principle is too general and needs Level 2 principles to articulate the detailed policies that give Level 1 specific meaning, as follows:

a. *Accountability philosophy:* "The board's fundamental accountability is to the shareholders."
b. *Social responsibility:* "Although the board accepts as its primary obligation to operate in the best interest of shareholders, that fidelity is tempered by an obligation to the social order and good citizenship."
c. *Governing style:* "The board will govern lawfully with an emphasis on (1) outward vision rather than internal preoccupation; (2) encouragement of diversity in viewpoints; (3) strategic leadership more than administrative detail; (4) clear distinction of board and Chief Executive roles; (5) collective rather than individual decisions; (6) future rather than past or present; and (7) proactivity rather than reactivity."
d. *Board job description:* "The specific job outputs of the board, as informed agent of the shareholders, are those that ensure an unbroken chain of accountability from shareholders to company performance."

e. *Board–shareholder linkage:* "As the representative of the share-holders' interests, the board will maintain a credible and continuing link between the owners and managers."

f. *Agenda planning:* "To accomplish its job, with products, with a governance style consistent with board policies, the board will follow an annual agenda that (1) completes re-exploration of Ends policies annually and (2) continually improves board performance through board education and enriched input and deliberation."

g. *Chair's role:* "The Chair assures the integrity of the board's process and, secondarily, occasionally represents the board to outside parties, including but not limited to shareholders."

h. *Directors' conduct:* "The board commits itself and its members to ethical, businesslike, and lawful conduct, including members' proper use of authority and appropriate decorum when acting as Directors."

i. *Committee principles:* "Board committees, when used, will be assigned so as to reinforce the wholeness of the board's job and so as never to interfere with delegations from board to CEO."

j. *Committee structure:* "Board committees are those set up by board action, along with their job products, time lines, and board-authorized use of funds and management time. Unless otherwise stated, a committee ceases to exist as soon as its task is complete."

k. *Cost of governance:* "The board will consciously invest in its ability to govern competently and wisely."[19]

Delivering Board–CEO Linkages[20]

The Level 1 statement of policy is as follows: "The board's sole official connection to the operational company, its achievements and its conduct, will be through a Chief Executive Officer (CEO)."

At Level 2 this translates into the following policies:

a. *Unity of control:* "Only officially passed motions of the board, speaking authoritatively as a group, are binding on the CEO."

b. *Accountability of the CEO:* "The CEO is the board's only link to operational achievement and conduct, so that all authority and accountability of staff, as far as the board is concerned, is considered the authority and accountability of the CEO."

c. *CEO delegation:* "The board will instruct the CEO through written policies that prescribe the organizational Ends to be achieved and describe organizational situations and actions to be avoided, allowing the CEO to use any reasonable interpretation of these policies."

d. *Monitoring CEO performance:* "Systematic and rigorous monitoring of CEO job performance will be solely against the only expected CEO job outputs: organizational accomplishment of board policies on Ends and organizational operation within the boundaries established in board policies on Executive Limitations."

e. *CEO remuneration:* "CEO remuneration will be decided by the board as a body and based on company performance and executive market conditions."

f. *CEO termination:* "CEO termination is an authority retained by the board, not delegated to any officer or committee."[21]

Having the appropriate information

Appropriate information can be categorized in three ways: it is based on a proper understanding of risks faced by the company, using stakeholder needs analysis to achieve this; it is translatable into appropriate KPIs; and it is of good quality.

Stakeholder needs-analysis-based information

Stakeholder needs analysis helps define what information is needed to align the company behind the agreed direction. Such an analysis will identify who the key stakeholders are; the business risks and opportunities arising from their needs (analysis and managing risk is covered in Chapter 6) and strategies for addressing them; and managing potential conflicting interests that may arise. It will also identify the KPIs used by the company to ensure that progress is being made and that the objectives, goals and milestones of the strategies are being met.

Appropriate KPIs

KPIs are high-level strategic performance indicators that show the links between the strategic drivers of the business with day-to-day operations. They should be designed to help the top management team and the board to keep their fingers on the pulse of the business.

KPIs come in three forms as illustrated below, using those of the Securities Industry Development Corporation (the training and development arm of the Securities Commission, Malaysia) as a model.

a. *Outcome KPIs represent a change in status for the organization*: "Our vision is to be recognized internationally as the leading training and development provider for Capital Markets in Asia Pacific." *SIDC Vision, SIDC Annual Report 2009.*

b. *Output KPIs are tangible things or results that have to happen so that the outcome KPIs can be achieved*, for example: "We will train 20,000 children, aged 10–12, in 2009 through our 'Kids and Cash' financial literacy program."

c. *Input KPIs are things that must happen along the project's critical path so that output KPIs can be created in time to meet the milestones on the route to achieving the desired outcomes*: "We will need to have trained 50 teachers to meet the target of teaching 20,000 children in 2009, by the end of Q2 2009."

To be effective, KPIs of any kind must be:

- *Reliable*—the process of gathering the data to derive the KPIs must be robust, lest it suffer from the "garbage in, garbage out" syndrome that will, at best, discredit the KPIs, and, at worst, lead to wrong decisions.
- *Balanced*—that is, they must include both financial and non-financial information, bearing in mind that most financial KPIs are lagging indicators, whereas the "soft" non-financial indicators tend to be leading indicators and drivers of performance.
- *Decision-driven*—allowing the linkages to be made explicit between input, output and outcome KPIs.
- *Actionable*—they must be strategic and actionable.
- *Simple*—easy to explain, easy to collate and limited in number.
- *Dynamic*—flexible and capable of change and improvement.

Table 5.2 reconciles a typical list of financial and non-financial KPIs that are normally used in Balanced Scorecards.[22]

TABLE 5.2 Reconciling Financial and Non-Financial KPIs

Financial KPIs: Lagging Indicators	Non-Financial KPIs: Performance Drivers

• Net Sales Revenue
  ($/per capita)
• Gross Margin
  ($/percent/per capita)
• Overheads
  ($/percent)
• EBIT (DA)
  ($/percent/per capita)
• PAT
  ($/percent/per capita)
• Interest cover
• Cash Flow
  – Free Cash flow
  – Sources and Uses of funds
• Working Capital Turn
  – Debtors ($/days/turn)
  – Stock ($/days/turn)
  – Creditors ($/days/turn
• Fixed Asset Turn
• Debt: Equity Ratio
• Market: Book
• P/E
• EVA
	• Brand equity
	• Market share
	  – Relative category penetration
	  – Relative frequency of purchase
	  – Relative volume and value purchased
	• Customer acquisition
	• Customer satisfaction
	• Customer retention
	• Customer profitability
	• Ability to innovate
	  – Number of patents
	  – Percent sales from new products
	  – Percent sales from proprietary products
	• Speed to market
	  – Compared with competition
	  – Time taken per generation
	• Product/process quality
	  – Process part-per-million defect rates
	  – Yields
	  – Waste/scrap
	  – Rework
	  – Returns
	• Manufacturing cycle effectiveness
	• Employee satisfaction
	• Employee retention
	• Employee productivity
	• Employee skills

Source: Kaplan, R.S and Norton, D.P, (1996), *The Balanced Scorecard,* (Boston: Harvard Business School Press).

Good-quality information

The characteristics of good-quality information are that it is:[23]

- *Relevant*—it should be focused on the overall objectives and strategy of the organization and presented in a concise and easy-to-read format. It should not be ambiguous and the salient points should not be clouded by irrelevant detail. However, the information should be sufficient to allow discussion and exploration of options so that impartial and good decisions can be taken.

- *Integrated*—when information is collated from different sources (external and internal) it should be integrated so that there are no inconsistencies between them. If there are discrepancies, there should be an integrated explanation of why these exist.

- *In perspective*—the information should provide the context, and the projections that are made should be plotted over time, so that meeting milestones and performance benchmarks have meaning and variances can be explained with corrective actions indicated. This applies to monitoring and controlling contracts, projects, revenues and expenses, the income statement, cash-flow projections and the balance sheet.

- *Timely*—it is vital that the information is timely and recent. Out-of-date information fails to give the board enough warning of problems to come, so that effective corrective action can be taken; or it may no longer be relevant, leading the board to focus on the wrong things.[24]

- *Frequent*—the monthly board report should contain information relating to the key processes identified by the board: the critical success factors and KPIs. The quarterly report should address wider areas of relevance, in particular the softer qualitative issues that act as performance drivers for the organization.

- *Reliable*—information should be of sufficiently high quality that board members can be confident when they make decisions based on it that they are not faced with "garbage in, garbage out."

- *Comparable*—performance covers all aspects of the organization, both financial and non-financial and needs to be structured in a way that allows comparisons to be highlighted for discussion at board meetings. Typical comparisons are plan or budget versus actual and/or actual current period with actual previous period.

- *Clear*—everyday language should be used wherever possible. Graphs and charts are useful for KPIs and also to identify and highlight trends.

Tables 5.3 and 5.4, based on the Chartered Institute of Management Accountants' "Performance Reporting to Boards," contrast good and bad practice.

TABLE 5.3 Principles and Characteristics of Good Information

The Principles	Good Practice	Poor Practice
Relevant	Succinct financial report, ideally no more than five pages in length.	A long and detailed report, in excess of 15 pages.
	A good report will summarize the issues and highlight the overall position, making use of graphs and charts.	Detailed and tedious description of all income and expenditure items and all variances.
	Narrative will focus on explaining why variances occurred.	Limited narrative actually explaining important items and why variances have occurred.
	Narrative will also suggest corrective actions.	No corrective actions identified.
Integrated	Activity data linked to financial performance. Variances calculated and explained. The report should integrate financial and non-financial reporting.	No activity data presented in the financial report. No balance between qualitative and quantitative factors.
	The report will include operational, compliance and financial KPIs.	Only financial KPIs provided.
Timely	Report available within five days following period end.	Information provided 28 days following period end.
Adequate	Abbreviated profit-and-loss account shows period and cumulative positions and highlights variances against budget.	Extremely detailed profit-and-loss account.
	Major variances are fully explained. Trend analysis is also valuable. Full-year projections updated.	Insufficient narrative to adequately explain key items and variances.
Reliable	All key issues identified with adequate explanation.	No key issues identified, or issues only spasmodically identified. Little or no explanation of why issues arose.

(continued)

The Principles	Good Practice	Poor Practice
Comparable	Use of consistent style. Use of consistent/ standard KPIs.	Inconsistent format and style of report. No use of KPIs, or KPIs not consistently provided.
Clear	Use of graphs; good use of color coding and clear chapter headings. Executive summary or synopsis provided.	Copious financial tables at the beginning of the report. No title or contents pages. Information presented in complex spreadsheets.

Source: Starovic, D., (2003), *Performance Reporting to Boards: A Guide to Good Practice*, (London: The Chartered Institute of Management Accountants): 12.

Table 5.4 shows examples of good and poor practice in relation to some of the key elements of the board report.

TABLE 5.4 Board Report and Practice

Element/section	Good Practice	Poor Practice
Executive Summary	All key issues identified in an upfront executive summary, with synopsis of KPIs.	No simple overview.
	Supporting documentation and appendices clearly referenced.	Information is there but in a confusing order with no cross-referencing. Typically excessive use of raw data or unrefined information.
Action plan	Corrective action specified with contingencies and sensitivity analysis showing best- and worst-case scenarios.	No action plan or only basic corrective actions identified. No consideration given to best/ worst-case scenarios.
Profit and Loss	Profit-and-loss account showing period and cumulative positions with highlighted variances against budget.	Cumulative income and expenditure account provided. Insufficient detail to support key issues.
	Major variances highlighted and adequately explained. Trend analysis shown graphically. Full-year projections.	Variances either not highlighted or not adequately explained.

(continued)

Element/section	Good Practice	Poor Practice
Cash flow	Profiled monthly cash flow summarizing actual and projected receipts, payments, and balances on a monthly basis to year-end.	No cash-flow information, or only historical information provided.
Capital program	Analysis of progress of major capital schemes showing percentage completion, current and projected expenditure, completion cost, and time scale.	No data provided, or only basic over/under budget details. No explanations for current status or corrective action plans provided.
Balance sheet	Indication of the working capital position, clearly presented in tabular format or using performance indicators; for example, debtor/creditor days.	No working capital information.

Source: Starovic (2003): 13.

Following is a simple checklist provided by Metapraxis, a management consultancy, to help directors assess the quality of the information being received:

- *Accuracy:* Can I trust the data?
- *Relevance:* Does it cover the critical issues?
- *Timeliness:* Is it sufficiently up to date?
- *Clarity:* Is it presented in such a way that I can digest it quickly?
- *Risk assessment:* Is the information purely historic or does it assess future risks?
- *Depth:* Do I receive only summaries or can I access individual reports?
- *Provision:* Can I access the data via a secure Internet connection?[25]

As far as financial information for external consumption is concerned, the Institute of Chartered Accountants of England and Wales (ICAEW) has this to say about what makes it useful:

Material

- It comprises only items of information whose size or nature mean that their misstatement or omission might reasonably be expected to influence the economic decision of investors.

Relevant

- It has the ability to influence the economic decision of investors.
- It is provided in time to influence the economic decision of investors.
- It has predictive value or, by helping to confirm or correct past evaluations or assessments, it has confirmatory value.

Reliable

- It can be depended on by investors as a faithful representation of what it purports to represent—or what it could reasonably be expected to represent.
- It is neutral, because it is free from deliberate or systematic bias intended to influence a decision or judgment to achieve a predetermined result.
- It is free from material error.
- It is complete within the bounds of what is material.
- It is prudent in that a degree of caution is applied in making judgments under conditions of uncertainty.

Comparable

- It can be compared with similar information for other periods and other entities so that similarities and differences can be discerned and evaluated.
- It reflects consistency of preparation and presentation, providing that this is not an impediment to improvements in practice.
- It is supported by the disclosure of the accounting policies used in its preparation.

Understandable

- It involves the characterization, aggregation and classification of transactions and other events in accordance with their substance and presentation in ways that enable the significance of information to be understood by users.
- It presumes that users have a reasonable knowledge of business and economic activities and accounting and have a willingness to study information with reasonable diligence.[26]

Getting the Best from Board Committees

It is worth repeating two of the Policy Governance® principles regarding the role and use of board committees.

Committee principles: "Board committees, when used, will be assigned so as to reinforce the wholeness of the board's job and so as never to interfere with delegations from board to CEO."

Committee structure: "Board committees are those set up by board action, along with their job products, time lines, and board-authorized use of funds and management time. Unless otherwise stated, a committee ceases to exist as soon as its task is complete."

The importance of these two principles comes from the need to protect the board from being disenfranchised by committees that take upon themselves the role of the board. Committees should only be formed if they are essential. They must not come between the board and management, and so must never judge management performance on the basis of their own criteria; they must use those of the board as a whole. (In most instances, committees do not go further than making recommendations to the board.) The existence of committees must not mislead directors who are on those committees that they are more equal than others who are not. Nor should directors fall into the trap of believing they are not accountable because they do not sit on a particular committee.

Typically, codes of CG focus on the three most important committees: the audit, nomination, and remuneration committees. Boards may sometimes choose to have additional committees such as an executive committee or a risk management committee.

The audit committee

The audit committee is required by law in many jurisdictions, including both Singapore and Malaysia. The Malaysian Revised Code (p.14) has this to say of its composition:

> The board should establish an audit committee comprising at least three members, a majority of whom are independent. All members of the audit committee should be non-executive directors . . .
>
> . . . All members of the audit committee should be financially literate and at least one should be a member of an accounting association or body.

The basic role of the audit committee is to assist the board in discharging its duties to shareholders and in helping improve board monitoring of the financial reporting process by liaising with management and the internal and external auditors. The audit committee is involved in the selection and assessment of external auditors.

In addition, the audit committee should supervise the review of the company's internal control framework and ensure the reliability of financial information for inclusion in the financial statements. An effective audit committee will, through its neutrality, add credibility to the board in its role of ensuring that management has a proper internal-control system in place.

To be effective, the audit committee must be able to work well with the CEO and CFO, to ensure that the committee gets the management's support and cooperation. It needs to operate under a charter which has been approved by the board and is reviewed annually to remain relevant.

It has been said that audit committees have been created to bolster the independence of the directors who could otherwise be dominated by management, and that therefore this is a second-best solution, with the best option being a truly independent board whose directors can constructively challenge what management is doing to protect the interests of shareholders. Such a board would be preferable to one where the directors are dependent, as in much of Asia, and the Audit Committee is the only way to achieve some independence of thinking.[27]

The nomination committee

The Malaysian Revised Code (p.11) recommends that: "The board of every company should appoint a committee of directors composed exclusively of non-executive directors, a majority of whom are independent, with the responsibility for proposing new nominees to the board and for assessing directors on an ongoing basis."

The role of the nomination committee has never been more important, as a company's performance depends on the quality of the people who lead it. Creating shareholder value depends not only on mastering the financials, but also on making the right decisions about which strategy to adopt, which markets to serve and what products to offer. This demands leadership qualities that ensure the company has the right talent in the right jobs at the right time.

The nomination committee's role is to make informed and objective recommendations on board appointments and re-elections, including to the board's committees. It also assesses the performance of each director and the board as a whole, making sure that independent directors are indeed independent.[28] The nomination committee also monitors the attendance of directors at board and committee meetings, checking on whether directors have too many directorships to allow them to contribute properly to the progress of the company.

The committee should also recommend who should be the Company Secretary and evaluate the incumbent's performance. In companies that have a formal succession-planning and talent-management process, the nomination committee will oversee the process.

The remuneration committee

The Malaysian Revised Code (p.14) says that a remuneration committee should consist "wholly or mainly of non-executive directors, to recommend to the board the remuneration of the executive directors in all its forms, drawing from outside advice as necessary."

The glare of adverse publicity concerning the remuneration of CEOs in the US and much of the West in general has never been greater. People cannot understand how CEOs can walk away with huge sums of money when they have been responsible for the failure of strategy or even the bankruptcy of the company. The bonuses paid out by Merrill Lynch to top managers just before it was taken over by Bank of America have caused widespread revulsion at the antics of Wall Street in general.[29]

As a result, the role of the remuneration committee will be in the spotlight in ways unimaginable before the recent excesses. Directors on the remuneration committee, whose specific job it is to determine on behalf of the board the terms of engagement and remuneration of the CEO and executive directors, will have to understand exactly the implications of the contracts they approve should things go wrong.

Recommendations should be performance-based and aligned to shareholders' interests, as in the case of stock options. However, in future, the recommendations will need to eliminate the gross asymmetries that have been the practice of the past, most particularly in financial services, where packages have rewarded senior executives for short-term risky upside behavior that has led to the claim that financial services' profits are privatized, while the losses are socialized.

Having said all this, however, remuneration committees do serve a useful purpose by:

- Determining the amount and composition of the CEO's package—provided they do not allow mutual back-scratching leading to inflated packages and ever-increasing awards.
- Determining whether other senior managers are paid in line with company's policies as agreed by the board.
- Understanding the options and their effect on the overall compensation, including when things go wrong.
- Operating any long-term, performance-related pay plan as it concerns the executive directors and all other managers who are affected by it.
- Determining matters of policy relating to the setting up and running of the company's pension scheme, of which the executive directors and senior managers are members.
- Nominating trustees of the pension plan, if there is one.

The executive committee (Exco)

Some companies set up Excos in order to evaluate the performance of the CEO; review the structure and effectiveness of the company's organizational design, and the systems for developing senior executives; determine the succession plan for the CEO and review the succession plan and talent management for the rest of the organization; and review other matters that may be required to be investigated by all of the INEDs.

Typically, membership of Excos comprises, a majority of INEDs, and while this may seem like a good approach, it is perhaps worth repeating John and Miriam Carver's words of warning:

We warn you about a particularly harmful committee—the executive committee—for it uniquely undermines both board and CEO authority. Since an executive committee is usually granted the authority to make board decisions when the board is not in session, its authority may in practice be more far-reaching than that of the board itself. Moreover it inserts itself in between the board and the CEO, making it difficult to tell exactly for whom the CEO works.[30]

Clearly the trick is to make sure that if the company has chosen to set up an executive committee, it does not disenfranchise the INEDs who are not on it, nor encourage them to think that they are no longer accountable for decisions made by that committee. They remain accountable as members of the board to which the Exco in fact reports.

The advisory committee

Some companies favor the use of advisory committees to help the board in certain areas of the business. However, given that managers and the board are capable of seeking the best advice available (which may not be present in the membership of the advisory committee), and given the potential for members of the advisory committee to become confused about their roles as advisors or directors, this practice is not recommended.

Conclusion

Usually, failures of CG are symptoms of other things that have gone wrong: strategies that were inappropriate (Marconi, UBS, AIG); or where people have taken gambles that were encouraged initially but in the end have not paid off (Société Générale, Barings); or where they made what seemed to be innocuous adjustments to the numbers that then grew bigger and bigger until the process went out of control (Xerox, WorldCom, Parmalat, Satyam). Only rarely are they the result of systematic plans by the CEO to plunder the company at the shareholders' expense.

What is crystal clear, however, is that whatever the cause, boards are accountable. They cannot blame the CEO or CFO and say they were misled, for it is their job to challenge the assumptions of the CEO.

Boards fail because they are overloaded with the wrong kind of information; have dominant CEOs who intimidate the INEDs (made worse when the Chair is weak); dysfunctional board dynamics or processes; and, above all, an inadequate understanding of risks faced by the company and how these might be changing over time.

As we have seen, the Policy Governance® approach makes it possible for boards to assess whether what is being proposed satisfies the agreed Ends of the organization and is within the boundaries set by the agreed Executive Limitations. This approach recognizes that the CEO and Chair have quite different roles and responsibilities.

To function effectively, boards must have all the appropriate information to enable them to make correct decisions. Such information will be based on a stakeholder needs analysis, which will highlight whether the organization has the necessary processes and information to capture the opportunities and mitigate the risks that present themselves. Once the board has identified what it needs to know, it must ensure that this information is of good quality and is translatable into appropriate key performance indicators.

Board committees should only be created if they are the most efficient way of carrying out the responsibilities of the board. To do this, their authority and terms of reference must be crystal clear and they must know whether they are supposed to report on behalf of the board, or whether they are expected to examine issues and report back to the board instead.

Many codes of CG stipulate that there should be an audit committee, a nomination committee and a remuneration committee, which have critical roles to play in helping the board do its job.

Endnotes

1 This was the case in the frauds that hit Barings, Parmalat and, apparently, Satyam.
2 Buffett, W. 1998, Chairman's Letter, Annual Report, Berkshire Hathaway:14–5; quoted in O'Sullivan, M. A. 2000, *Contests for Corporate Control: Corporate Governance And Economic Performance In The United States And Germany*, Oxford: Oxford University Press: 203.
3 "Kerviel says SocGen superiors encouraged his trading risks," Viscusi, G., *Edge Financial Daily*, February 10, 2009: 16.
4 Speech to the Directors' College, Stanford Law School, Stanford University, March 22, 1999, quoted in O'Sullivan, op. cit.: 203.
5 "Xerox hit a record high of nearly US$64 a share in May 1999, just three weeks after Thoman replaced Allaire as CEO. Today, the stock trades around US$7, a few dollars above the price at which it listed on the New York Stock Exchange in 1961. The evisceration of US$38 billion in shareholder wealth already qualifies Xerox as a corporate catastrophe of the first order." "Xerox: The Downfall: The Inside Story of the Management Fiasco at Xerox," *BusinessWeek* Online, March 5, 2001.
6 Ibid.
7 "In mid-December, Allaire circulated a memo to senior management affirming his support of Thoman. The board is 'unanimously supportive of Rick' despite the 'clearly disappointing performance of the

company,' he wrote. Behind the scenes, though, Romeril, Buehler, and other executives were coming to Allaire and threatening to resign unless Thoman was removed. In the first quarter of 2000, Xerox actually exceeded the Street's expectations, modest though they were. But the die was cast. 'There was no last straw, no flash of lightning, no thunder,' Allaire says. 'Rick had clearly lost the confidence of the board, his extended management team, and me. When that happens, you have to make a change.'" Ibid.

8 In their research on CG, IMD found that about 90 percent of board members claimed to be well informed about the organization's business strategy, with 70 percent still claiming to be well informed when it came to the HR strategy. Two-thirds felt they were well informed regarding the company's markets and related political, legal and societal issues. However, one-third felt uninformed about competitors, market dynamics and industry trends. As far as technology, innovation and manufacturing operations were concerned, more than half claimed to have at best a rough understanding; and for strategic R&D, more than half said they were poorly informed. See Steger, U. and Amann, W. 2008, *Corporate Governance: How To Add Value*, Chichester: John Wiley & Sons: 92.

9 Ibid.: 93.

10 Ibid.: 95–6.

11 "Meetings, Bloody Meetings" and "More Bloody Meetings" (developed by John Cleese's Video Arts) are two of the best training materials on how to run meetings effectively, and are equally applicable to board meetings.

12 See Pfeffer, J. and Sutton, R. I. 2000, *The Knowing–Doing Gap: How Smart Companies Turn Knowledge Into Action*, Boston: Harvard Business School Press.

13 Revised Malaysian Code of Corporate Governance 2007; Zinkin, J.,"Corporate Governance: Where are we going?" MICPA-Bursa Malaysia Business Forum 2008: "Reinventing for Success," Kuala Lumpur, October 20, 2008.

14 Wallace, P. and Zinkin, J. 2005, *Corporate Governance*, Singapore: John Wiley & Sons: 59.

15 That this was the case was acknowledged by the prosecution: "'Third-party facilitators have played a critical role in allowing corporate misconduct to happen, whether it be outside counsel, accountants, advisors, or, as we see in this case, a bank whose financing schemes fuelled Enron's misdeeds,' said Deputy Attorney General James B. Comey Jr." "CIBC Agrees to US$80 Million Enron Penalty," *Wall Street Journal Asia*, December 24, 2003. According to the same report, Canadian Imperial Bank of Commerce agreed to pay US$80 million to settle civil charges brought against it by the SEC over Enron; JPMorgan Chase

agreed to pay US$162.5 million: Citigroup agreed to pay US$126.8 million in civil settlements with the SEC, the bank regulators, and the Manhattan District Attorney's Office.

16 See Wallace and Zinkin, op. cit.: 60–1.

17 For more detailed policies affecting the CEO's Executive Limitations, see Appendix 2.1: "Sample Board Policies: Executive Limitations on the CEO," Wallace and Zinkin 2005, op. cit.: 78–82.

18 Ibid.: 65–7.

19 Ibid.: 82–90.

20 Ibid.: 69–71.

21 For still more detailed policies affecting board–CEO linkages, see Wallace and Zinkin 2005, op. cit.: 90–3.

22 See Kaplan, R. S. and Norton, D. P. 1996, *The Balanced Scorecard*, Boston: Harvard Business School Press.

23 Wallace and Zinkin 2005, op. cit.: 191–3.

24 "Marconi is often cited as an example of a company that failed partly because its board didn't receive timely information. In other words, it wasn't simply a case of incompetence or flawed risk assessment, as is often stated. The simple truth is that the company's directors may not have had the chance to act, because they didn't find out what was going on until it was too late." Starovic, D. 2003, *Performance Reporting to Boards: A Guide to Good Practice*, London: The Chartered Institute of Management Accountants: 7.

25 Quoted in Starovic 2003, op cit.: 9.

26 Ibid.

27 For a full discussion of the role of the audit committee, including a sample audit committee charter and evaluation form, see Wallace and Zinkin, 2005: 207–55.

28 For a detailed discussion of board evaluation, including alternative evaluation forms, see Wallace and Zinkin 2005: 279–327.

29 See, for example, "Cuomo Reveals 4 Top Merrill Lynch Execs Grabbed Big Bucks Just Before Government-financed Takeover," *New York Daily News*, February 12, 2009.

30 Carver, J. and Carver, M. M. 1998, *Reinventing Your Board*, San Francisco: Jossey-Bass: 51.

6

FROM GOOD GOVERNANCE TO GOOD RESULTS

This chapter discusses the four factors boards must consider for moving from good governance to good results: effecting right strategy; making informed decisions; managing change and converting strategy into action; and implementing effective succession planning.

The reason why there is often a disconnect between good governance, from a regulatory perspective, and good results lies in the difficulties of getting strategy right in the first place and then implementing it effectively. Effective implementation requires informed decision-making and the ability to convert strategy into action, which in turn depends in large part on having the right people in the right place at the right time—which is achieved through good succession planning and talent management.

Getting Strategy Right

This first stage in the road to good results is closely linked with defining the organization's Ends: the difference its existence will make to its beneficiaries and the costs and return implied by such activity. This is, however, not the same as determining what the Ends of the organization are.

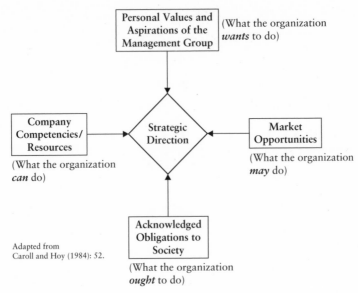

FIGURE 6.1 Setting strategic direction

Introducing the ethical dimension

Figure 6.1[1] provides a useful framework for the first steps in deciding what the organization's strategy should be. First, it captures the
ethical dimension by recognizing that organizations are driven by
the personal values and aspirations of the top management team
and that therefore, for any strategy to work, it must be aligned with
them. Once these aspirations have been decided, the top management team must then form a view of the company's likely obligations
to society, framed in terms of what it ought to do to maintain its
long-term license to operate. Assuming that there is no irreconcilable
conflict between what the firm wants to do and what it ought to do,
then the third step is to establish whether it is worth doing—whether
the market opportunity is large enough to warrant the investment of
time, energy and money. The final step is to determine whether the
company has the competencies, resources and capabilities to make a
sustainable success of serving that market.

Choosing the "resource-based" view or "strategy as stretch"

Another way of looking at the same exercise, but without the ethical
dimension outlined above, is to merely look at the market opportunities and see whether the organization has resources to allocate to

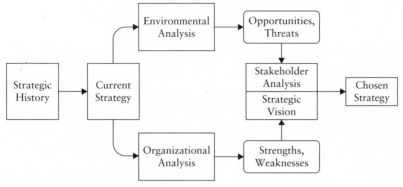

Adapted from Dobson, Starkey and Richards (2004).

FIGURE 6.2 Improving the game: The resource-based view

match these. This type of approach—often called the "resource-based view" of strategy—is rational, economic and seeks only to maximize returns. Figure 6.2[2] shows how this is done.

In determining future strategy, the company recognizes its strategic history or legacy effects as its starting point. This legacy sets boundaries around the current strategy which is then reviewed using organizational analysis that covers all the resources inside the firm: people, money, plant and equipment, intellectual property, brands, and patents.

At the same time, planners will analyze the political, economic, social and technical (PEST) trends affecting the firm and its products. They may add in analysis of the legislative and ecological trends and may also use Michael Porter's "Five Forces" that drive strategic competitive advantage as well. From this they can derive the opportunities and threats that exist outside the firm and match them to the strengths and weaknesses inside the firm. The integration of these fact-based analyses allows the articulation of the strategic vision and the chosen strategy. The key point about this approach is that the driver of strategy starts with the past legacy that constrains the firm and limits its degrees of strategic freedom.

Typically such an approach is to be found in firms that are probably past/present market leaders. They think in terms of the resources and competencies they own when allocating resources and setting priorities.

New entrants, interested in changing the game, as opposed to improving the game, are likely to approach strategy differently, as is shown in Figure 6.3.

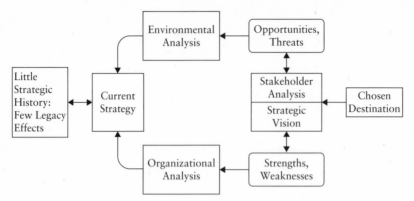

Adapted from Dobson, Starkey and Richards (2004).

FIGURE 6.3 Changing the game: Strategy as stretch

The only difference between strategy as stretch (SAS) and the resource-based view (RBV) of strategy is the starting point. SAS starts with the future and therefore is not constrained by the past. Typically, companies adopting SAS are new players who want to change the game, for to do otherwise is to play to the strengths of the incumbents.

For example, the full-service airlines in the US, Europe and, to a lesser extent, Asia were tied to a hub-and-spoke strategy, with small regional feeder planes flying into major airports where passengers disembarked and then got onto wide-body planes for the connecting medium- and long-haul flights. This strategy was designed to maximize the utilization of the wide-body planes, at the expense of passenger convenience. As the hub airports became ever-more congested, the downtime of planes flying in and out began to undermine the very efficiencies that the hub-and-spoke system was supposed to deliver. Planes spent too much time waiting to take off or land. Travel became more unpleasant, with passengers having to wait longer than ever in planes at crowded airports, where often they had to walk long distances to make the connections. The landing rights and slots became more expensive as a result of scarcity, further undermining the economics of the system.

Then along came the low-cost carriers (LCCs) with their strategy of flying medium-sized planes point to point. This had the advantage of saving passengers a great deal of time and inconvenience as well as allowing very quick turnaround times because the airports they frequented were not congested. In addition, the landing rights were much cheaper. The owners of the LCCs established systems that minimized the cost of flying by cutting services to the bone, and some of the key cost benefits they had came from the fact that they did not use the hub airports. The faster turnaround times were critical because they reduced the overhead burden represented by depreciation by allowing the planes to be in the air earning for longer than the full-cost carriers.

What stopped the full-service airlines matching what the LCCs were doing was their legacy: they were locked into the hub-and-spoke system. If they started to migrate away from the hubs, they lost the critical mass that was the original justification for the model; so they had to stay. Also, by moving away they risked diluting the connectivity of the system which was supposed to be a source of competitive advantage when competing with LCCs.

PC manufacturers found themselves with a similar dilemma when Dell developed its direct distribution system, bypassing the resellers. Acer, H-P, Compaq, and IBM had invested a great deal of time, effort and money building up third-party distribution which was supposed to give them sustainable barriers to entry. Dell developed a game-changing distribution system that did away with third-party distribution. This gave it significantly lower costs and it was not faced with inventory blockages in the distribution pipeline because it only made and sold to order. For years, Acer, H-P, Compaq, and IBM were handicapped by their investment in third-party distribution. They had too much invested in the system to abandon it and switch over to copy Dell. For any one of them to contemplate doing so could lead to dealer defections to the others; so none did. Meanwhile Dell profited handsomely at their expense.

Just as the LCCs had made a virtue of not being invested in legacy arrangements in hub airports, so Dell made a virtue of not being invested in third-party distribution. By changing the game, they were able to turn previous sources of strength in the incumbents' business models into sources of weakness.

Recognizing strategies have "sell-by dates"

One of the biggest risks companies face is to continue with successful strategies without asking whether the sources of the success have become obsolete. The "if it ain't broke, don't fix it" mindset is dangerous for it breeds complacency and reinforces an inward-looking mentality that fails to spot early-warning signals of impending change externally that could make the strategy worse than irrelevant.

External change in the form of new competitive business models, changes in technology, or sociopolitical considerations all may serve to take a successful strategy past its sell-by date.[3] Unrecognized new forms of competition may render the company's offerings obsolete or, worse still, put the company out of business. This can happen when the board does not see or understand how these new forms are in fact not head-to-head competitors but, rather, substitutes for the product category as a whole. This particular type of threat is termed "disruptive technology" and it destroys entire markets.

There are countless examples of strategies that went past their sell-by date. For instance, when digital cameras and digital files destroyed the market for analog cameras and film, strategies that had served Kodak so well for a hundred years became irrelevant. When planes became powerful and reliable enough to carry passengers across the Atlantic, the luxury liners that had spent years competing with each other in the Blue Riband race across the Atlantic went out of business. Their focus on the race created a demand for speed which aircraft were better placed to satisfy than ships, and so one by one the great transatlantic liners and their companies disappeared after the Second World War.

Why does this kind of blind spot to strategic obsolescence happen in industry after industry? The answer is that incumbents are locked into a mindset based on past success that becomes difficult to change and, as a result, boards no longer understand what it is that their customers are really buying. This can be the result of disruptive technology or social change: "foresight is a real problem; the usefulness of the change may be hidden; there may be a need for complementary inventions or infrastructure for the change to get traction; it may require a recombination of existing technologies in unusual ways for the hidden needs to be met."[4]

Foresight was certainly a problem for Thomas Watson, the founder of IBM, who, at the end of the Second World War, predicted world demand for computers would reach no higher than five. Marconi foresaw radio for ship-to-ship and ship-to-shore communication, but never saw the potential for broadcasting. Bell Labs did not apply for laser patents in telecoms, where they made a huge difference. Nor did it see the potential of transistors; Sony did.

Sometimes before an invention can become an innovation, its usefulness is hidden because of the need for either complementary inventions or investment infrastructure to make it work. For example, for lasers to make a difference in telecoms, there needs to be investment in fiber-optic backbones—the one is unable to deliver value without the other. Faxes and phones were useless unless they had other machines with which they communicated and, for this to work, achieving critical mass was essential. The impact of so-called network effects cannot be overstated. Without the network, the Internet is pointless.

The problem of network effects is that they take a long time to be achieved, and often gestation is not under the company's control, as it may depend on third parties to do the investing in the network. IBM's failure to appreciate the network effect when launching its incompatible OS2 operating system meant that the existing network of developers who were writing applications using Microsoft's MS-DOS as their platform prevented IBM from commercializing OS2. To build an equivalent network would have taken too long. It took much longer for the telephone to spread than the fax; and for the fax than the Internet. The reason for this is simple: phone companies had to build the infrastructure; faxes and the Internet were able to leverage off that existing infrastructure without having to invest in developing it.

Recombining existing technologies can create powerful new applications that were not foreseeable, using normal frames of reference. Sony's Walkman and all the personal portable digital-sound systems that descended from it are a case in point. All of the necessary technologies existed. It just took the genius of Sony's engineers to put them together into a new package that created new possibilities. They were then followed by Nokia and others with mobile phones and Apple with the iPod.

Another celebrated example is the nuclear submarine. The elements that made it unique and different all existed: submarines were already standard in many navies; the Russians and Americans had ICBMs targeted at each other's cities and nuclear reactors to generate power were well-established. Precisely because the technologies were tested and mature, it was possible for Admiral Hyman Rickover to come up with the revolutionary idea of combining them.[5] The result changed the face of nuclear warfare. Nuclear submarines can hide in the ocean for years and because they carry ICBMs they guarantee the second-strike capability of both the Americans and Russians. By guaranteeing Armageddon, they made nuclear annihilation unlikely.

Making Informed Decisions

Informed business decisions have five elements in common: they frame the issue appropriately; reflect the values of the organization; generate creative alternatives; are based on meaningful and reliable information; and create clear tradeoffs, based on logical, correct reasoning.

Framing issues appropriately

The key to making well-informed and relevant decisions is making sure that the problem to be solved has been framed correctly in the first place.[6] If it is wrongly framed, there is a great risk that the wrong problem is being addressed: however excellent the solution, it will not help if it is tackling symptoms rather than causes.

Consequently it is important to understand the objective of the decision-making exercise before it is undertaken. Is it strategic or operational in scope? What are the assumptions underlying the issue as it is understood? Three questions that must be answered are: What is the company trying to achieve? Why? How will it know if it has succeeded?

Once these questions have been answered, the company can proceed to use Motorola's Six Sigma techniques to get at underlying root causes. Figure 6.4 below shows how using Toyota's "Five Whys" technique (by being confronted with the question "Why?" five times, the person answering is forced to go down a level each time to finally get at the root cause) in combination with the "Ishikawa Fishbone" is very useful for getting beyond symptoms to analyze cause and effect.

It is not the job of the board to get into the details of a Six Sigma process; it is the job of the management and the CEO to ensure that such a process has been adopted so that what is presented to the board is based on solving the problems.

The board needs to distinguish between strategic and operational issues. If the issue in question is one that requires a fundamental re-examination of the way business is done, it is likely to be strategic and the role of the board; if it is operational then it is the responsibility of line management. In any event, the business model and behavioral assumptions must be clearly articulated and agreed at the board as part of the strategic planning process.

When discussing business model assumptions it is important to recognize that:

- Deciding on what to offer may no longer depend on either the product or market characteristics, but on the customer.
- The market itself may no longer be either domestic or regional, but global.
- Instead of focusing on features and quality, the emphasis may now be on speed, flexibility and "just-in-time" approaches.

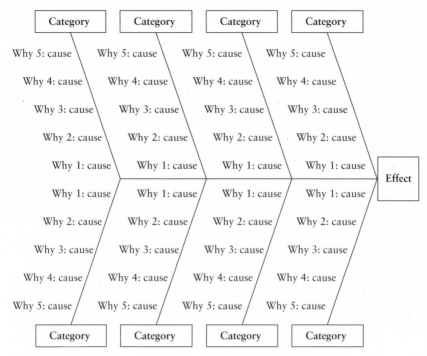

FIGURE 6.4 Ishikawa Fishbone using Five Why technique

- Marketing may have moved from a mass-marketing approach through segmented marketing to niche marketing or mass customization.
- Instead of benchmarking competitors, success may only be assured by leapfrogging them.
- Instead of adopting an adversarial approach to suppliers, companies may have to move toward building a limited number of quality relationships based on trusted suppliers.
- It may be necessary to move from a "command and control" attitude to information and business processes, to a new model of networked core competences[7] and smart partnerships.
- The measures that are needed have changed over the past 30 years as boards have come to recognize the limitations of traditional data and understand the importance of Six Sigma and Balanced Scorecards in addition to financial data.[8]

The behavioral assumptions managers make must be made explicit. This is particularly important if the company operates in more than one country, so that misunderstandings about behavioral outcomes and the meanings of behavior are avoided.[9]

Framing issues correctly can bring to the surface communication problems caused by differing assumptions about what matters which are the result of divergent cultural axioms about how to behave. Often people fail to convince each other because they have different mental models and corresponding ladders of inference that make them quite literally "talk past each other."[10]

Reflecting organizational values

In addition to ensuring that the organization has a strategy whose aspirations and personal values are acceptable to the top management team, there are serious operational issues to consider as well, usually reflected in the company's code of conduct.

Values matter. A focus on Ends values alone at the expense of Means values suggests to staff that the ends justify the means and that anything goes. If companies are to pay attention to Means values they must spell out what is acceptable and what is not. Once these values have been articulated, they must be monitored, measured and rewarded, with deviations punished.

But business is about getting things done and boards and companies must find the right balance between ends and means. The following four-stage model may help in this regard.

Stage 1: End-result ethics: Here the primary test is whether whatever is decided will deliver results. By itself, such an approach is Machiavellian: anything goes, as long as the desired outcome is achieved. This is the first step in any determination of policy, since there is no point in adopting a course of action that is ineffective. However, this is not enough. Boards and the top management team need to go to the second stage to ensure that the company is not put at risk through failure of procedure or process.

Stage 2: Rule-based ethics: Here the primary test is whether the action indicated by Stage 1 violates company rules and procedures. If it does, it should not be allowed because the long-term damage to the organization from having no clear rules, policies and procedures will outweigh any short-term benefits. This particular perspective—namely, that policies and procedures are important—is one of the factors that differentiate first-world and third-world economies. Too often in developing countries, decisions are taken in violation of agreed procedures, encouraging a "grace and favor" approach to decision-making that promotes unpredictable outcomes and corruption.

Stage 3: Social-contract ethics: Assuming the proposed decision has passed the tests in Stages 1 and 2, here the test is really about how the proposed decision will affect other people. Will adopting the proposed course of action have consequences for society as a whole and for other stakeholders within the organization? If so, have those consequences been taken into account? Perhaps the best way to characterize these factors is to use a couple of simple guides: How will it look if it appears in tomorrow's newspaper? Will the decision stand the test of time; will it still seem appropriate with the benefit of hindsight? If the answer to either question is "No," then it would be prudent not to take that decision.

Stage 4: Personal ethics: Finally there is the simple test of how the decision makes each individual feel. Can he or she sleep at night knowing the full consequences of the decision?

Decisions that pass all four stages are right/good decisions because they take into account the values of the organization, of society and of the individual, and are also effective, achieving the desired outcomes.

Generating creative alternatives

Boards must avoid being presented with a single option by line management. Being presented with only one case leaves two unattractive outcomes: if they accept, they run the risk of becoming a cipher, rubber-stamping what management proposed; if they reject the proposal, they run the risk of de-motivating managers who may have put a great deal of time, thought and effort into the proposal.

To enable the board to make informed choices, it is suggested that it should be presented with a number of alternatives to review:

- *One requiring a substantial increase in the budget*, but that delivers correspondingly more in view of the increased risk.
- *One requiring a substantial reduction in the budget*, but that delivers correspondingly less in view of the reduced risk.
- *Continue with the budget as is.*
- *Stop the project and preserve its salvage value.*[11]

Creativity is a systematic activity that can be trained. It begins with brainstorming designed to maximize divergent thinking. Only when a large list of unfiltered ideas has been generated does the process of screening begin, as the team tries to create convergence in their thinking without creating "groupthink." The techniques designed to encourage a diversity of ideas include:

- *Playing Devil's advocate*, where questions focus on the opposite outcomes of what is held to be likely. This allows managers to "think the unthinkable" and to create scenarios that prepare them for the unexpected.
- *Arguing by analogy* allows managers to see whether solutions to problems in other environments have possible application to the problem they currently face. Benchmarking is a formalized way of doing this.
- *Putting oneself on the other side of the table* allows managers to see how the offer, proposition or argument feels to the person to whom it is being made and whether it is convincing when seen from the other side of the table. More valuable still, once they have put themselves in the shoes of a customer, they can develop a different route to breakthrough results by recognizing the missing conditions and rectifying the problem.
- *Imagining "desired states,"* where a different and desirable future outcome for the company is imagined, with the team then working back from there to current reality and assuming ways to bridge the gap. By defining the gaps, managers then have a good idea of what needs to be done. This, in turn, helps them develop an action plan with milestones and accountabilities to create what has been assumed to exist, but which is not yet in place.[12]
- *Avoiding "black hats,"* which are the judgments passed on ideas generated in all the creative processes. These normally take the form of objections that might look helpful, but they are designed to kill off the ideas. Typical black-hat objections include phrases such as "We tried that before and it did not work;" "Great idea, but we don't have the resources;" "We need to spend more time to make it perfect;" and so on.

  Rather than allowing such objections to kill off ideas, the top management team should seek ways of making them practicable by asking questions such as "How can we make this more relevant?" "What kinds of resources do we need to follow up on this idea?" "If we had unlimited resources, what should we do, and in what order, to make this happen?"

The interaction of each step with the other steps and the options available within each provide a range of "what-if" scenarios, all of which have their own individual outcomes. In making its decision, the board will need to assess each outcome to determine whether it is actionable in the real world and which delivers the best returns, after allowing for the risk profile and appetite of the company. When testing and refining these options, the board should seek expert opinion from outside, as well as using sources inside the company.[13]

Using meaningful and reliable information

Given that there are no facts about the future, the board needs to look for information that will yield insights into the future so that it can understand what tomorrow's business will look like, while still doing today's. Doing this effectively requires the board to put aside comfortable assumptions about how the business operates. It might be useful, in this regard, to use Donald Rumsfeld's famous "Known Knowns" framework to categorize information.[14] In developing this information it is essential to recognize that traditional forecasting is not enough; to adopt an "outside-in" rather than "inside-out" approach; and to access the right "outside in" information.

Typical errors involved in traditional forecasting include assuming that there is a technical approach that will work; looking at historical data and projecting from these without recognizing that the past is at best an imperfect predictor of the future; adjusting the assumptions until a positive net present value is obtained; and believing that the numbers are real.

The effectiveness of an "outside-in" approach will depend on accessing the right information. This is a combination of facts (past observable data) and judgment (justifiable perspectives of future possibilities) made possible by:

- *staying close to customers*, using focus groups, surveys and informal feedback. It is important to remember, however, that staying close to customers has not helped firms that were hit by disruptive technological change.
- *involving supply-chain members*, where upstream and downstream partners can be useful sources of information and ideas because they know about impending changes in their own customers' uses of technology, about changes in processes or new products in the pipeline and, in particular, how these will affect the competitiveness of the company's offers.

- *involving industry experts*, who may include government regulators and legislators, to obtain early-warning signals of changes in impending regulations and legislation that could adversely affect the company's license to operate, as well as academics, consultants and investment analysts, who all bring a different perspective to bear on how the company is doing, where it is going and whether or not that makes sense.[15]

Creating logical tradeoffs

Western tradition demands that we use fact-based reasoning to create and evaluate alternatives facing the company. This requires modeling alternative outcomes so the board is able to shift its sights from the present to the future: from the world it knows to the world it seeks to know and understand. Traditional financial analysis goes only so far. It must be supplemented with an understanding of the sources of uncertainty surrounding decisions, and this must then be quantified. To do this well, the board must be sure it has adopted a process that:

- *Expresses uncertainty in terms of probabilities:* Managers normally create a "point estimate" for each item being reviewed—for example, "the cost of launching product X will be US$5 million." This spurious accuracy affects the thought process. A more appropriate way of thinking about uncertainty is to recognize that all the important values lie along a range, which reflects judgments about the likely sources of uncertainty. In these circumstances it is better to say "The cost of launching product X will be in the range of US$3.5 million to US$6 million." Yet most people will not do this for fear of appearing too vague and therefore not on top of their subject.[16] Rather than try to create spurious accuracy, today's cheap computing power allows managers to do Monte Carlo simulations[17] covering all the different ranges of possible outcome, allowing quantification of the likely profile of the envelope of risks.
- *Avoids bias:* Individuals try to make things more concrete and certain when faced with uncertainty and then they suffer from overconfidence bias, which encourages people to make the twin mistake of selecting a point estimate, and choosing too narrow a range—which means that the actual results fall outside the expected range. The most pernicious element in the process is the use of an "anchor" reference point around which people then

build their assumptions regarding the appropriate range. The presence of the "anchor" affects them in the first instance, allowing them to fall into the trap of setting the range too narrowly as a result of their overconfidence in their judgment.[18] Experts are no better because they do not get punished for being wrong: all that matters is that they speak with authority.[19]

Another form of bias that can affect the process is confirmation bias, which has its source in selective memory. People remember and are likely to believe evidence that confirms their current beliefs and selectively forget or downplay anything that does not.

- *Makes explicit what is **not** known:* Repeatable bias[20] leads people to misconstrue uncertainty or avoid dealing with it altogether.[21] Even so, the organization must plan for the future and there are no facts about the future, only hypotheses:

> A smart organization learns how to work with uncertainty in its decision process, identifying what it knows and does not know. It makes decisions without sweeping uncertainty under the rug. It identifies the key sources of uncertainty, assesses them as well as possible, and then creates strategies with the best balance of risk and return. It recognizes it can hedge and manage uncertainty, but never eliminate it.[22]

The resulting information allows the company to assess upsides and downsides and see how they fit with the company's and its shareholders' risk appetite.

Even the simplest models create several alternatives between the financial flows over different time horizons, with different market sizes, shares, margins, competitor reactions, inflation, interest and tax rates, with several hurdle rates reflecting varied assumptions about risk and the risk-free rate of return. Monte Carlo simulations allow a much wider and richer set of analyses to generate likely scenarios, which need to be matched with the company's particular risk–reward profile.

This way of analyzing the options is impersonal so that there are no positions to defend or face to be saved. All that is needed is to examine the sensitivities and the size of their impact; the time at which they become critical to the outcome; and the level of risk they reflect, and whether this is acceptable for the company. To do this, there needs to be clarity about the possible tradeoffs the board must consider and these tradeoffs relate to the Ends issues of the organization and to the Executive Limitations placed on the CEO.

Ends issues tradeoffs might include such things as customer value versus shareholder value; earnings versus corporate social responsibility; long-term versus short-term results (the exact definition of long-term and short-term will differ by industry, but the tension will always exist); and revenue growth versus profit growth.

Executive limitations tradeoffs might include cash flow versus profit—the timing and use to which the cash flows are put (for example, reinvestment versus dividends or share buyback). They might also include the impact of a project on the sources and uses of funds, whether the company is going to need debt or equity financing and the effect this might have on its credit rating, cost of capital and risk profile. Other points to consider in this regard relate to the company's exposure to sovereign risk and its potential effect on exchange rates; the risk to assets and people resulting from changes in policy; and the possible adverse impact on the company's reputation that involvement in a particular type of business might have, including issues of ethics, integrity, and corruption.[23]

Ten Steps from Strategy to Action

Strategy must be connected to action via effective implementation. There is no such thing as a great strategy that is poorly executed. If it was poorly executed, it was a poor strategy because conception must include effective execution. On the other hand, it is possible to have a poorly conceived strategy well executed, and experience shows that this will deliver better results than the former, for the simple reason that 90 percent of strategic success lies in its implementation.

There is often a disconnect between strategy development and action: many companies know what ought to be done, but do not do it.[24] There are many reasons for this inertia, but perhaps the most important is that senior managers believe that merely by analyzing and discussing an issue they have made something happen, when nothing has in fact changed. Also they often believe that because a decision has been taken at the board, it has been transmitted effectively to the rest of the organization to the people who will implement it. There is a very real risk that during the process of transmission from the board to the employees who make it real, the message will get distorted or sabotaged as it passes through what Niall Fitzgerald, when he was chairman of Unilever Ltd, called the "marshmallow layer of management."

Well-executed strategic decisions recognize the different levels and roles involved in implementing decisions. Any decision that fails to take into account the feelings and vested interests of all involved in making the decision work, will not be a good decision.

To avoid such failures of implementation, it helps to recognize that from the conception of a strategy to its effective execution there are 10 steps:

1. Decide on the Ends of the business.
2. Articulate the business mission.
3. Create a compelling vision.
4. Set the over-riding business objective.
5. Agree the subordinate business objectives.
6. Align the strategic enablers.
7. Define the "desired states."
8. Agree the gaps.
9. Agree the action plan.
10. Commit to action, recognizing the importance of "buy-in."

The first three steps were covered in Chapter 2, so we'll start here with Step 4.

Step 4: Setting the overriding business objective (OBO)

The OBO must capture in a single memorable phrase the purpose of the business and be:

- *A call to action*: It must be simple enough for the most junior person to grasp; unifying across all divisions and departments; and supported and reinforced by subordinate objectives.
- *An explanation of why people come to work every day*: Everybody in the organization must understand where their individual role fits in delivering the OBO. It gives meaning to their work, no matter how menial the task, and as a result allows them to take pride in belonging to the organization.

Step 5: Agreeing the subordinate business objectives (SBOs)

Doing this requires that the value chain is divided up into discrete elements, each with its own key objective that:

- *Supports the OBO:* It makes sense that the SBOs should derive their legitimacy from the OBO; otherwise there is a risk that a part of the value chain may be at odds with the direction of the company as a whole. This is why organizational alignment is so important.

- *Is consistent with SBOs of other elements in the value chain:* Sometimes there is what appears to be a legitimate inconsistency between the SBO of one department and that of another. By articulating formally what the SBOs of each element are supposed to be, it becomes possible to avoid internal contradictions through careful negotiation. For example, the sales force always wants to maximize the number of SKUs it can offer and wants as much stock available so that customers are not inconvenienced. The finance function, on the other hand, wants to keep working capital to a minimum and this means minimizing the numbers of SKUs and the amount of inventory the company has to hold. Obviously these two approaches contradict, and unless there is a mature conversation and negotiation between the two departments, there will be conflict at the expense of achieving the OBO.

- *Creates synergy between the different parts of the value chain:* The whole idea behind business process re-engineering and Six Sigma is to reduce the problems of hand-off (that is, finishing one stage in the process and passing the semi-finished product to someone else at the next step in the process). By cutting down on the number of hand-offs, quality is improved greatly and costs are reduced through simplification and a corresponding reduction in the need for expensive rework. The same logic applies for the value chain as a whole.

Step 6: Aligning the strategic enablers

The strategic enablers are McKinsey's famous "Seven S" framework plus two more Ss: sequence and significance.

Figure 6.5 shows the importance of achieving alignment in the seven elements if the mission and the vision and also the OBO (which is a distillation of the two into one memorable call to action) are to be achieved.

The framework shows that at the heart of delivering the OBO are the shared values of the organization: what kind of business it is; how people within the organization will behave toward each other and their external stakeholders; and what things it will not do and what behaviors it will not tolerate.

This then drives the strategy of the organization: what it is trying to achieve and how it will do that. The strategy in turn defines the structures of the organization: how resources are to be allocated and who is accountable for them.

Structure in turn has a powerful influence on the design and implementation of systems: how information flows, when and to whom; and how people will be rewarded and recognized for the work they have done. It affects all the informal feedback mechanisms as well as the formal ones.

Strategy, structure and systems all affect how the tasks will be performed and therefore what staffing levels are needed. However, staffing on its own is only the raw material; people need to have the required competencies and skills to do the jobs well, and so desired skills are affected by all of the preceding elements. Finally, style is about behavior.

Figure 6.5 shows through the direction of the dotted lines that there is a preferred sequence in which the seven enablers need to be put in place. The solid lines show that there is interdependency between all seven, so that it is not enough simply to implement them

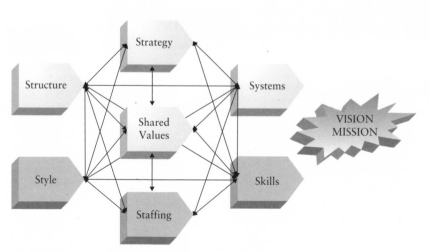

FIGURE 6.5 **Importance of alignment to deliver Vision and Mission**
Based on McKinsey's 7S framework.

in the right order, but that implementation has to take into account their impact on each other.

In addition to thinking about the sequencing of implementation, we need to think about the relative significance of the elements and which, if not done, will hold up implementation and have adverse effects on the other elements, perhaps leading to overall failure.

Figure 6.6 shows how a company that sets itself the OBO of achieving market leadership might go about this. The illustrative value chain is broken into seven constituent parts—each with its subordinate objectives which are designed to help it achieve the OBO. The strategic enablers on the right-hand side follow the same sequence as the "7S" framework except that there is no strategy. Instead, strategy is shown as the vector that is the sum of each of the other 6 Ss, allowing for both sequence and significance.

Step 7: Defining the "desired states"

In Figure 6.6, at each intersection of strategy and the enablers there is a series of crosses to represent the required "desired states" necessary for the subordinate business objectives to be realized. A couple of examples will help:

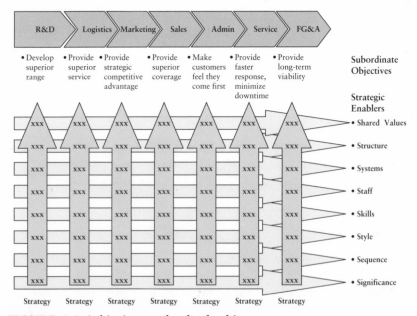

FIGURE 6.6 Achieving market leadership

- *Skills:* where "Never lose a sale through poor salesmanship" is the desired outcome at the intersection of "Selling" and "Skills." Such an outcome can only be achieved if, for example, the "desired states" stipulate that the following skills must exist in the sales force: listening skills; closing skills for small orders; consultative selling skills for large orders where the buyer takes a significant personal risk in making the decisions; account-strategy development skills; planning and goal-setting skills and good time management.

- *Style:* where *"Make customers feel they come first"* is the desired outcome at the intersection of "Style" and "Customer administration." Such an outcome can only be achieved if, for example, the "desired states" stipulate that the following behaviors must exist in customer administration: the customer is treated as a friend and not as a problem; phones are answered within three rings; callers are never left hanging in the system; and everybody in the company recognizes they are a part of the frontline.[25]

Step 8: Agreeing the gaps

Once the "desired states" have been defined, the next stage is to decide where the company stands. This requires an objective analysis of current resources, competencies, capabilities and attitudes and how they affect the development of strategy, structure, systems, and so on. The differences between the current state of play and the future "desired states" define the gaps to be closed while achieving the subordinate business objectives.

Step 9: Agreeing the action plan

As soon as it is evident that there are gaps, the top management team needs to agree to an action plan to bridge them.

In order to avoid falling into the "Knowing-Doing" trap that so many companies suffer from, the board must make sure the CEO gains the motivation and commitment to action from internal stakeholders. The most effective way to do this is to get them involved in the process of defining the desired states and the ensuing gap analysis (that is, in Steps 7–9). Most critically, they must not just be partners in developing the action plan, they must also be owners of the timelines and the need to achieve the key milestones, so that they can influence others to do what is required.

The most effective way to get this essential buy-in is to follow a two-step process:

- *Identify the critical obstacles:* The CEO, as "owner" of the decision, must determine, along with the most senior managers who are going to have to deliver the results, the three to five biggest obstacles to success. Brainstorming techniques will no doubt produce a long list and it is then up to the top management team to determine the most critical and set the others aside to be dealt with at a later date.
- *Identify the best way to overcome these obstacles:* The CEO must work with the most senior managers affected by the decision to establish a range of solutions to the key obstacles identified. Again, the process is the same. Once the most urgent and important solutions to the key problems have been voted upon, tabled and agreed, the others are set aside for implementation at a later date.

Following these two steps enables the top management team to know what needs to be done and when. What is now needed is commitment to action.

Step 10: Committing to action

Every person involved in the identification of the solutions in Step 9 must commit personally to doing something measurable by a self-appointed and agreed due date. Everybody involved will be held accountable for the parts they have agreed. Formal action plans are then drawn up, with due dates, and names against each milestone, and all team members formally sign off on the master planning document, which serves to reinforce their individual and collective accountability.

If the process requires a change in the way business is done or in mindset, then the board and CEO must set up a communication process that allows people to come to terms with the need for change, as illustrated in Figure 6.7.

Internal stakeholders must be made aware of the need for change and this must be communicated from the top. The appropriate way to do this is to show that the drivers of change are external to the organization and that if the organization does not change under its own steam, it will be changed by others from outside. Once people

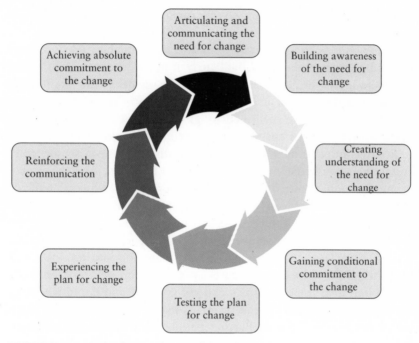

FIGURE 6.7 **Articulating the need for change**

in the company begin to understand the need for change it becomes possible to gain conditional commitment and in those circumstances the top management team and the key opinion formers in the organization can get employees to start testing the plan for change by targeting the areas where results will be more easily achieved, and then celebrating each success so that employees become less nervous about the implications of change.

The Role of the Board in Succession Planning and Talent Management

France's President De Gaulle is reputed to have said the cemeteries of the world are filled with the graves of indispensable men. The sad truth is that nobody is indispensable and therefore succession planning is critical to the sustained success of any organization. Yet time and again, boards fail to plan succession effectively.

In case boards think that succession planning is an operational problem or is too sensitive an issue for them to become involved in, directors must remember that it is, in fact, one of the six principal responsibilities of a board, as we saw outlined earlier in the Malaysian Code of Corporate Governance.[25]

Many boards do a good job of finding and replacing CEOs. Many fewer, however, understand the bench of talent below the CEO—the members of the organization's senior management who are its first and second line. Yet it is their responsibility to know these people well enough to make informed judgments when their names come up for review and for ensuring that they are fit for key roles.

Boards must understand the responsibilities these senior roles entail: the skills and competencies required to do the jobs; the appropriate personality attributes and, of course, the required balance between Ends and Means values. They must have a clear picture of how each candidate for the jobs in question fits these parameters. Do they have the necessary skills and competencies? If not, can they acquire them in the time available before moving into the job? Will they strike the right balance between getting the job done ethically and in line with the company's code of conduct and doing whatever it takes to achieve the desired results? Finally, do they have the right temperament for the job? Putting people with the wrong temperament into key jobs can be a guarantee of failure, even if they appear to have the right skills and competencies.

Using the analogy of a ship to help determine leadership qualities in succession planning, there are three types of leader: captains, navigators, and shipbuilders. They have quite different skills and temperaments.

Captains are good at deciding where they are going, when they will leave port and when they need to arrive and, at allocating crew responsibilities accordingly. They are in their element when the ocean gets really rough and unpredictable. They are highly skilled at energizing the crew to do the right things at the right moment, and this is never more important than in a typhoon that risks sinking the ship. It goes without saying that captains must be good communicators.

Navigators are skilled at plotting courses once they know where they are going and how long they have to get there. They will evaluate all the options and advise their captains on the best route to take, what course corrections are likely to be needed and they track progress continuously to make sure that when the typhoon strikes, they can take avoiding action and still get back on course. From a technical perspective, navigators need higher levels of skill than captains, though their interpersonal skills need not be as highly developed.

Like captains, navigators must keep calm in typhoons and work out alternative courses of action for their captains to take.

Thus good captains need good navigators to succeed. Yet both need good shipbuilders, for if the ship is poorly built, it will not respond to the navigator's course corrections or to the captain's directions. So shipbuilders are essential. But we need to remember that good shipbuilders build ships in dry dock. Temperamentally, they are not good at dealing with typhoons. They need the certainty of dry land and are less good at handling the uncertainty of the ocean. They may be great project managers but putting a good shipbuilder in the role of a captain or navigator in a typhoon is asking for trouble.

Successful companies need these three types of leader at all levels and they must be able to work together. Boards must recognize this and understand which type of leader they are dealing with in succession planning lest they choose wrongly and risk sinking the ship.

Finally, while it is true that the operational responsibility for effective talent management sits with the CEO and line management, supported by HR, it is the responsibility of the board to ensure that the right talent strategy is in place: one that recognizes that the unique portfolio of talents needed for the organization to thrive will change over time in an increasingly competitive world where the key success factors are determined by a dynamic combination of external and internal forces.

At the heart of successful talent management is the recognition that yesterday's skills, knowledge and attitudes may not be what are needed today and most probably are not what will be appropriate for tomorrow's successful business.

This recognition requires directors to review the existing talent-management strategy annually to confirm the critical positions throughout the organization as they change with business growth and evolving external threats and opportunities. However, directors must not only know which positions are critical to the success of the organization, they must also understand the required competencies for those positions; and this in turn means that the board must review and approve the competency models being used by HR to ensure they remain aligned to changing business needs.

Too often, talent management only looks at technical competencies—be they related to subject matter or interpersonal skills—without integrating them with the organization's values. Yet, the values of the organization are vital as they are the unchanging glue that binds everybody together. Above all, it is the board's responsibility to ensure that people moving up the talent pipeline, or recruited from outside, live those values. The board must ensure that expediency in filling vacant positions does not override the principles of how people should behave. "Fitting in or falling out" is an essential part of moving up the talent-management pipeline. The failures of talented people hired from outside can often be attributed to their inability to come to terms with the values of the organization they joined.

Boards must also understand the need for the right mix of specialists (people who "know more and more about less and less") and generalists, who are able to integrate what the specialists are doing and so prevent divisive silo thinking. This usually means having two career ladders: a management ladder that depends on the generalist leadership and people-management skills being developed appropriately, and a specialist technical ladder that promotes people for their technical contributions. Too often, companies have only the one career ladder, forcing people who are great technicians to move into management positions for which they may be temperamentally unsuited. Thus, the organization is harmed twice over: through the loss of applied technical skills, and through the mismanagement of subordinates.

Endnotes

1 Carroll, A.B. and Hoy, F. 1984, "Integrating Corporate Social Policy into Strategic Management," *Journal of Business Strategy* 4 (3): 52.
2 Dobson, P., Starkey, K. and Richards, J. 2004, *Strategic Management and the Search for Competitive Advantage*, Oxford: Blackwell Publishing.
3 For a full discussion of the strategic threats posed by political, economic, social and technological change, see Zinkin, J. 2003, *What CEOs Must Do to Succeed*, Kuala Lumpur: Prentice Hall: 2–19, 62–155.
4 Ibid.: 107–28; See also Rosenberg, N. 1995, "Innovation's Uncertain Terrain," *McKinsey Quarterly* 3.
5 http://inventors.about.com/od/militaryhistoryinventions/a/Military_Subs_3.htm, visited on February 22, 2009.
6 A good technique to check this is to draft a press release for each of the affected constituencies, even if it is not needed. This allows the story to be reviewed through multiple lenses. See Pollard, I. 2009, *Investing in Your Life*, Queensland: John Wiley & Sons Australia: 332.

7 See Prahalad, C. K. and Hamel, G. 1990, "The Core Competence of the Corporation," *Harvard Business Review*, May–June.

8 Wallace and Zinkin 2005, *Corporate Governance*, Singapore: John Wiley & Sons: 130–1.

9 See Zinkin 2003, op. cit.: 280–98.

10 Senge, P. 1990, *The Fifth Discipline: The Art and Practice Of The Learning Organization*, New York: Doubleday.

11 This suggested approach is based on one developed for R&D investments in Matheson, D. and Matheson, J. 1998, *The Smart Organization—Creating Value through Strategic R&D*, Boston: Harvard Business Press: 40–1.

12 For a full discussion of how to use "Desired States," see Zinkin 2003, op. cit.: 197–200.

13 This section is based on Wallace and Zinkin 2005, op. cit.: 133–6.

14 In a Department of Defense Briefing on February 12, 2002, Rumsfeld said: "Reports that say that something hasn't happened are always interesting to me, because as we know, there are known knowns; there are things we know we know. We also know there are known unknowns; that is to say we know there are some things we do not know. But there are also unknown unknowns—the ones we don't know we don't know. And if one looks throughout the history of our country and other free countries, it is the latter category that tends to be the difficult ones."

15 This section is based on Wallace and Zinkin 2005, op. cit.: 136–8.

16 Matheson and Matheson 1998, op. cit.: 43–4.

17 "A problem-solving technique used to approximate the probability of certain outcomes by running multiple trial runs, called simulations, using random variables." See: http://www.investopedia.com/terms/m/montecarlosimulation.asp.

18 Overconfidence is a general phenomenon and is critical when a company is trying to do something it has never done before. Some examples of the level of overconfidence are useful as a warning:

- The employees of a chemical company thought they would only get 10 percent of general business facts wrong. In fact they got 50 percent wrong. As far as company-related facts were concerned they thought they might get 50 percent wrong. In fact it was 79 percent.

- In another, computer-related, company, they thought they would get only 5 percent of general business facts wrong. In fact it was 80 percent. With regard to their own company, they estimated would get 5 percent wrong, but got 58 percent wrong.

- Even physicians got the probability that a patient has pneumonia wrong: 82 percent, against their own estimates of 0–20 percent.

See Russo, J. E. and Schoemaker, P. J. H. 1989, *Decision Traps—The Ten Barriers To Brilliant Decision-Making and How To Avoid Them*, New York: Fireside Book, Simon and Schuster: 2.

19 Ibid.: 73.

20 The inability to repeat a test is often a good guide to the poorness of the validity of the prediction. However, the fact that a test is repeatable is not a guarantee of the validity of the outcomes.

21 Kahnaman, D., Slovic, P. and Tversky, A. (eds) 1986, *Judgment Under Uncertainty: Heuristics and Biases*, Cambridge, UK: Cambridge University Press.

22 Matheson and Matheson 1998, op. cit.: 125.

23 This section is based on Wallace and Zinkin 2005, op. cit.:138–42.

24 Pfeffer, J. and Sutton, R. I. 2000, *The Knowing-Doing Gap—How Smart Companies Turn Knowledge Into Action*, Boston: Harvard Business School Press.

25 For more detailed examples across all the elements of the value chain, see Zinkin 2003 op. cit.:197–200.

26 This is reinforced in "Catalyzing GLC Transformation: Green Book Enhancing Board Effectiveness," Asian Roundtable on Corporate Governance, Cebu, Philippines, April 18–20, 2007; available at: http:// www.oecd.org/dataoecd/22/9/40792765.pdf.

7

MANAGING RISK

This chapter explores the different types of external risk that companies face. It then looks at the internal risks and explores the characteristics of an effective risk management system. It outlines the stages involved in matching the company's risk profile to the risk appetite of its shareholders.

A company's ability to manage risk affects not only its share price but its long-term ability to survive and prosper. Risk arises in three ways: externally, internally and in its impact on the company's risk profile compared to the risk appetite of shareholders.

In thinking about risk, it may be helpful to picture the organization as an inverted pyramid—a structure with a broad top, consisting of all the day-to-day operations, each one of which has associated risks, but none of which on its own is likely to bring down the edifice. At the very narrow base—the foundation of the edifice—is systemic risk, which, if it materializes, will by itself bring down the entire edifice at the same time as it breaks the system. Yet precisely because it is hidden from view, it is ignored, until it is too late and the organization's ability to exist is destroyed. In between the two extremes lie strategic and business risks. These are shown in Figure 7.1.

The sources of risk can be either external or internal and it is vital that boards understand how to manage external risks, over which they have no control, as well as the internal ones, over which they have control. They will be held accountable for how well they do

FIGURE 7.1: Organizational risk needs to be managed at four levels

both and it is imperative therefore that responsibility for managing risk is clearly recognized in the board—with the "voice" of risk management being given equal weight with that of revenue generation. A large part of the failure to manage systemic risk in Wall Street arose from the fact that boards were only listening to those who were responsible for revenue and profit growth, ignoring the advice of those who recognized the risks posed by such activities.

Managing External Risks

A failure to understand external risk can lead to crippling problems—from the destruction of demand to disruption of supply at either end of the wealth-creating value chain. It can lead to destructive stresses being put on the balance sheet as a result of assets being written down, either because they have become worthless or because of systemic failure. This can lead to a collapse of the market so that mark-to-market rules force asset values into a vicious downward spiral, eroding the balance sheet to the point of bankruptcy. It can turn assets into liabilities as inventories and debtors go bad when a product becomes obsolete or debtors fail to pay up. Poor business choices can destroy company and brand reputations and as a result damage the valuations placed on the intangible element in market capitalization. Disproportionate dependence on one customer or one product line carries serious risks should they get into trouble for any reason.

Typically when people refer to external risks they mean risks that are political, economic, financial, socio-cultural, technological or competitive. Rarely, however, do they think of systemic risks. Yet, in today's world, it is systemic risks that are the most serious— specifically, those in the global financial system and the eco-systemic risk posed by climate change. We will begin, though, by dealing with the six external risks listed, before discussing the financial systemic risks (which incorporate elements of these six) in more detail.

Political risk

Political risk is often overlooked in mature democratic societies where changes of government come and go without causing too much disruption. Yet even in these societies, lobbying is regarded as a critically important activity to ensure that politicians and legislators understand the impact of the laws they propose.

In less democratic and less transparent societies, where politics and business are intertwined, political risk is extremely important as changes in the political power structure have serious knock-on effects in respect of who gets contracts, which industries are favored, and so on. Not so long ago changes of government in the UK or France meant that completely different industrial policies were adopted, depending on whether the incoming government was conservative or socialist. It is possible that the same may be about to apply in the US with the new Obama Administration, which has a different attitude to the role of government from its predecessor. Healthcare providers, for example, will have a very different political environment under the new administration.

It is therefore extremely important for the board to understand the political agendas of both the government and the opposition, and what effect they will have on the company's strategic freedom and, ultimately, on its ability to prosper.

Changes in legislation can affect terms and conditions of employment through defining the numbers of hours to be worked or imposing a minimum wage; they can affect the freedom of movement of people through immigration policies designed to promote or hinder freer labor markets; they can affect the tax regimes that companies work under through changes in corporation tax, goods and services tax, national insurance levies, exchange rates, and so on. It is therefore vital that boards understand what drives the political and legislative agendas and how these can affect how the company does business.

The excesses of Wall Street were only possible as a result of decisions made by politicians: the repeal of the Glass-Steagall Act in 1999; the promotion of affordable housing that led to the subprime crisis; the pressure on the SEC not to regulate hedge funds and to let the market self-regulate, when it was clearly incapable of doing so. Of course, they were also helped by poor judgment calls by regulators: the SEC not pursuing "Red Flags" suggesting that Bernard Madoff was running the biggest Ponzi scheme of all time; the naïve belief that markets can be trusted to do the right thing; Alan Greenspan forgetting the existence of the Kondratieff Wave, with its 40–60-year cycles, in the buildup of excess credit and repudiation of debt (shown in Figure 7.2).

However, there is a basic problem in dealing with political agendas: politics reflect vested interests that may not be able to coalesce in a way that makes sense to the company. As a result, boards must pay attention to stakeholder analysis, understanding where different constituencies stand on issues that affect the firm and its license to operate, as these constituencies will bring pressure to bear on politicians and the legislative agenda.

In dealing with these issues, boards would do well to remember that politicians are sovereign and hold levers of power that companies cannot match. People are beginning to realize this as a result of the economic crisis we have entered, with companies looking to governments and taxpayers to help them out of their difficulties.[1]

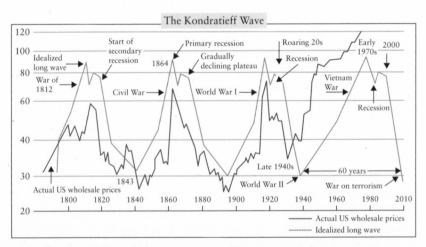

FIGURE 7.2 Kondratieff Wave shows there are 40–60-year cycles
Source: http://www.angelfire.com/or/truthfinder/index22.html.

In thinking about these issues it is important for boards to remember two cardinal subjects: first, the interplay between governments, business and civil society; second, what can happen to companies operating in more than one jurisdiction.

Interplay between government, business and civil society

Figure 7.3 shows three conditions where the relationship between government, business and civil society can be depicted as a series of circles of political influence. In the first case, in a totalitarian society like North Korea or Cuba (or, in the past, the Soviet Union and Maoist China), the government subsumes both civil society and business. There is no room for any political role outside government; government literally swallows everything. In the second case—the mixed economy such as exists in Malaysia or Singapore—the government is still the most important factor in the polity, represented by the relative size of its circle and the fact that business and civil society circles have relatively little independent space outside the government circle. This shows the importance of government in its political impact on business and the relative quiescence of civil society. In the third case, we see business as the dominant circle, with civil society the next largest and government in retreat as the smallest. This could have been the case of the US or the UK before the economic meltdown.

The key point to note is that the political dynamics and the interplay of the three actors are different in the three conditions because of the different power relationships they represent.

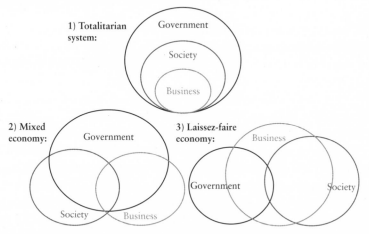

FIGURE 7.3 Interplay between government, business and civil society

As economies transition from one state to the next—or revert, as was being suggested by GE chairman and CEO Jeffrey Immelt,[2] from a US-type laissez-faire economy to a mixed economy more typical of Malaysia, Singapore, and France—boards need to understand what is happening and how the transitions will affect their strategic freedom.

If the company is operating in more than one country, it is even more important for the board to understand whether the conditions prevailing abroad are the same as those in the home country, as this will affect the way the politics is handled. Many Western companies have entered markets in countries like China or Vietnam without understanding the underlying political forces, only to find they have backed the wrong people who promised them access to markets or influential people, and then failed to deliver.

State-owned enterprises and sovereign wealth funds from China, Singapore or the Middle East have gone West only to discover that pluralistic societies with vociferous lobbies and free media are quite different places to do business. The failures of CNOOC to buy Unocal[3] or Dubai Ports to keep the US port operations of P&O[4] are good cases in point.

Jurisdictional crossfire

When companies are caught between competing interpretations of the law, boards have to tread doubly carefully. They cannot afford to alienate the political establishment in either country, and yet sometimes they have to make choices between the lesser of two evils. Subsidiaries of UK and US companies had to make difficult choices during the Apartheid regime in South Africa. Some like Shell, BP and Unilever elected to stay and break South African laws, while respecting US and UK laws, arguing that by remaining engaged they would do more good than harm. Others chose to leave so as not to get in trouble back home. The same issues apply today for multinationals that do business with Zimbabwe, Myanmar and, to a lesser extent, Iran. Many multinationals with codes of conduct that forbid discrimination in employment of any kind have found the past affirmative-action policies of the Malaysian government problematic, and either lobbied for exemptions (which were often granted) or else chose to invest elsewhere.

Boards must remember that political risk translates into legislative and regulatory action, which can either severely limit the freedom to do business or forbid it altogether. Consequently, boards must be constantly alert to the pressures politicians face and the ways they are likely to respond to those pressures and form a view of the possible effect such reactions may have on the company.

For example, few in financial services would have predicted in 2007 that the regulatory regimes would become more restrictive. Yet the colossal failures of regulation in the US and UK and their disastrous consequences, combined with a change of government in the US, have completely changed the climate of opinion regarding financial regulation. Add to this a change of key players at the top and any board should realize the pendulum will swing back to re-regulation and that the days of "light touch" regulation favored by London are over—with enormous consequences for how financial services business will be done in the future.[5]

Economic risk

Boards must understand what is happening in the economy as a whole—nationally and internationally, even if their business is only domestic.

The latest financial and economic crises have set to rest any theories about Asia and emerging markets being decoupled from the US and Europe. Clearly, destruction of demand in the developed economies has had a devastating effect on the export-oriented economies of Asia, leading to stunning declines in exports and GDP in the last quarter of 2008 and first quarter of 2009. These falls in turn have cut the growth rates of the domestic economies of exporting countries so that companies that only do business in their home countries still need to watch what is happening elsewhere in the world.

Such disruptions do not just affect demand, they also affect currencies and the cost of money in ways that may have unforeseen consequences. At the beginning of 2009 it seemed likely that the US and Europe would export deflation to Asia, in particular, as a result of the downturns they created. It seems that this has only really happened in Japan. However, they are also involved in unprecedented levels of fiscal and monetary stimulus, with near-zero interest rates and "quantitative easing" by the Federal Reserve and the Bank of England. These measures may stop the precipitous declines in demand, but they will have long-term inflationary effects, whose timing and consequences are hard to predict. As Nuriel Roubini has argued, the Fed's policies create the "mother of all carry trades" out of the US dollar into higher-yielding assets, leading to further asset bubbles elsewhere in the global economy—bubbles which will burst in due course, with terrible results.[6]

Boards must understand the vastly different effects that growing, stagnating and declining economies have on business prospects, as well as the impact inflation and deflation have on financial strategy and risk.

Rising demand

Boards need to ask in times of overall rising demand whether the rates of growth are sustainable or merely creating an asset bubble, which will have to be unwound painfully later. If an asset bubble is being created, the board must be able to take a view on how long it could last and, more importantly, know how the company will be affected when it finally bursts, and therefore prepare for it.

Boards will need early-warning indicators of what is happening to rates of productivity and attendant inflation. This will help them know whether they will be short of scarce resources at critical times and whether they can raise prices if necessary to compensate for increased costs. This, in turn, will depend on whether or not customers are resistant to price increases. By looking ahead, boards can get management to think of actions that will help them get access to scarce resources and talent in boom times and, equally important, to think about holding on to talent rather than losing it to other companies.

In thinking about how consumers will react, it is vital for boards to understand whether it is domestic suppliers that are satisfying the pent-up demand or whether it is importers who are bringing in goods from low-cost economies such as China and Vietnam. This matters, because one of the most important reasons why the world had rapid growth without inflation in the 1990s and the first years of this century was the entry of huge pools of cheap and skilled labor into the global economy when China and Eastern European countries gave up Communism and India turned its back on autarky.

A key lesson from the years of the dot.com boom was that the tech sector lost control of its inventories and its credit as a result of over-optimistic sales forecasts that the boom would go on forever, financed by vendor credits that turned into losses caused by bad debts. It is a lesson that is being repeated again in 2009 as companies across a huge range of industries and sectors discover to their horror that the boom years have led them to invest in excess capacity that will have to exit the market somehow if the economy is to find its footing once more.

Stagnant demand

Times of stagnant demand may not seem to be problematic, but they are, because shareholders continue to expect high yield and double-digit growth. Increasing revenues in a stagnant market must come at the expense of someone else's market share and that is more difficult to do than in a growing market. This puts extra pressure on the need to save costs, and as cost savings are passed back down the supply chain, one company's savings becomes another company's fall in revenues, thus exacerbating the need to cut costs further. It is this dynamic that means markets rarely stay static for long. They either recover their ability to grow or else are tipped into demand destruction.

Declining demand

Times of demand destruction are the hardest to deal with, especially in today's world of extended supply chains where management are often faced simultaneously with the problems of selling to people who are too scared to buy and the problems caused by disruptions to integrated supply chains.[7]

In these circumstances the key questions boards must answer relate to the company's survival: Is the balance sheet strong enough to continue operating independently? If not, the company must look for a savior or else be prepared to file for Chapter 11 bankruptcy. However, if the balance sheet is strong, there is an opportunity to acquire distressed assets cheaply.

Above all the company will need to think about how to minimize its indebtedness as the real cost of borrowings in a deflationary environment is very high.

After the economy hits bottom, it always turns round. The question is when, and will the company be prepared for the upturn? That again is for the board to consider, so that the company does not miss out on future growth because of excessive cost-cutting and disposal in the short term to keep its head above water.

Financial risk

Financial risk can be both externally caused and the result of poor internal controls. For the moment, we are only concerned with the financial risk that comes from outside—the internal financial issues are covered in the appendices for this chapter.

There are at least three external factors that create serious financial risk: a change in the cost of money; a change in exchange rates; and a general collapse in liquidity. Any one of these, singly or in combination, will affect the risk inherent in the funding structure of the company. When deciding on how to finance a company it is not enough to think solely about the cost of capital and relate it to the discounted net present value of cash streams. The board also has to think carefully about the risk dynamic that a financing strategy brings with it, which can change the risks presented by a given debt-to-equity profile.

Cost of money

As interest rates change, so does the viability of projects. But that is not all; the change in the interest cover may not affect the debt/equity ratio or any margin in it, but lead directly to a downgrade in the company's rating. This in turn will affect the cost of money for the company. We have only to remember what happened to AIG when the rating agencies downgraded the company's rating, leading to the biggest bust of all time.

Boards therefore must pay careful attention to what central bankers are doing. They may raise interest rates to choke off excessive demand, curb the growth of asset bubbles or protect the exchange rate. These actions will hurt the company in three ways: first, by slowing growth; second, by raising the cost of finance, making marginal investment projects uneconomic; and third, simultaneously making it harder for the company to cover its existing interest costs. Obviously the reverse is also true. Lowering interest rates to stimulate the economy or weaken the exchange rate will help the company in the short term, though the inflationary effect of these actions in the long term may have unintended consequences.

Exchange rates

Exchange rates are volatile since most countries no longer have fixed exchange rates (though some, like Hong Kong, are pegged to the US dollar). The demand for currencies is now less about financing trade than about carry trades. The desperate need at the end of 2008 to repatriate dollars to the US was purely to cope with the unprecedented de-leveraging in the second half of 2008. Investors had to get out of commodities, equities and emerging markets all at the same time as a result of the credit crunch, driving down the prices of all asset classes, except for gold. This had the perverse effect of pushing up the price of the dollar when the US economy was at its weakest in decades. As people realized what was happening, the demand for dollars turned into a flight to quality as countries dependent on exports saw their markets collapse.

Liquidity

Perhaps the most important external factor to consider is what is happening to liquidity. Each time the credit markets seize up, the resulting recessions are longer, deeper, and more painful than if they were just part of the normal business cycle. What is perhaps more serious is that boards must remember that we seem never to learn from the mistakes of the past.

Credit crises have been crossing borders since at least 1720 (South Sea Bubble), maybe even earlier if the currency devaluation of the Holy Roman Empire in 1618 is considered. Moreover the US has been the source of contagion since at least 1857, every crisis being worse than the last and the numbers getting steadily bigger.[8] They are always caused by excessive availability of credit leading to speculation; bubbles followed by debt repudiation bringing down the whole house of cards, or in the words of Larry Summers: "Money borrowed in excess and used badly."[9]

What we experienced in 2008–09 is not very different from the Long Term Capital Management Crisis in 1998. In both cases, the mathematical models were found to be wanting and the financial engineers were shown to be people who created no sustainable long-term value and whose hubris was such that they believed their models covered all likely events, except for the Black Swans which, as we saw in Chapter 3, were assumed, incorrectly, to be impossibly rare and therefore could be safely ignored.

Socio-cultural risk

As discussed in an earlier chapter, there are many social trends which boards need to consider because they affect the risk posed to their business by changes in socio-cultural assumptions.

The rise of civil society, with greater press freedom and better education and healthcare, has meant companies have had to take health-and-safety matters and environmental protection much more seriously than before. The growth of the middle class in the BRIC[10] economies is having a huge impact on how people in those countries live and what they will tolerate with regard to product safety and quality.

Usually, socio-cultural change takes a long time, long enough for boards to see it coming. The changing demographics in the developed world that will lead to people living longer and needing different types of healthcare and ways of spending their leisure time should be clear to anyone who spends a little time thinking about such things.

As societies get richer and people work shorter hours, it is almost inevitable that they will want to spend those extra hours of free time seeing their friends and visiting other parts of the world. The boom in tourism, making it the biggest employer worldwide, is not just the result of cheap and safe air transportation (important though that is), but also of the fact that people in the developed world have the time to travel, and to watch TV and read books about the natural, cultural and culinary wonders of different countries.

Technological risk

Coping with technological risk is not just about responding to the creation of new products and services; it is also about recognizing that technology can change processes dramatically so that the adoption of the process by others is what creates new threats to the business.

The Internet is a new technology whose effect on the way we live and do business is still evolving. However, it is the use of the Internet combined with the downturn in consumer demand that has bankrupted electrical-goods retailer Circuit City.[11] Circuit City tried to cut costs by getting rid of experienced staff who gave advice, replacing them with rude, inexperienced staff that cared little about customers. As a result, customers no longer wanted or needed to go into its stores. It was simpler to buy on-line and this change in the way business was done gave its creditors the justification to call in their loans.

For many years Dell was the best-performing PC vendor. This was not the result of superior products or service but, rather, the use of technology to develop a totally different supply and value chain. Dell used the Internet to allow buyers, who now knew enough about PCs, to make bespoke purchases on line. The benefits of this technological innovation in process included better margins for Dell (by cutting out middlemen); satisfied customers who bought exactly what they wanted; negative working capital as Dell only assembled to order after being paid; and practically no obsolescent stock in the pipeline, allowing Dell to introduce upgrades immediately without having to wait to clear inventories. This was such a powerful and patented use of process technology that it took IBM and H-P years to work out the right response to this threat.

Competitive risk

Most boards understand clearly who their direct competitors, who pose real risks to the business and market share, are and will review plans to deal with them. Such risks are overt and therefore it is easier to understand that boards need to be reassured that management has plans in place to deal with them.

The covert competitive risks are more difficult to deal with, though Michael Porter's Five Forces framework does provide useful insight. Figure 7.4 shows how there are different competitors for market margin, as opposed to just market share, and how they constrain the company from maximizing its share of total market margin.[12]

As Figure 7.4 shows, there are more sources of competition for market margin than just head-to-head competitors. These include:

Suppliers

In addition to how many and how strong they are, suppliers' ability to capture more than their fair share of the market margin depends

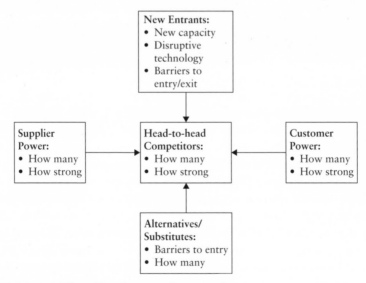

FIGURE 7.4 The "Five Forces" framework
Source: Based on Michael Porter's Five Forces model.
http://www.valuebasedmanagement.net/methods_porter_five_forces.html.

on the number of stages or processes of transformation; the number of intermediaries; the price sensitivity of customers; and the competitive intensity of supply; and whether the product is a small but vital ingredient in an expensive value chain. For example, because platinum is an essential catalyst in refining, oil companies are willing to pay high prices to keep expensive refineries going.

New entrants

New entrants affect market margin through introducing additional capacity which tends to reduce prices and therefore margins, or, worse still, by introducing new rules of the game through disruptive technology. The impact of this additional capacity or different ways of doing business will depend critically on whether there are high barriers to entry and, more importantly, to exit. If it is difficult for excess capacity to exit, the market will suffer from endless price wars.

Customers

Customers place a ceiling on market margin through their willingness to pay, which is affected by relative supply and demand, and their bargaining power, which is influenced by whether there are only a few big customers (like the retail chains in Europe) or many competing to buy the same goods and services, where they sit in the supply chain and whether they are competitors as well as customers.

Alternatives and substitutes

The availability of alternatives and substitutes also places a ceiling on the price by offering wider choice—for example, high-speed trains in Europe and Japan compete with planes, and low-cost airlines in Asia outside Japan compete with buses and cars. Here again the question is: How strong are the barriers to entry and exit? For example, aluminum and copper are substitutes. Copper is the better conductor, but when it gets too expensive, aluminum will do. Yet, once the switch has been made, it may be irreversible. When it was first introduced, photocopying was seen as an alternative to copy-typing. However, once companies switched to photocopying, there was no chance for copy-typists to stay in their former occupation, regardless of how much or how little they cost.

Intermediaries

Though intermediaries are not shown as a separate group in the Five
Forces, they are nevertheless effectively the sixth force; they need
to be rewarded for the value they add, and so, in a sense, they too
compete for market margin.

Systemic risk

Systemic risk in many ways incorporates the risks discussed above.
It often manifests itself in a deterioration of both the economic and
financial outlook because it affects both. As a result, it also ampli-
fies financial risks, as the current economic and financial crisis is
showing only too clearly. It often happens as a result of a combination of trends in the socio-cultural, technical, and competitive
environments coming together in unexpected ways that drastically
undermine the received wisdom and assumptions on which business
as usual are premised—the so-called Black Swans.

The present financial and economic crisis represents perhaps
the biggest systemic risk since the Second World War, along with the
potentially existential threat posed by climate change (which we
will look at in more detail in Chapter 8).

The financial crisis is the result of several trends combining globally
to take human greed and excesses to new levels, as outlined below:[13]

Wage arbitrage

The first mega-trend was the appearance in 1989 of a labor force of
nearly three billion who entered the global marketplace when China
and the countries of the former Soviet Union in Europe turned their
backs on Communism and India abandoned its policy of autarky.
This produced a flood of cheap goods and services, resulting in low
inflation for two decades.

Financial arbitrage

The second mega-trend was the rise of almost interest-free Yen loans
globally, creating the famous Yen carry-trade. This allowed people
to arbitrage the differences in national interest rates and exchange
rates, with Western economies finally adopting Japan's zero or near-
zero interest rate policies (ZIRP). The supply of almost interest-free
funding in Japan in an attempt to deal with its deflationary problems

in the 1990s allowed the rise of financial engineering—a response to unlimited credit and low interest rates that forced investors and pension funds to focus on yield achieved through leverage.

Knowledge arbitrage

The third mega-trend was the rise of financial engineers—scientists and physicists—who applied their technical and statistical skills to financial markets, without understanding the limitations inherent in what they were doing. The rise of financial models would not have been possible without unlimited cheap computing power. Despite the computing power and the intellectual horsepower of the financial engineers, their models suffered from severe limitations. These limitations were technical, and best expressed in the concept of Black Swans.[14]

Regulatory arbitrage

The last mega-trend was deregulation globally, from the lowering of tariffs under the WTO, the freeing up of capital controls under the IMF and the Friedmanite belief that the market was the best setter of prices and that competition would increase efficiency worldwide. Minimalist thinking regarding regulation had become fashionable since the days of Ronald Reagan and Margaret Thatcher, who had started the rollback of the state and regulatory supervision.

The result of these converging trends was to convert national markets into a networked global market for goods and services and money. The crucial flaw in the approach was that there was no global regulator, and so the system failed.[15]

This failure was all the more serious because American and European banking had changed from being essentially retail-based into a new wholesale banking model that amplified the consequences of the search for yield—itself the result of excessively loose monetary policy (the so-called Greenspan put), low interest rates and the ensuing carry trades. Improved telecommunications and cheap computing power drove the market away from conservative buy-and-hold policies adopted by retail investors and pension funds to the highly risky, over-leveraged dynamic trades using real-time information to extract the maximum advantage from information asymmetry. This in turn led to the creation of new products that turned out to be toxic:

> Four elements of financial innovation and deregulation came together to create the toxic products that were at the root

of the current crisis. The first was plain vanilla residential mortgages that were securitized into mortgage-backed papers by government mortgage institutions such as Fannie Mae and Freddie Mac . . . The second was that accounting and regulatory standards permitted such potential liabilities to be moved off the balance sheet so that the banks benefited from "capital efficiency," meaning that leverage could increase using the same level of capital. The third was the use of insurance companies and the newly evolved credit default swap (CDS) markets to enhance credit quality of the underlying paper. If the underlying assets looked weak, the purchase of credit default swaps sold by AAA insurers such as AIG enhanced their credit quality. The fourth sweetener was the willingness of the credit rating agencies to give these structured products AAA ratings, for a fee.

By slicing the traditional mortgages into different tranches of credit quality, collateralizing each tranche with various guarantees or assets, the financial engineers "structured" collateralized debt obligations (CDOs) that felt and smelt like very safe AAA products with higher yields than boring government treasury bonds. What investors did not realize was that these products carried embedded leverage that could unravel under certain circumstances. . .

It looked too good to be true, even to the regulators, but they were assured when the market kept on growing. [Emphasis added] Time and again, Greenspan and others commented on the potential risks, but at the same time remarked that risks were being distributed outside the banking system.[16]

Systemic risk is caused by a failure of its weakest link when individual actors all behave in a way that is rational as individuals, but dangerous when they are all doing the same thing at the same time. In these conditions, "the [system] is only as safe as its weakest link and if one part of the [system] is taking higher and higher leverage to increase its profitability, it is doing so at the expense of the rest of the [system]."[17] This is the so-called tragedy of the commons.

Managing Internal Risks

Risk also manifests itself internally, which is why internal control systems are so important, and why most codes of CG emphasize the need for a sound system of internal control in managing a company's business risks.

It is important to realize that internal control is a process that is a means to an end, not an end in itself, and that it is undertaken by people. So it is not just about having the right policy manual and forms. As a result it cannot guarantee the board absolute assurance, only reasonable assurance that things are being done properly. Internal control systems are necessary because the environment in which the company operates is evolving all the time and it is the role of the internal control system to make sure that the company's objectives are not jeopardized through inappropriate or improper activities. Essentially, "a system of internal control is necessary in order to safeguard shareholders' investment and the Company's assets."[18]

A sound system of internal control must be risk-based; embedded in the operations of the company; supported by risk management functions and appropriate tools and technologies, with regular independent assurance that the system is meeting its objectives; and it must be reviewed regularly by the board. Such a system depends on a thorough and regular evaluation of the nature and extent of the risks to which the company is exposed. Since profits are, in part, the reward for successful risk taking in business, the purpose of internal control is to help manage and control risk appropriately, rather than to eliminate it. Figure 7.5 shows the four characteristics of an effective internal control system:

- *a problems-focused system* consists of the following processes: timely and integrated identification and evaluation of key problems to corporate objectives; appropriate risk treatment; ownership and responsibility for risks (see Appendix D);
- *an embedded system* (see Appendix E) is part of the company's operational and strategic business activities. It communicates control expectations; ensures capability exists for risk treatment and monitoring; monitors progress using early-warning systems (see Appendix F); and implements corrective actions;
- *an assured system*, which provides a structure of assurance of functions; management reporting and oversight; and independent assurance operations;
- *a reviewed system*, which consists of regular monitoring; annual board review of control effectiveness; and refinement and adaptation.

Tables 7.1 and 7.2 show the key questions boards must ask to ensure there is an effective internal control system.

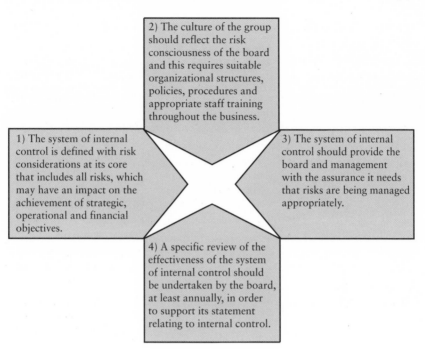

FIGURE 7.5: Key characteristics of an internal control system

TABLE 7.1 Key Questions Boards Must Ask

1) Risk-based	Do we know the main business risks? Do we understand their implications across the scope of the company's interests and how likely they are to occur? Do we have control procedures to manage these risks? Are they effective?
2) Embedded	Have we got action plans where needed? Are controls supported by management, processes and technology? Do the creators of risk take responsibility for managing it?
3) Assured	Are our internal functions adequate to provide sufficient assurance? Is their approach based on the risks and controls assessed by the business?
4) Reviewed	Is the review of risk a specific board activity?

(*continued*)

TABLE 7.1 (continued)

Are we taking the *right risks?*	Are we taking the *right amount of risk?*	Do we have *the right processes to manage risks?*
1. How are the risks we take related to our objectives and strategies? 2. Do we know the significant risks we are taking? 3. Do the risks we take give us competitive advantage? 4. How are the risks we take related to the activities that create value? 5. Do we recognize that business is about taking risks and do we make conscious choices concerning these risks?	1. Are we getting a return that is consistent with our overall level of risk? 2. Does our organizational culture promote or discourage the right level of risk taking? 3. Do we have a well-defined organizational risk appetite? 4. Has our risk appetite been quantified in aggregate and per occurrence? 5. Is our actual risk level consistent with our risk appetite?	1. Is our risk management process aligned with our decision-making process and existing performance measures? 2. Is our risk management process coordinated and consistent across the entire enterprise? Does everyone use the same definition of risk? 3. Do we have gaps and/or overlaps in our risk coverage? 4. Is our risk management process cost-effective?

Based on Wallace and Zinkin (2005): 148.

TABLE 7.2 Ten Practical Steps to Manage Risk

Steps	Checklist Questions
1) Ensure right levels of authority	Do risk professionals have appropriate authority? Will issues affecting reputation be raised to the right level? Does the company strike the right balance between authority for risk management and making profit?
2) Risk management must be led from the top	Is there the right "Tone at the Top"? Are there relevant independent committees responsible for overall risk management? Is there an individual with overall responsibility for risk management? Should the organization recruit a chief risk officer?

Steps	Checklist Questions
3) Ensure right levels of risk expertise	Does senior management understand the risks facing the organization and their potential impact? Does the executive team come from a diverse background? Is the top management team at risk of misunderstanding the nature and level of risk because of information filtering lower down the hierarchy?
4) Ensure data are reliable	What are the sources of information used to gain an understanding of risk? How reliable are these sources and are they tested against other sources? Does the organization rely on purely historical data? Is the organization using the right mix of quantitative and qualitative risk inputs? Does the organization consider Black Swans?
5) Ensure stress testing and scenario planning take place	Does senior management set aside time to discuss different scenarios and their likely impact? To what extent are different scenarios considered when setting long-term strategy? Does senior management seek a range of views and perspectives to test assumptions? Does it allow for Black Swans?
6) Ensure incentives reward long-term stability not short-term profit	Are CG processes robust enough to ensure remuneration will not cause reputation risk? Is there a qualified remuneration committee in place to review and approve policies? What is the link between performance and reward? Are incentive programs designed to motivate and reward, without encouraging behavior that creates organizational or systemic risk?

(*continued*)

TABLE 7.2 *(continued)*

Steps	Checklist Questions
7) Consolidate risk factors across the organization	Does the company understand the interaction between different risk categories and how an event in one part of the business can have a knock-on effect elsewhere? Is there a common language of risk to ensure clarity and understanding across the organization? Do the data and IT infrastructure support aggregation and communication of risk information?
8) Avoid excessive reliance on external data providers	To what extent does the organization rely on external sources of information? How robust is this and how often is it cross-checked? Does the organization really understand the methodology used by external providers? Are the limitations understood?
9) Achieve balance between centralized and decentralized risk	What is the standing of risk management in the organization? Is risk management seen as a support function and cost center or as a protector of long-term profit? Does it form part of the strategic considerations? Are risks identified and aggregated centrally and subject to an enterprise-wide review?
10) Ensure risk management is adaptive	How frequently does the organization review and update its risk assumptions? Is it often enough to take into account changed external circumstances? How is information about changes in the risk environment and risk profile communicated to senior management? To what extent do changes in the risk environment lead to changes in risk management priorities or processes?

Source: Ross (2009).[19]

It is important to realize that risks are not just financial. Financials are lagging indicators, whereas KPIs are leading indicators, and the eight areas that investors look at most often KPIs are:

- *Execution of corporate strategy*: How well does management leverage its skills and experience and stay aligned with shareholder interests?
- *Quality of strategy*: Does management have a vision for the future? Can it make tough decisions and quickly seize opportunities? How well does it allocate resources?
- *Ability to innovate*: Is the company a trendsetter or a follower? What is in the R&D pipeline? How readily does the company adapt to changing technologies and markets?
- *Ability to attract talented people*: Is the company able to hire and retain the very best people? Does it reward them appropriately? Is it training the talent it will need tomorrow?
- *Market share*: Is the company capturing the value of the current market? Is it well positioned to expand that value in the future?
- *Quality of executive compensation*: Is executive pay tied to strategic goals? How well is it gauged to the creation of shareholder value?
- *Quality of major processes*: Does the organization reduce risk and enhance return through the deft execution of its current operations? Is the transition seamless in changing conditions?
- *Research leadership*: How well does management understand the link between creating knowledge and using it?

The implications of this are significant. The manner in which the company manages key non-financial areas of performance and then communicates related successes to key stakeholders, in particular the investment community, has a powerful effect on how they are valued.[20]

Shareholders and investors are still interested in the financial metrics, but they now appreciate that these are often no more than lagging indicators, which only tell them what a company has done in the past, not what it is going to do in the future. As a result, these groups are seeking a balanced report or balanced scorecard on the hard numbers *and* the "intangibles" that will protect and create value in the future.

Matching Risk Profiles to Shareholder Risk Appetites

The relationship between value and risk has become an increasingly important consideration in the strategic decision-making process. This is, in part, recognition of the impact risk has on an organization's strategies, stakeholders and processes—the drivers of value creation. Capitalizing upon the value/risk relationship—through management of risks to value creation—can maximize shareholder value.

Shareholder value is defined as the static net present value of the firm as it exists plus the net present value of the future growth options that are represented by its new investments and ideas.

By linking risk management to what the shareholders consider vital to the success of the business, the company provides shareholders with certainty that what they value is protected. The four key stages in understanding and managing the link between risk and shareholder value are:

- Establishing what shareholders value about the company.
- Identifying the risks around the key drivers of shareholder value.
- Determining the preferred treatment for the risks.
- Communicating risk treatments to shareholders.

These four stages are discussed further below.

Stage 1: Establish what shareholders value about the company

The first stage of connecting risk management activity to shareholder value is to determine the specifics of what shareholders value in the company and the corporate processes contributing to that value. The most important processes are the drivers of shareholder value. By actively engaging the investment community—equity analysts, institutional investors, and the like—in systematic discussions, the company can achieve a shared understanding of the four key drivers, which are:

1. The way the company allocates capital between projects and between the present and future earning streams.
2. The company's efficiency, measured via its ability to control costs.
3. The company's record of innovation, which is critical to building its future income streams.
4. The company's ability to execute—that is, to turn great ideas into profitable operations.

In assessing the company's market value, directors need to think carefully about balancing the value created by the company as it currently exists and the additional value to be derived from future new activities and investments it is likely to undertake. Traditionally, risk management has only sought to protect the former.

Based on the definition of shareholder value (the net present value of the firm as it exists) and the value of future growth options, the board may choose two different strategies to increase shareholder value:

- Minimize risks around its present business model to protect and guarantee existing income streams, thus increasing the perceived current value to shareholders because there is less risk; or
- At the same time, generate the maximum number of future growth options so some will ultimately be converted into additional shareholder value over what is currently being generated. However, in so doing the board is increasing the risk and uncertainty faced by the company and the tradeoff may be appropriate as a result of the extra future value these risky options deliver.

This means that the board must be able to explain to shareholders the strategies it has to reconcile present profits with future cash flows, as illustrated in Figure 7.6.

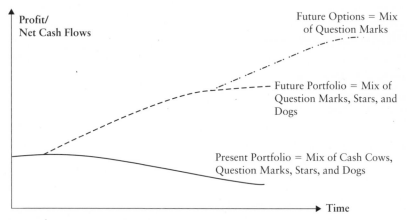

FIGURE 7.6 Reconciling present profits with future cash flows

Stage 2: Identify the risks around the key drivers of shareholder value

Next, the company must consider risks that may have an impact on each of the drivers of shareholder value. Risks stem from many areas—business environment, governance, operations, financial information and transaction. All areas of risk should be assessed across the entire company.[21]

The investment community has a role in developing this framework—discussions with them should determine their views on risks to the company's drivers of value as well as the drivers themselves. In many cases, the capital markets will have a great deal of insight into industry risk and may have certain expectations of the risk the business should accept. The shareholders and the company should view themselves as partners in this exercise. Many leading analysts already use intangible parameters to determine their overall assessment of a company's value in response to growing pressure to establish new types of market indices, which take into consideration non-financial measures, including quality of managing risk to protect and grow shareholder value.

Stage 3: Determine the preferred risk treatment

Once the board has identified the risks to each of the drivers, it should then determine what shareholders would accept as suitable risk treatments. Risk treatment can be defined as any strategy which affects the amount of risk being taken. This might mean avoiding the risk, managing it, insuring it, hedging it, or using a combination of these.

The board must recognize that its choice will affect the value to shareholders because it will have changed the impact of the potential risk on the business. The board will have its own views on the best form of risk treatment. However, equity analysts, institutional investors, and similar groups will also have valuable insights and preferences as to how to treat a particular risk to their satisfaction. The board should take these opinions into account when agreeing the approach. Where differences are evident, the challenge for the board is to convince the investment community that its suggested risk treatments are the most appropriate and effective.

Stage 4: Communicate risk treatments to the shareholders

The company has a vested interest in informing shareholders of its value-creation plans, how it intends to execute them and any significant events that may affect their investment. It is important for the long-term growth of the company that shareholders are well informed and that their view of the company is a positive one. Access to the markets is based on this shared vision of value—both present and future. But it is also based on the perceived risks to that value, and how those risks are being managed. Good risk management is part of the shared vision.

In deciding how best to communicate with shareholders, the board must establish the shareholders' views on the company's value, the risks to that value, and appropriate risk treatments. The ensuing communication should go beyond mere reporting to the markets. Indeed, effective communication in itself is a form of risk management. During periods of adverse market conditions for a particular industry, markets can often react unfavorably to all companies in the sector. Proactive communications can lessen, and perhaps, eliminate such negative effects on the company's valuation.

Conclusion

A failure to understand external risk—political, economic, financial, socio-cultural, technological, competitive or systemic—can lead to crippling problems at either end of the wealth-creating value chain. It can lead to destructive stresses being put on the balance sheet and can turn assets into liabilities when products become obsolete or debtors fail to pay up. Poor business choices can destroy company and brand reputations.

As well as managing the full range of external risks, boards must also manage internal risks. Having sound systems of internal control in place is essential in this regard.

Risk also manifests itself internally which is why systems of internal control are so important. By linking risk management activity to what the shareholders consider vital to the success of the business, the company provides shareholders with certainty that what they value is protected.

Endnotes

1 See, for example, "GE's Immelt Accepts Blame Amid 'Opportunity of a Lifetime,'" by R. Lyne, in *The Edge Financial Daily*, March 3, 2009: 18, which had the following: "'We intend to reset this business to be smaller, less volatile and more connected to the GE core,' Immelt wrote of GE Capital. As for the economy, 'we are going through more than

a cycle. The global economy and capitalism will be "reset" in several important ways. The interaction between government and business will change forever. In a reset economy, the government will be a regulator; and also an industry policy champion, a financier and a key partner.'"

2 See quote above.

3 For details, see "Is CNOOC's Bid for Unocal a Threat to America?" *Knowledge@Wharton*, November 21, 2005.

4 See, for example, "Dubai Ports World Deal for P&O Draws Fire from US Lawmakers," *Outsourced Logistics*, February 21, 2006.

5 Turner, A. 2009, "The Financial Crisis and the Future of Financial Regulation," *The Economist*'s Inaugural City Lecture, January 21, 2009.

6 See "Roubini Says Carry Trades Fueling 'Huge' Asset Bubble (Update3)," Patterson, M., Bloomberg, October 27, 2009, http://www.bloomberg.com/apps/news?pid=newsarchive&sid=atlyygQuBLUl.

7 Toyota US testified in Congress asking Congress to help GM and Chrysler, even though they were competitors, because their exit would cripple its supply chain, because many of Toyota's suppliers were their suppliers too. See "Why Toyota Wants GM to be Saved: A GM Failure would Cause Production Problems, Crush already Weak Demand and Potentially Open the Door to Low-cost Competitors," CNN Money.com, December 16, 2008.

8 Kindleberger, C. P. 1996, *Manias, Panics, and Crashes: A History of Financial Crises*, Chichester: John Wiley & Sons: 194–5.

9 In "Riding to the Rescue," *Newsweek*, February 2, 1998: 39; as quoted by Sheng, A. in "From Asian to Global Financial Crisis," Third K. B. Lall Memorial Lecture at The Indian Council on International Economic Relations, New Delhi, February 7, 2009.

10 The acronym for Brazil, Russia, India and China.

11 See "All Circuit City Stores Set To Close Tomorrow," by A. Yoskowitz, Afterdawn.com, March 7, 2009 at: http://www.afterdawn.com/news/archive/17191.cfm.

12 Market margin is the total added value available to market participants between the extraction of raw materials or primary ingredients, their conversion into goods and services, their distribution and retailing and the final price that the final end-user or customer is prepared to pay.

13 Sheng, op. cit.: 4.

14 Ibid.: "The world of risk was a bell-shaped statistical curve that ignored the long-tailed Black Swan risk. It was the underestimation of the once-in-400-year risks that proved their undoing."

15 Ibid.: 5: "Under universal banking, commercial banks began to network with securities business, mutual funds, insurance and even hedge funds, because under Metcalfe's Law, the value of the network increases exponentially with the number of users. Hence, business geography melded to become market space—enabling banks to become financial Wal-Marts providing the whole range of financial services.

But what the free market economists, financial engineers and their regulators did not realize was that networks are linked both ways—benefits come with risks. *The more the networks expanded, the higher the risks of contagion. In a sense, the network is only as safe as its weakest link and if one part of the network is taking higher and higher leverage to increase its profitability, it is doing so at the expense of the rest of the network. Interconnectivity has win-win positive feedbacks, but also lose-lose negative feedbacks, which explain the way markets overshoot in both directions.* [emphasis added]

Unfortunately, the four arbitrages also led to four excesses that were the hallmark of the present crisis—excess liquidity, excess leverage, excess complexity, and excess greed. Note that complexity creates opacity and therefore grand opportunities for fraud."

16 Ibid.: 8–9.
17 Ibid.: 4.
18 Statement on Internal Control—Guidance for Directors of Public Listed Companies, KLSE, 2000.
19 Ross, A., 2009, "Managing Risk in Perilous Times: Practical Steps to Accelerate Recovery," Economist Intelligence Unit.
20 See, for example, "An Integrated Framework of Corporate Governance and Firm Valuation" by Beiner *et al.*, *European Financial Management,* March 2006; and "Corporate Governance and Equity Prices" by Gompers *et al.*, *Quarterly Journal of Economics,* February 2003.
21 For a full discussion, see Wallace and Zinkin 2005, *Corporate Governance,* Singapore: John Wiley & Sons: 161–71.

8

WHAT WE MEASURE
AND REWARD

The late Peter Drucker observed that what is measured gets managed. This chapter will make the case that we often measure and reward the wrong things. The resulting measures and their associated rewards promote irresponsible behavior by CEOs and their top management team, leading to a failure to assess long-term risk to the company or the system in which it operates. Existing measures also fail completely to take into account the social, environmental, and human costs of companies' actions that damage social and environmental ecosystems.

Peter Drucker once famously observed that only things that are measured are managed. He was right. But that puts a serious onus on the people who determine the metrics used to ensure that not just the right things are being measured, but that they are being measured in the right way, especially if the measures determine rewards and remuneration. This measurement problem comes in two parts: (i) an inadequate emphasis on right behaviors and values (the "soft" measures, as opposed to looking at the "hard" metrics) and (ii) excessive importance being placed on financial information at the expense of other indicators of an organization's health.

Inadequate Emphasis on Right Behaviors

I always worry when senior managers or CEOs say proudly that their company is results-driven (as opposed to performance-driven). An excessive focus on results leaves people open to the risk of adopting the "do whatever it takes" approach we spoke of earlier—an approach that undermines the moral compass of the company.

Yet if boards do not get the CEO and the top management to focus on results, nothing will happen. A results orientation is therefore essential, but it should not be at the expense of the firm's moral compass, and it should somehow take into account the effect the company has on its environment. The problem is that there are no easy ways to measure behavior that affects either of these crucial considerations.

The need for a moral compass

A moral compass matters because it gives meaning to what people do. It informs the Tone at the Top, which matters because leaders must lead by example and live the values they profess. However, in coming to terms with the concept of a moral compass in business, it is important to understand the underlying axioms about motivation we hold to be true. Unfortunately, there are two competing world-views—those of rational "Economic Man" and irrational "Thymotic Man"—which assume quite different things. The failure to recognize this has unfortunate consequences for business.

Rational Economic Man

This is perhaps the single most pressing area where correction to the single-minded Anglo-Saxon focus on results is needed. Underlying the way much of management is taught and practiced are some key assumptions about what makes humanity work, as discussed in Chapter 2. At the heart of the argument presented by laissez-faire liberals is the belief that people are utilitarian, maximizing pleasure, and minimizing pain, and that as long as we can appeal to this motivation we will improve our lot. This view can be summed up in the concept of "rational economic man." The idea of "Economic Man" lies at the heart of the Anglo-Saxon world-view. Economic Man is a rational utility maximizer, seeking to maximize happiness—an idea captured in the famous phrase from the American Declaration of Independence: "We hold these truths to be self-evident, that all men are created equal, that they are endowed by their Creator with certain unalienable Rights, that among these are Life, Liberty and the pursuit of Happiness."

Irrational "Thymotic Man"

The utilitarian approach ignores another view of what drives us as human beings—an approach endorsed by all leading religions, and by Plato, Hegel, and Kant—which suggests that people are emotional and more concerned with protecting or preserving their dignity, sometimes even at the cost of their lives. Such "thymotic" people are unlikely to respond well to utilitarian arguments. (For a longer discussion of what is meant by the term "thymotic" and how Thymotic Man behaves, see Appendix G.)

Interestingly, in the Declaration of Independence there is no claim to the right to be respected, to be treated with dignity, to be allowed to feel important. Yet, as Plato observed, this need to be respected is a fundamental driver of the human condition. The utilitarian view of the world has no room for the person who swims into rough seas to rescue a stranger; the soldier who storms an enemy machine-gun nest to save his mates; the fireman or policeman who risks his life to help those in peril. It cannot begin to comprehend the suicide bomber.

This failure to recognize that people can be driven by motives other than utility maximization may lie at the heart of the approach to workers that has dehumanized work, deskilling it and destroying self-respect. It is perhaps why Anglo-Saxon firms tend to be instrumental in nature, whereas Asian and Latin firms tend to be social in nature, where the social aspects of work, the relationships between people, matter as much as getting the work done.

Perhaps it is this lack of a social dimension, with the emphasis instead being placed on the legal and contractual aspects of fulfilling a task, that has created what many see as the emptiness of Western acquisitive society, where conspicuous consumption seems to be the way of conferring meaning and justification for actions that often appear to ignore moral or social norms.

There is a world of business—popularized on TV by Donald Trump's "The Apprentice"—which is shallow, self-serving and devoid of either meaning or morality. Indeed, people watching the program might be justified in concluding that the only way to succeed in business is to cheat, lie, and stab others in the back. Moreover, all that seems to matter to many of America's top executives is where they rank in the Forbes list of wealthy people and in being able to say that they have more possessions than their peers. This need to have more as a measure of individual worth and significance may explain the absurd levels of remuneration American CEOs and their top management demand these days. It is perhaps no accident that in the earlier days of American capitalism, founder-CEOs knew they were doing something valuable—contributing to the well-being of society—and felt rewarded by their achievement so that they did not need to demand the incredible levels of remuneration that now prevail.

This change in values has worried John Bogle, the founder of the Vanguard investment management group, so much so that he has written a book that deals specifically with this.[1] It may also explain how people like Sir Fred Goodwin can hold on to a pension of £700,000 (US$1 million-plus) per year at the age of 50 after presiding over the collapse of Royal Bank of Scotland. (To get rid of him, the board used taxpayers' money to fund the pension, whereas if the bank had been allowed to fail—as a consequence of his poor decision-making—he would only have been entitled to an annual pension of £28,000—some US$42,000—at the age of 65.)[2] Perhaps it is also why AIG had to pay US$165 million to the management team in London that destroyed the company, or Merrill Lynch paid its top managers US$3.6 billion in bonuses after they had presided over losses of nearly US$28 billion.[3] In all of these cases, the justification given was the letter of the contracts, not the spirit.

The moral purpose of the business also matters. The success and failure of Marks & Spencer in the UK helps make the point. When its founders set out to build their business, they did not set out to build a retail chain. Rather, their mission was to subvert the British class structure, perhaps because the founders were immigrant Jews, outsiders with no vested interest in preserving the British class structure.[4]

Marks & Spencer was incredibly successful until the end of the twentieth century, and then somehow lost its magic. While it is true that British consumers changed and that Marks & Spencer appeared unable to adapt to these changes, I believe that there are two other reasons for this. The first is that Marks & Spencer was too successful in its mission to create a social revolution: people were no longer immediately identifiable as belonging to a particular class because of the clothes they wore or the food they ate. Like NASA, the company needs a new mission; it has to find a new driving moral purpose around which all employees can align. The second is that the firm is no longer managed by the founders and their families, but by professional managers who are members of the establishment and perhaps cannot relate to the original mission and sense of moral purpose.

If this is correct, then Marks & Spencer will only regain its iconic status when it finds a new and equally compelling sense of moral purpose. It is not enough to aim to be the best or most profitable department store in the world.

How, then, do boards measure the importance of moral compass and the Tone at the Top? How do they measure and reward CEOs and the top management team for creating such a purpose; for treating employees with respect and dignity; for making work well done an act of worship?

Perhaps the only way to deal with this problem is to ensure that any statement of values is translated into behaviors that are measurable and rewardable, that can be broken down into KPIs for each job description so that employees understand that they are assessed on their ability to live the values of the organization. Naturally, the people for whom this will matter most are the most senior in the organization as they must set an example that others can follow. This means that when considering statements of values, boards must ensure that such values are internally consistent and measurable.

The importance of values as the glue that holds people together was reinforced when I was running a workshop in Cambodia for Vietnamese capital-market regulators. I was explaining that unlike an organization's vision and mission, values do not change over time. To make the point, I was describing how the values that had been agreed by the management team in SIDC when I first joined it as the new CEO are what drive who we recruit, who we promote and who we terminate as part of an explicit commitment to the need to "Fit In or Fall Out" (FIFO). Just as important, they are the only thing that the four ethnic groups and the three generations in SIDC really have in common, as underlying assumptions about how to behave and what defines performance differ by ethnic group and generation.[5]

Externalities and Systemic Risk

At an ACCA conference on climate change in Hong Kong in 2007, Al Gore gave the accounting profession a challenge: find a way of measuring the impact of company activities on the environment and charge it to the income statement. His argument was that, without such a set of measures, companies would not know what harm they were inflicting on the environment, nor would they care, because it cost them nothing.

For the individual firm, it is true that externalities do not appear to cost their creators anything. However, this ceases to be true once a large number of individuals or companies adopt the same course of action. Traffic congestion, pollution and now global warming are all examples of this. The combined actions of groups of individuals can create a situation where all end up suffering inconvenience at best and serious economic consequences at worst.

The tragedy of the commons,[6] as this problem is called, exists because accountants have yet to find a good way of capturing and recording the costs arising from collective action. Externalities are a real issue. Traffic jams, for example, cost companies and economies millions of dollars in lost productivity every day, and yet they are not shown on income statements. In the end, though, someone has to foot the bill.

Until the latest financial crisis, it was always assumed that the problem really only existed in the physical domain, where the limits placed upon our collective existences by the fact that we share finite natural resources forced us to restrict our individual freedom to damage the environment.[7]

The financial crisis created by subprime mortgages and structured products nobody really understood is but another example of the tragedy of the commons. The disaster in this case was that it paid individuals so handsomely to be totally irresponsible. People in Wall Street, and the mortgage brokers who originated the toxic assets, were richly rewarded for putting the system at risk. As long as only a few firms were operating on the "originate-package-distribute" model the collective impact of their actions was too small to pose a systemic risk to everybody. However, as soon as it became apparent that it paid so well to be irresponsible, the growing number of participants and the size and number of their collective transactions nearly destroyed the system for everybody.

Participants in such dubious activities were caught in something of a double-bind, a situation described by Chuck Prince, a former CEO of Citigroup, as "dancing": everybody was expected to do it, because nobody wanted to spoil the party, even though they all knew it could not go on forever, and those who did not join in would be called fools.[8]

Saving the system has created moral hazard because, rather than being punished, those organizations responsible for jeopardizing the system are now being bailed out with taxpayers' money. A proper accounting that showed the costs to the system of this financial tragedy of the commons might have saved the world from the recession it entered in 2008. The fact that we are capable of creating a tragedy of this magnitude[9] is argument enough for the need to regulate the system rather than relying on the market to self-regulate, as the double-bind problem will always haunt an unregulated system— meaning that we cannot rely on conscience to prevent actions that hurt everybody while benefiting individuals.

This is also true of companies that bribe and suborn government officials so that they can continue to break the law or obtain privileged access to contracts at rigged prices. The individual "cost of doing business" is less than the benefit accruing to the "technical know-who," as it is sometimes called. So there are always some companies that will try to bribe officials. As long as it is only a few, they may gain significant competitive advantage at relatively little cost to the economy. As soon as the practice becomes the norm, however, the competitive advantage falls and the "costs of doing business" rise—in some economies as high as 20 percent of GDP. Once corruption is endemic, it poses a systemic risk to everybody, in much the same way as subprime undermined the financial system. People find themselves in a double-bind: "Others are doing it; and even though it is wrong, I cannot afford not to join in," the reasoning goes. (To counteract this, John Bogle asserts, "Our society cannot and should not tolerate the substitution of moral relativism for a certain form of moral absolutism, and its debasement in the ethical standards of commerce.")[10] So not just the cost of doing business goes up for all, but respect for the law and institutions of governance are undermined, making it not just less profitable, but also more risky and uncertain. In an environment where there is no respect for the law every business is vulnerable to arbitrary actions by unscrupulous politicians. Those who undermined respect for the system though bribery and corruption probably forgot to factor in the systemic risk of the collapse in law and order that occurs in failed states.

In the final analysis, the reason why people keep creating the tragedy of the commons is because there are no adequate or appropriate reward and punishment systems to stop them from doing so as individuals. Even if there are penalties, they may not be severe enough to deter them from seeking personal gain at the expense of the collective, and this is made more difficult to handle because there are no effective pricing systems to deal with externalities.

Excessive Importance Placed on Financial Information

Compared with market-based metrics or ethical measures designed to track and reward performance, financial information is much easier to collect. It also seems to be more robust; it is after all "hard" data and therefore, at first sight, less subject to manipulation and subjective interpretation. This is, in part, illusion, because there are real problems with financials, which often are not quite what they seem—hence the term "creative accounting."

The real issue with financial information is that it represents only one facet of the organization's health and this is why the concept of the Balanced Scorecard was created. Moreover, financial information deals with lagging indicators, whereas the other factors measured in the Balanced Scorecard approach are leading indicators that provide early warning of how the organization will do in the future, as opposed to being indicators of the past.

Traditionally, measures of company performance have focused on financial information and, in particular, on profit and profit-related ratios such as Return on Assets, Return on Capital Employed, and Return on Sales. These are then translated into Earnings per Share (EPS) and Price-Earning (P/E) ratios and used as external yardsticks of how well a company is doing and whether or not to buy its shares.

Unfortunately, there are a number of problems with traditional financial information and the way in which it is collected and interpreted. These problems are operational as well as philosophical; and they do matter, because people assume that if management has gone to all the trouble to collect and collate data, what they are measuring must be important. As with all systems, people learn to "game" the system: to make it work to their advantage while at the same time undermining the purpose the system was set up to serve. Observing form rather than content, letter rather than spirit, are behavioral problems as old as humanity.

The problems associated with traditional financial data are set out below.

Financial information is focused on the past and inward-looking

An important weakness in financial information is, to paraphrase Professor Moshe Rubinstein, that "It brings the past to the present, when what boards need is to bring the future to the present."[11] When accounting bodies like CIMA talk of quality information, typically they talk of it being produced within a week of the previous month's end. That is fast, but it is still firmly rooted in the past.

The second problem with financial information is that it is, by definition, inward-looking. Generally, only the numbers inside the firm are recorded. The one exception to this rule is sales revenue, which records how the outside world is responding to the company and its offers. However, even this does not really tell the board what it needs to know about the suitability of the offer in the marketplace. To get that information, the board needs market share by volume as well as value and, for it to be a meaningful guide to the desirability and sustainability of the offer, the board needs to understand how that market share was achieved.[12] Two brands can have the same overall market share, but the way it has been achieved may be very different, and these differences determine the health of the brand.

For example, brand A may have very high relative market penetration, but be bought very infrequently, while brand B may have very few people buying it (low penetration) but they buy it many times more often than those who buy brand A. Assuming price and volume effects are identical, brand A is a weak brand. It has been tried by nearly everybody, but they do not buy it often, suggesting low levels of loyalty. Brand B has the same market share, but its dynamics are quite different. Not many people buy it, but they are devoted to it. It has very high loyalty. To grow the business, each brand will have to follow a different strategy. Brand B only has to increase penetration; whereas brand A must work on its performance attributes and value proposition to become more attractive to users so that their repeat-purchase rates meet the average for the category. Brand B's task is much easier than brand A's.

I am not suggesting here that the board needs to get involved in the computation of market share, but I am suggesting that it needs to be able to have a conversation with line management that shows it understands how the outside world affects the key determinants of purchase and loyalty.

From my experience of having run many workshops for directors of public-listed companies in Malaysia, I am also suggesting that it is a problem if the board spends too much time reviewing the financials, because they are about the past and they focus attention inwards. Boards meet infrequently and for not very long. It is a pity if they spend 75–80 percent of their time reviewing the numbers, as this takes their focus away from the job of direction, which, by definition, must be forward-looking and outwardly focused. This is akin to a driver spending the vast majority of the time looking in the rear-view mirror rather than at the road ahead. When the driver's attention is focused on where he has been rather than on where he is going, there is bound to be an accident.

Traditional accounting data do not measure the right costs

The second problem boards encounter when focusing excessively on financial information is that traditional accounting data are periodic and do not capture the most important cost of doing business—the costs created by activities. Nor do they record the differences in profitability by customer.

Accounting data are periodic

Accounting records, whether they are cost accounting, management accounting or financial accounting, are periodic in nature: monthly, quarterly, and annual. Even though business and customer relationships are not discontinuous, as financial periods imply, companies find themselves having to make operating adjustments with financial implications just to meet the analysts' expectations for the quarter or the financial year end. Such window-dressing maneuvers may cause problems for suppliers, whose payments are held up just to get the payables right, or sometimes, for customers, who are asked to pay earlier or to bring forward purchases to reduce payables and inventories, especially at year end. These requests are disruptive and, in the overall scheme of things, unnecessary, occurring only because of artificially imposed periodic boundaries.

Activity-based costing

Companies that do not use activity-based costing do not really know how much it costs to do business. Traditional accounting aggregates costs by categories into various "buckets," such as labor, raw materials, utilities, and so on. These totals are then divided over the numbers of units of production, sales, and so on. They are not tagged to individual activities as and when they occur. Yet it is the activities that consume the raw materials and use labor, both directly and, more important, indirectly. Each time a sale happens, a salesman has called on a prospective buyer a number of times, finally achieving a close; an invoice is raised; goods are moved out of inventory and delivered to the customer; the transaction has to be followed up; and payment received and logged. Based on the need to replace the inventory, an order is placed on the factory, which in turn causes an order to be placed on suppliers for the necessary components; production plans are set in train; manufacturing schedules are updated and workers make the product. This set of activities cuts across the entire value chain, which is not the way accounting records are kept, unless they are activity-based.

Peter Drucker characterizes the difference between traditional accounting and activity-based costing this way:

> Traditional cost accounting measures what it costs to *do* something. Activity-based costing also records the cost of *not doing* . . . The *costs of not doing*, which traditional cost accounting cannot and does not record, often equal and sometimes even exceed the cost of doing. Activity-based costing therefore gives not only much better cost control, it gives *result control* . . . Activity-based costing asks, "Does it have to be done? If so, where is it best done?" Activity-based costing integrates what were once several procedures—value analysis, process analysis, quality management and costing—into one analysis.[13]

Customer profitability

If a company does not have activity-based costing it is really difficult to assess how much profit any individual customer brings to the company. Yet if boards are to ensure that the assets for which they are responsible do not get wasted in a profitless chase for market share, they must find a way of reconciling customer value with shareholder value.

Not all customers are equally valuable, according to Professors Cooper and Kaplan of the Harvard Business School, who argue that

20 percent of customers account for 225 percent of the profits, and 80 percent lose 125 percent of the profits.[14] The discipline of requiring the creation of shareholder value acts as a good regulator on the sales perspective that seeks to capture as many customers as possible, regardless of their effect on profits and, more important, cash flows. It forces marketers to think carefully about why they wish to have the customer portfolio they aspire to, just as it forces them to reconsider the extent to which they will go in segmenting the market into its constituent elements and how many variants and SKUs they need to produce to serve those segments.

Other research divides customers into four groups:

- Those who are easy to acquire and retain—32 percent of the sample but only 20 percent of the profit.
- Those who are expensive to acquire but easy to retain—15 percent of the sample but 40 percent of the profits.
- Those who are difficult to acquire and retain—28 percent of the sample but only 25 percent of the profits.
- Those who are easy to acquire but difficult to retain—25 percent of the sample, but only 15 percent of the profits.

The researchers conclude:

If retention efforts simply focus on keeping the most customers, companies will not only waste money trying to retain the loyal unprofitable group but will also vainly throw money after the profitable transient group. What's worse, those funds won't be spent on attracting potentially highly profitable customers who are hard to acquire.[15]

The problem for most boards remains that traditional financial information they receive does not help them understand the real costs of doing business nor the value of customers. This is critical, because *without customer profitability there can be no brand or company profitability* (see Appendix H).

Two boards that understood the importance of customer-based thinking in driving profits were GE and Coca-Cola, which both worked on increasing the "profit zone"[16] of their businesses:

GE's strategy, as illustrated in Figure 8.1, was to move from box selling, which was focused only on selling the product and its performance attributes, to solution-selling, which was based on the understanding that the product was only part of a wider customer need. Industrial products come with a variety of options and accessories designed to meet specific situations; their purchases need to be financed and then serviced, for equipment is only valuable to its user if it is working. GE's move into financial services was a master-stroke at the time, though it has now become a liability as the financial-services industry struggles with the aftermath of the global financial crisis. As Figure 8.2 shows, Coca-Cola moved down the value chain toward its final consumers to capture the margin between itself as a simple supplier of syrup and the profits accruing to the intermediate activities.

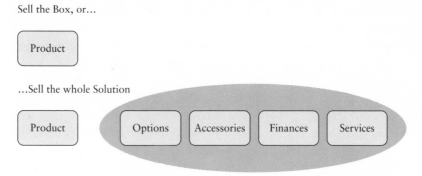

FIGURE 8.1 GE adopted solution-selling to increase its "profit zone"
Source: Slywotzky *et al.* (2002): 74.

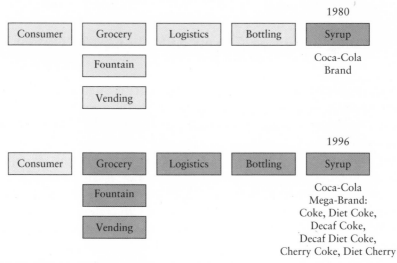

FIGURE 8.2 Coca-Cola moved down the value chain to increase its "profit zone"
Source: Slywotzky *et al.* (2002): 139.

Neither board would have been able to work out what they should do if they had relied on traditional accounting data, as it would have been limited to internal numbers only.

Profits are an Accounting Fiction—Only Cash is a Fact

Given the attention analysts pay to earnings (profits) and the fact that many commentators believe that the responsibility of the board is to maximize profits, it is surprising that profits are such a flawed measure.

Anyone who has been exposed to finance knows that profits depend on conventions and treatments; and accountants are skilled at deciding what level of profits will be reported depending on what they are asked to do. The only thing that cannot be massaged is cash, which is why cash is king. Predicting profits is also an art rather than a science, as profits are a small residual number based on the difference between two very big numbers: revenues and costs.

It is not just that profits are an accounting convention, but also that an excessive focus on profits, as opposed to cash generation, will mislead the board and, at worst, can lead the company to bankruptcy. What matters is the firm's working capital cycle. If there is a long cash-to-cash cycle, rapid and apparently profitable growth will lead to the company running out of cash, and it is with cash that bills and interest are paid, not profits.

Comparing Return on Capital with the Cost of Capital is not Comparing Like with Like

People assume that if the return on capital is greater than the cost of capital, it must make sense to invest in the project or do the deal. While this may be a reasonable assumption, it is based on a misunderstanding; namely, that what is being compared is indeed truly comparable. This is, in fact, wrong because returns on capital are not cash, but profits, which as we have seen are merely an accounting convention, whereas the cost of capital is cash-based. What should be compared are cash inflows with cash outflows; what matters is that, given that a particular cost of capital is used as the company discount rate, the net present value (NPV) is positive.

The company's cost of capital is, however, not as simple as it seems at first sight. It needs to reflect the risk profile of the portfolio of assets and businesses in which the company is engaged, as each line of business has its own risk profile. It matters that the risk-adjusted cost of capital reflects the risk profile accurately. This is the weighted average cost of capital (WACC). However, if assets are depleting, as is the case in extractive industries, then the WACC is not appropriate. Even if it were, changes in circumstances affect credit ratings and downgrades increase the cost of capital. It was a rating downgrade that brought AIG to its knees at the end of 2008, precipitating the greatest losses in history.

Discounted Cash Flow (DCF) Sacrifices the Future for the Present

Discounted cash flow is a good way of assessing whether an investment makes sense, assuming that the correct cost of capital has been used as the discount factor. However, it suffers from two problems: it sacrifices the future for the present, and adjusted present value (APV) is a better way of assessing whether or not a project is worth doing.

Sacrificing the future for the present raises important questions of inter-generational equity. The problem arises because discounting to get to net present value puts a low value on any financial streams in the future. For example, if a 10 percent discount rate is used, after just one generation (25 years) the weight given to US$1 in today's money is only US9.2 cents. Financial decisions about the future effectively give someone born in 25 years time only 9.2 percent of the importance of someone living today. It is the financial equivalent of Groucho Marx's famous comment: "Why should I care about posterity? What's posterity ever done for me?"

Yet, as human beings we feel we are responsible for the quality of life of our children and grandchildren—an idea captured in the concept of trusteeship which exists in all the great religions, and well expressed in the words of Julius Sterling Morton: "Each generation takes the earth as trustees. We ought to bequeath to posterity as many forests and orchards as we have exhausted and consumed."[17]

DCF and the time value of money encourage today's generation to consume, deplete and pollute at the expense of the next generation, violating the concept of stewardship, the essence of which is to leave the world in better condition than we found it. The quantification offered by DCF provides us with one set of measures that are deeply flawed because they ignore the moral rights of the unborn to enjoy the fruits of the earth.

Endnotes

1 Bogle, J. 2009, *Enough: True Measures of Money, Business, and Life*, Hoboken, NJ: John Wiley & Sons.

2 "Scapegoat Millionaire," *The Economist*, March 7, 2009: 18.

3 See "The Real Harm Caused by the AIG Bonuses," by Newman, R., *Money and Business*, US News and World Report, March 16, 2009.

4 See Drucker, P. F. 1999, *Management Challenges for the 21st Century*, Oxford: Butterworth Heinemann, which has the following to say about M&S: "The business of Marks and Spencer, they decided, was not retailing. It was social revolution . . . to subvert the class structure of nineteenth-century England by making available to working and lower-middle-class customers upper-class goods in superior quality but at a price the customers could afford . . . This then yielded specific marketing and innovation objectives, and also objectives in respect to productivity, to people and social responsibilities." (pp.86, 93–4)

5 The staff of SIDC are Malay, Chinese and Indians, with me as an Anglo-Saxon CEO. Our underlying assumptions about what matters in life differ. The same applies to the fact that I am the only baby-boomer in a company that is made up of Generation X and, increasingly, Gen Y, who often have difficulties understanding each other. By focusing on our five values and translating them into KPIs and observable, reward-able and punishable behaviors, we have managed to create a sense of unity, fairness and coherence that would not have been possible otherwise.

6 So called after a 1968 article of the same name by Garrett Hardin (*Science* 162: 1,243–48) in which he outlines a scenario in which multiple individuals, acting independently, and rationally and self-interestedly, will ultimately deplete a shared limited resource even when it is clear that it is not in anyone's long-term interest for this to happen. Hardin concludes: "Ruin is the destination toward which all men rush, each pursuing his own best interest in a society that believes in the freedom of the commons. Freedom in a commons brings ruin to all."

7 On this point Hardin says that "we are locked into a system of 'fouling our own nest,' so long as we behave only as independent, rational, free enterprisers."

8 "Citigroup Chief Stays Bullish on Buy-outs," by Michiyo Nakamoto in Tokyo and David Wighton in New York, *Financial Times*, July 9, 2007.

9 Bloomberg News, April 21, 2009, reported that according to the IMF "The Worldwide losses tied to distressed loans and securitized assets may reach $4.1 trillion by the end of 2010 as the recession and credit crisis exact a higher toll on financial institutions."

10 Bogle 2009, op. cit.: 139.

11 Rubinstein, M. F. and Firstenberg, I. R. 1999, *The Minding Organization: Bring the Future to the Present And Turn Creative Ideas Into Business Solutions*, Chichester: John Wiley & Sons.

12 Market share = $(P_b/P_c \times F_b/F_c \times W_b/W_c \times V_b/V_c)$, where:

P_b is the percentage penetration of the company's brand—that is, the percentage of the total universe who buy the brand; P_c is the percentage penetration of the category—that is, the percentage of the total universe who buy the category;

F_b is the average frequency with which the company's brand is bought and F_c is the average frequency with which the category is bought;

W_b is the average weight or volume purchased of the company's brand and W_c is the average weight or volume purchased for the category;

V_b is the average value paid for the company's brand and V_c is the average value paid for the category.

13 Drucker 1999, op. cit.: 111–2.

14 Doyle, P. 2000, *Value Based Marketing: Marketing Strategies for Corporate Growth and Shareholder Value*, Chichester: John Wiley & Sons: 87.

15 Thomas, J. S., Reinartz, W. and Kumar, V. 2004, "Getting the Most Out of All Your Customers," *Harvard Business Review*, July–August: 116–23.

16 Slywotzky A., *et al.* 1997, *The Profit Zone*, New York: Crown Business.

17 Julius Sterling Morton (1832–1902) was US President Grover Cleveland's Secretary of Agriculture. He introduced Arbor Day so that people and organizations could plant trees. Originating in Nebraska, the idea has spread to other countries.

9

SAVING CAPITALISM FROM THE CAPITALISTS[1]

This chapter looks at the failure of modern Anglo-Saxon capitalism and concludes that there is a better way forward which can maintain the unrivalled success of capitalism in raising standards of living, but without its excesses.

I begin this chapter with the following quote by Felix Rohatyn, the former managing director of Lazard Frères, as it expresses concisely the problem capitalism faces:

> I am . . . a capitalist and believe that market capitalism is the best economic system ever invented. But it must be fair, *it must be regulated* [emphasis added], and it must be ethical. The last few years have shown that excesses can come about when finance capitalism and modern technology are abused in the service of naked greed. Only capitalists can kill capitalism, but our system cannot stand much more abuse of the type we have witnessed recently, nor can it stand much more of the financial and social polarization we are seeing today.[2]

These words, originally spoken in 2002, sadly remain just as true in 2009. Despite his warning, nothing changed in the intervening years because of vested interests in Wall Street.

History has proved Karl Marx wrong in many ways. However, he was right about globalization and the interconnectedness created by modern capitalism.[3] He was also right to foresee national vested interests would find it difficult to come to terms with the changes brought about by free markets globally. What he may not have been able to foresee, even though he understood very well the role of speculation in capitalism, was just how important it would become in modern developed economies.

The financial speculation and its immoral excesses that have been the signature of the years after Reagan in the US and Thatcher in the UK could have been avoided if the system of regulation put in place under Presidents Roosevelt and Truman had not been foolishly dismantled in the name of free markets.[4]

Perhaps the most distressing and sickening feature of this failure of American capitalism is that it could have been avoided because it was a repeat of what had gone before, both politically and economically. These events had even been predicted as long ago as 1989 by Lawrence Summers, who—ironically—was himself one of the architects of Wall Street-friendly deregulation.[5]

The extent to which what is happening in America is a replay of the events of 1929–1932 is best shown by the fact that President Roosevelt's inaugural address in 1933 deals with exactly the same issues faced by President Obama in 2009:

> Yet our distress comes from no failure of substance . . . Plenty is at our doorstep, but a generous use of it languishes in the very sight of the supply. *Primarily this is because rulers of the exchange of mankind's goods have failed through their own stubbornness and their own incompetence, have admitted their failure, and have abdicated. Practices of the unscrupulous money changers stand indicted in the court of public opinion, rejected by the hearts and minds of men.*
>
> True they have tried, but their efforts have been cast in the pattern of an outworn tradition. *Faced by failure of credit they have proposed only the lending of more money. Stripped of the lure of profit by which to induce our people to follow their false leadership, they have resorted to exhortations, pleading tearfully for restored confidence. They know only the rules of a generation of self-seekers.* They have no vision, and when there is no vision the people perish . . .
>
> Happiness lies not in the mere possession of money; it lies in the joy of achievement, in the thrill of creative effort. *The joy and moral stimulation of work no longer must be forgotten in*

the mad chase of evanescent profits. These dark days will be worth all they cost us if they teach us that our true destiny is not to be ministered unto but to minister to ourselves and to our fellow men.

Recognition of the falsity of material wealth as the standard of success goes hand in hand with the abandonment of the false belief that public office and high political position are to be valued only by the standards of pride of place and personal profit; and there must be an end to a conduct in banking and in business which too often has given to a sacred trust the likeness of callous and selfish wrongdoing. Small wonder that confidence languishes, for it thrives only on honesty, on honor, on the sacredness of obligations, on faithful protection, on unselfish performance; without them it cannot live.[6] [Emphasis added]

How little has changed! We seem to have forgotten that happiness is not guaranteed by more money. We no longer know when enough is enough and in part the media are to blame for this with their mindless promotion of celebrities and their ranking of the wealthy.

If capitalism is to regain its rightful place in the hearts and minds of people it must do three things: neutralize the amorality of financial services; rediscover the moral purpose in business and end the alienation of key stakeholders. If it does this, it will be recognized as: the best system yet devised to raise the standards of living of all people and it will overcome the resistance of vested interests who seek to protect their rent-seeking in the name of national identity and the preservation of unique cultural values and heritage.

Neutralizing the Amorality of Financial Services

The importance of financial services is, in the main, an Anglo-Saxon phenomenon. New York and London dwarf all other financial centers. Of all the G20 economies, it is only in the US and the UK that they represent such a large part of the economy.[7] So in a real sense, the present crisis of capitalism from which we must be saved if capitalism is to remain acceptable, is Anglo-Saxon, with a dysfunctional and amoral core in Wall Street and the City of London.

People with a sense of vocation do not appear to enter financial services: they become doctors, nurses, teachers, architects instead. People with ideas of how to change the world become entrepreneurs. These days, the motivation for entering financial services seems to be the overwhelming desire to make a great deal of money. There seems to be an endless supply of the brightest, but not necessarily the best, willing to work in Wall Street,[8] provided by business schools that propagate a view of work that is devoid of the values around which our society was founded.[9]

Almost uniquely, financial services are driven by greed and fear. Building cities, making environmentally friendly cars, designing aircraft, providing food for the tables of the world are not driven by these motives. Also almost uniquely, traders really do live in a real zero-sum world where one side of the trade is a gain at the other side's cost.[10] "Win-lose" is second nature. Yet in every other business enterprise, there is always an opportunity to create win-win partnerships, and before the days when banking and insurance became embroiled in wheeling and dealing and speculation, they too were able to create mutually beneficial opportunities.

If this is correct, then financial services may be filled with self-selecting people whose moral compass and sense of moral purpose in business is not the same as in other spheres of human enterprise—a difference in philosophy perhaps immortalized in the film "Wall Street."

Moreover, regulators the world over will need to be careful how they respond to the blandishments and special pleading of Wall Street. In a provocative article,[11] Simon Johnson, a former chief economist at the IMF, argues that the cult of money-making seeped into the culture at large, serving to increase Wall Street's mystique even further. According to Johnson, the vested interests in Wall Street have taken the US government captive in much the same way as the oligarchs did with the Russian government or the rich in the Argentine and business elites in Southeast Asia.[12]

Given this, it is all the more important that financial services are re-regulated properly along the lines originally envisaged by President Roosevelt and now Lord Turner of the UK's Financial Services Authority (FSA). Moreover, the tragedy of the commons and the double-bind phenomenon discussed in Chapter 7 provide two more compelling reasons why people in financial markets must be regulated.

An excellent example of the double-bind at work was evident during the dot.com boom in the behavior of the all-important analysts who unashamedly pumped up shares they knew were not performing. Jack Grubman of Citibank, for example, justified his behavior as follows: "I did my work as an analyst within a widely understood framework consistent with industry practice that is now being extensively second guessed"[13]—which is not very different from justifying theft on the grounds that others do it too.

Regulators must neutralize the tendency to amorality of the capital markets by creating the appropriate regulatory framework within which the capital market can flourish, recognizing that it cannot be trusted to look after itself.

Where exactly those boundaries are going to be drawn, both at a national and international level, will be determined in the next few years, and, if Lord Turner is right, we can expect much tighter regulation of anything that "looks like a bank, acts like a bank"—so all near banks, shadow banks, and financial intermediaries can expect a tougher regime and higher levels of capitalization. Gone are the frothy days of unlimited liquidity from the global imbalances created by Asian exporters and oil producers financing the unsustainable consumption of the US and UK, supporting inappropriate securitization and lunatic levels of leverage.

Regulators in emerging markets must remember that the Anglo-Saxon regulatory frameworks reflect the conditions prevailing in Anglo-Saxon capital markets and that what is suitable in those markets may not be appropriate in markets where the state has a large involvement in the leading enterprises listed on the stock market.

Anglo-Saxon capitalism is only one way to create a developed economy. There are others: Japanese and Korean capitalism with their interlinked companies with cross shareholdings and a bank at the centre; French and German capitalism, where industrial banks play a much greater role and in the case of France, where there are state-controlled enterprises, reminiscent of Singapore's and Malaysia's GLCs. The Chinese have yet another system. All of them have their merits and drawbacks. So regulators will need to remember that one size does not fit all and that "cut-and-paste" regimes are not necessarily the right answer.

The key to neutralizing the destabilizing effect of self-serving financial services is to find a way to reduce systemic risk without creating moral hazard. Here I find myself in agreement with Paul Krugman on the need to limit the role of securitization and the use of credit to finance levels of leverage that put the entire system at risk. This will inevitably mean cutting the financial-services industry down to size, forcing it to rediscover its real role as an enabler, rather than as an industry in its own right. Lord Turner of the FSA has produced a report designed to do just that.[14]

A key point underlying Lord Turner's recommendations is that financial institutions are a public good as well as being private entities and therefore cannot be treated as private property in the way vested interests in Wall Street and London are arguing. This is even truer if they are "too big to fail." In those circumstances everybody has an interest in their success and survival and they should therefore be treated as regulated utilities in which the government has a legitimate interest, as opposed to private entities designed to maximize shareholder value.

As for reviewing the way rating agencies are paid, it goes without saying that a system that rewards conflicts of interest must be changed.

The Turner report also recognizes that no regime is an island; this requires that all jurisdictions work together in coordinated fashion, to prevent companies from playing them off against each other in a regulatory "race to the bottom."

Rediscovering Moral Purpose in Business

If we go back to the roots of business, it was originally a communitarian activity as opposed to private enterprise. As such, it had a wider sense of purpose—creating value for the community as a whole.

The first businesses, in the West at least, belonged to the Roman Catholic Church which began the process of industrializing agriculture through monasteries that needed sources of income to finance their religious activities. Creating value and a surplus was literally God's business, for without them the monks and nuns would not be able to do God's work.

Thus from the outset there was a sense of a wider purpose than just making money. Enterprise existed to create benefit for the community as a whole, through the gains in agriculture by improving livestock bloodlines, making water safe to drink by turning it into beer, and so on.

This sense of wider moral purpose was perhaps lost when capitalism was born because it privatized assets that had originally served the community as a whole, either through guilds or the monastic orders,[15] and it rewarded speculation. Moreover, the creation of the firm turned it into an identifiable property unit so that the means of production and workers became legal objects, as opposed to social communities. In addition, the law defined the firm as an entity subject to private ownership through shares—removing the firm from the social arena and placing it in the economic arena instead.[16]

As with all private property, owners had absolute rights over their property as long as the law was obeyed and public order maintained. As a result, society was transformed from a society of community to a society of contracts by the invention of the firm. Consequently, it was argued that it was in the interest of the owners, as the residual claimants of firm profits, to optimize firm management by maximizing profits as this enhanced overall efficiency.[17] And so the debate moved from the social arena with its moral considerations to the economic arena where maximizing efficiency became the goal, regardless of its social and systemic costs caused by externalities. It is hardly surprising, therefore, that business began to lose its sense of moral purpose and moral worth, replacing it with soulless profit maximization.

More seriously, the emphasis on making money only legitimized the rent-seeking that business elites have practiced in much of the developing world. In parts of Asia and Latin America, powerful family businesses are rent-seekers of one kind or another, benefiting from the granting of licenses to make money by government in return for a close client–patron relationship where vested interests get the license, and politicians share in the resulting economic benefits.

In Northeast Asia, however, these same vested interests have chosen to do something extra to justify their existence. Japanese conglomerates, and Taiwanese and Korean family firms chose to develop technology, build brands and add value by making better products at lower prices to capture global market by taking the world's best head-on on a level playing field. As a result these three countries have created world-class brands and have been able to progress beyond "technology-less industrialization."[18]

If we compare the business purpose of Western and Asian companies, we can see that there is often a stronger, broader sense of moral purpose in the Asian company mission statements, as shown in Table 9.1.

The contrast is perhaps at its most extreme at Honda (see Appendix I), where respect for the individual is the cardinal principle that forms the basis for initiative, equality, and trust between employees but, more important, between the company and its customers. It's fundamental philosophy is captured in the concept of "The Three Joys"—of buying, of selling, and of producing—which emphasize its commitment to exceeding its customers' expectations, creating personal relationships with them, and creating products in which the company take pride and which generate "joy for society as a whole."

TABLE 9.1 Business Purpose Compared

Western Company	Asian Company
Food Kraft: "Helping People Around the World Eat and Live Better." Unilever: "Unilever's mission is to add Vitality to life. We meet every-day needs for nutrition, hygiene and personal care with brands that help people feel good, look good, and get more out of life."	**Meiji:** "We utilize the gentleness and strength hidden in nature's rich store-houses to create good-tasting food people can trust and to ensure sound health . . . As a source provider of new food experiences, we give our customers a bright and lively new day every day."
Engineering Conglomerates **General Electric:** "For GE, the big question has a simple answer: We exist to solve problems—for our customers, our communities and societies, and for ourselves."	**Samsung:** "We will devote our human resources and technology to create superior products and services, thereby contributing to a better global society . . . Our management philoso-phy represents our strong determi-nation to contribute directly to the prosperity of people all over the world. The talent, creativity, and dedication of our people are key fac-tors to our efforts, and the strides we've made in technology offer endless possibilities to achieve higher stan-dards of living everywhere . . . Our goal is to create the future with our customers."
Office Products **Xerox:** "Our strategic intent is to help people find better ways to do great work—by constantly leading in document technologies, products, and services that improve our customers' work processes and business results."	**Ricoh:** "The Ricoh Group's corporate philosophy is based on three Founding Principles laid down by our founder, Kiyoshi Ichimura. He summarized his thinking as follows: Love your neighbor Love your country Love your work."
	Canon: "The corporate philosophy of Canon is *kyosei*. A concise defini-tion of this word would be 'Living and working together for the com-mon good,' but our definition is broader: 'All people, regardless of race, religion or culture, harmoni-ously living and working together into the future.'

Western Company	Asian Company
	Truly global companies must foster good relations, not only with their customers and the communities in which they operate, but also with nations and the environment. They must also bear the responsibility for the impact of their activities on society. For this reason, Canon's goal is to contribute to global prosperity and the well-being of mankind, which will lead to continuing growth and bring the world closer to achieving *kyosei*."
Cosmetics **L'Oréal:** "At L'Oréal, we believe that everyone aspires to beauty. Our mission is to help men and women around the world realize that aspiration, and express their individual personalities to the full. This is what gives meaning and value to our business, and to the working lives of our employees. We are proud of our work."	**Shiseido:** "We seek to identify new, richer sources of value and use them to create a beautiful lifestyle."

Source: Respective company home pages.

Searching General Motors' or Ford's website does not yield statements of this kind; there, the focus is on profitability and shareholder value; and yet these are two of the most unprofitable car manufacturers on the planet. Perhaps it is no coincidence that they both have had enormous problems with their workers, since, rather than regarding work well done as worship (the Islamic perspective) or believing in the joy of producing (the Honda perspective), both companies subscribe to the doctrines of Taylor and Ford, which deskill labor and destroy the dignity of work.

If only boards can rediscover a sense of moral purpose in the activities of their companies, a large part of the problem of capitalism begins to disappear. Once an organization has a sense of purpose and a morally meaningful mission, the people who work for it will feel quite differently about spending so much of their waking hours at the office or factory. If they can relate to why the company exists, and if they can identify with the outcomes it creates, then half the battle is won.

This sense of purpose and mission must appeal to the heart as well as to the mind and pocket. It really is not enough to put "maximizing shareholder value" at the heart of the capitalist enterprise. People do not identify with profits or shareholder value. They can, however, identify with the kinds of business purpose adopted by Asian companies illustrated in Table 9.1, because they can visualize the results of their efforts. Once they can do that, they will work hard; they will have pride in what they do; and they will willingly go the extra mile. This requires creating a clear line of sight between the vision and mission and the everyday activities of the humblest of employees. As the tale of the two quarry workers in Chapter 2 demonstrates, having a sense of purpose produces vastly different attitudes to work.

Yet capitalism as a whole does not lack that sense of purpose entirely. The Japanese and, to a lesser extent, the Germans, for example, trust their employees to come up with ways of improving the business. When German companies delegate authority to their foremen and the Japanese look to all of their staff to come up with ways of continuously improving operations, there is an implicit trust that goes both ways—a trust that is notably lacking in Anglo-Saxon firms that adopted Taylor and Fordist principles of so-called scientific management.[19]

There is also the question of loyalty, but the importance of loyalty being a two-way street needs to be reaffirmed:

Rare is the high-ranking corporate officer who doesn't call on his or her workforce to display loyalty, but too many managers stop there. The best leaders, however, make certain they give loyalty back in equal measure . . . It really is incredible that it has taken most American companies so long to realize that it is simply *not right* to ask those who do the daily work to be loyal to the corporation without making the same commitment, with the same fervor, that the corporation will be loyal to them in return.[20]

Emphasizing trust and loyalty is not moralistic posturing because they are effective ways of keeping down the frictional costs of doing business, and allow companies to grow beyond the narrow boundaries of blood or clan into global organizations.[21]

Yet giving commitment to the workforce requires a change in the attitude of business leaders. It requires them to recognize that most people are emotional and need to be treated with respect, if they are to reciprocate. This means moving away from the legalistic and instrumental Anglo-Saxon approach to business that regards the firm as a *legal nexus* of contracts towards the Asian communitarian approach, which values the *social nexus* of relationships at work and between organizations as they do deals.

This is not to suggest that legal contracts and performance contracts do not matter. Clearly they do. It is, rather, to suggest that they must be supplemented by an appreciation of the fact that people should be treated with respect for their abilities and creativity, recognizing that everyone, no matter how junior, can contribute to improving the way work is done.

John Bogle has some useful pointers as to how to get this right: "A great workforce must be managed as a long-term asset . . . Some guidelines: Avoid layoffs in temporary downturns; beware of excessive stringency in compensation; don't slash benefits to meet short-term budgetary constraints, and never demand that some arbitrary percentage of the workforce must unilaterally be rated unsatisfactory. *Never!*"[22]

Stop Alienating Key Stakeholders

Capitalism must recognize that it is answerable to more than just shareholders. Companies are not islands: they exist in a social context; they serve members of the community; they draw their employees from the community and the pay taxes to the community. So they, like individuals, must recognize their responsibilities as citizens, for if they fail to do so, society will, in the end, tire of them and remove their license to operate.

Yet for boards to focus on their companies becoming responsible citizens three things must happen: first, shareholders must change their expectations of business so that boards can once again direct their companies to deliver long-term and real economic value; second, the idea that firms are answerable to society if they wish to continue to operate must continue to gain ground; third, reward, remuneration and recognition of senior managers, and CEOs in particular, cannot continue to be a source of understandable outrage and grievance.

Shareholders must change expectations

Investing is about long-term ownership where value and wealth are created gradually by businesses which have the ability to provide the goods and services customers want, without breaking the law or creating systemic risks that destroy the system itself.

This long-term approach to the creation of wealth has worked regardless of whether the sources of funds have come from equity (as in the Anglo-Saxon model), bank finance (the French, German, Japanese model), government intervention (the French, Korean, Singaporean, Malaysian, and Chinese model) or family and trade finance (unlisted family-firm model). The reason is simple: the approach assumes that shareholders will hold onto what they have because they are interested in what Keynes called the "prospective yield of an asset over its entire life."[23]

But that is not what drives shareholders today. Instead, we see the froth of speculation, driven by analysts' forecasts of what the next 90 days is likely to bring. Stock markets have become places where people trade shares, options and derivatives, not on their intrinsic value but on their view of whether they will rise or fall in value more than other comparable instruments. This is the exact opposite of looking at the long-term "yield of an asset over its entire life."

This switch from investment to speculation by the major participants in the capital market is neither healthy nor sensible, as Bogle points out:

> In the long run, stock returns have depended almost entirely on the *reality* of the relatively predictable investment returns earned by *business*. The totally unpredictable *perceptions* of market participants reflected in momentary stock process and in the changing multiples that drive speculative returns, essentially have counted for nothing. It is *economics* that controls long-term equity returns; the impact of emotions, so dominant in the short term, dissolves. Therefore . . . the stock market is a giant distraction from the business of investing.[24]

In fact, the stock market today is worse than a distraction because it gives wrong signals to boards and CEOs, who then feel forced to work to the short-term time horizon of speculators instead of remembering that they are stewards, responsible for the long-term value of the business.

Only when shareholders remember that they are investors, and not speculators, will they have the right expectations of business; and only when these expectations have been corrected will stock markets send the right signals to boards, allowing them to do their jobs properly. Until that time, there will be an inevitable and unhealthy contradiction between the demands of shareholders as speculators and boards as custodians and stewards of the long-term health and value of the business.

Maintaining the license to operate

Once shareholders remember they are investors, boards can focus on the most important job of all: acting as stewards, responsible for the long-term viability of their companies.

Companies must, in the first instance, serve an economic purpose, otherwise they waste scarce resources. However, boards must actively think about the fact that what was acceptable in the past may no longer be so; and so they must spend time "thinking the unthinkable," focusing on what could destroy their license to operate and what they need to do to maintain it in the future.

Society's tolerance of company activities changes over time as a result of better understanding of the interconnectedness of activities and the systemic risks they pose to the environment, to the fabric of society, or to the financial system as a whole.

Nowhere in the world is it acceptable to pollute the environment in ways that were commonplace in the early days of the Industrial Revolution. Pollution that leads to a serious medical emergency like that at Love Canal in New York State in 1978[25] is unlikely to occur again anywhere in the world where there is good, democratically elected government. Mercury poisoning like that in Minamata is also extremely unlikely and the original attempts by the company and the Japanese government to cover up the facts over a period of years in order to protect profits would not be acceptable in today's Japan.[26] Climate change and the green agenda are here to stay and their implications must be taken into account by boards when they make investment decisions.

Equally, the use of child labor is now contentious everywhere, as Nike's disastrous experience of the adverse publicity of children making footballs proved. Yet it was perfectly acceptable to have eight-year-olds pulling coal carts a mile underground in Victorian England.

Society's acceptance of products also changes as a result of better understanding of the health and safety implications of consuming products which are harmful to health. The change in the status of tobacco and alcohol companies is a reflection of society's increasing disapproval of the products they market as the health costs become better recognized. The same is true of fast-food and soda companies, and food companies like Unilever and Nestlé worry a great deal that the conflicting evidence on food safety will restrict their license to operate in the future. Food safety is a highly charged issue everywhere in the world, as the Chinese learned to their cost with melamine-tainted milk products.[27]

As far as financial services are concerned, the crisis that started with subprime in August 2007 will raise many questions about what they can be allowed to do in the future and how they will be regulated. The irresponsibility of Wall Street will inevitably lead to restrictions on its future operations.

Rewarding top management appropriately

Boards have a fundamental responsibility to ensure that CEOs and the top management team are properly rewarded.

Any package should reinforce the right tone at the top. It should also be seen to be fair, both in the differential that is paid to the top management team and in rewarding superior performance and penalizing poor performance.

Everything about effective governance depends on having the right tone at the top. Companies can tick boxes to demonstrate that they are well governed and are behaving responsibly but if the tone at the top is wrong, the letter of the law is respected, but not its spirit. Boards must therefore ensure that CEO remuneration rewards correct behavior rather than encouraging risky behavior that jeopardizes the company's long-term interests, either through fraud or through decisions where CEOs are rewarded for short-term gain without taking into account the long-term impact.

Boards that rewarded CEOs at the expense of shareholders in the name of aligned incentives were negligent at best, liable for encouraging theft at worst. Yet this was the way stock options were handed out in the US in the 1990s, despite warnings from the likes of Warren Buffett and Joseph Stiglitz.[28]

These scandalous packages awarded to so many incompetent or crooked CEOs and their top management teams since the 1980s caused shareholders to suffer three times over: first, from the poor decisions taken at the expense of the long-term viability of the company; second, through the payouts of excessive benefits for mediocre or poor performance; and third for the costs and settlements of any ensuing lawsuits, which were paid by the companies involved.

This gross misallocation of resources by boards undermines capitalism in a number of critical ways. It perpetuates the myth of the superstar, celebrity CEO and devalues the results of the rest of the workforce. There is no way that the job of CEOs in the US has become 20 times more difficult than it was in Alfred Sloan's day or 10 times more difficult than it was in the 1970s, and yet the packages suggest precisely that. It is not just that money is taken from shareholders; just as important, it takes money away from R&D, from creating better customer value, from better terms and conditions for the rest of the workforce, and even from the government in the form of lower taxes as a result of excessive CEO pay. CEOs may be important, but they are not that important; and it is a signal failure of American boards to cut the "imperial CEO" down to size.

Even if the levels of pay given to CEOs are justified, the failure of boards to ensure that they reflect the individual CEO's ability to create value and wealth is egregious. When CEOs walk off into the sunset with huge settlements, regardless of their performance, it is a signal to the rest of the world that there are two standards by which performance is judged: pay-for-performance for ordinary people; and pay for non-performance for the CEO suite. This is so manifestly wrong that it eats at the heart of capitalism[29] and is even more corrosive when the money comes from the taxpayers' pocket to make good catastrophic errors of judgment by CEOs who believe their own PR. This point is well recognized by Jeffrey Immelt, chairman and CEO of GE:

> I think we are at the end of a difficult generation of business leadership, and maybe leadership in general. Tough-mindedness, a good trait, was replaced by meanness and greed, both terrible traits. Rewards became perverted. The richest people made the most mistakes with the least accountability. In too many situations, leaders divided us instead of bringing us together. As a result, the bottom 24 percent of the American population is poorer than they were 25 years ago. That is just wrong.
>
> At the same time, ethically, leaders do share a common responsibility to narrow the gap between the weak and the strong. The residue of the past was a more individualistic "win-lose" game. The twenty-first century is about building bigger and diverse teams: teams that accomplish tough measures with a culture of respect.[30]

Thus if companies are to regain the trust of regulators and the man in the street, boards must ensure that their remuneration committees understand exactly what packages they are offering to CEOs, including their upsides and downsides. Boards can no longer hide behind the claim that they did not understand the fine print of the package put together by corporate headhunters; nor should they trust headhunters to have the interests of the company and its stakeholders at heart. Just as ratings agencies have failed boards who believed they were neutral, so have headhunters.

Fortunately, the problem of ridiculous levels of CEO remuneration is one that is mainly confined to North America, though it has the potential to affect the rest of the world through the argument that CEOs in Europe and Asia must be paid the same as the going rate in the US if those economies are to attract and retain talent.

Conclusion

There are serious defects in Anglo-Saxon capitalism: the importance and amorality of financial services with its excessive securitization and leverage; the apparent lack of moral purpose in so many Western enterprises; the belief that the purpose of business is to maximize shareholder value without paying adequate attention to other stakeholders; the view that a firm is an economic nexus of legal contracts, ignoring the social nexus of emotional contracts; the excessive pay of CEOs that appears to be disconnected from performance; the principal-agent conflict exacerbated by the fact that too many shareholders have become speculators rather than owners or investors.

These all must be rectified if capitalism is to win the hearts and minds of the people it affects every day. Asia has four distinct advantages over the West in creating a new, gentler, less-speculative capitalism:

- Financial services play a much smaller part in the economies of Asia, which are still geared to producing goods as opposed to services, some of which are of questionable value in creating real, sustainable, long-term wealth.
- Many Japanese and Korean companies, in particular, have not forgotten the importance of having a moral purpose that takes into account the wider needs of all stakeholders, allowing a deeper sense of engagement and alignment by the workforce with the objectives of the company.

- The communitarian nature of many Asian societies and the fact that, in many Asian companies, dominant shareholders are either families with long-term "skin in the game" or governments with a long-term view of the business purpose of the firms in which they have a stake, means that there is less principal-agent conflict than in Anglo-Saxon markets. In this sense, in much of Asia business is still community based rather than being truly private. Moreover, equity markets are less important as sources of capital—therefore reducing the risk of the stock market acting as a distraction from investment.
- The fact that in the majority of Asian cultures the firm is seen as a nexus of social relationships that matter as much as (if not more than) the nexus of legal, instrumental and contractual relationships means that there is greater room for the loyalty that John Bogle regards as key for the long-term survival of firms. The same applies to relationships between enterprises, where legalistic contracts are not regarded as paramount, while preserving relationships is.

This is not to say that Asian governance is perfect. It is not. Minority shareholders are regularly mistreated. It is extremely difficult for independent non-executive directors to do their jobs, given both the concentrated structure of ownership and the cultural constraints within which they must work. Families make wrong investment decisions and governments are not very good at picking winners over the long term. On the other hand, no Asian CEO is paid the way American CEOs are, and so there is less risk to the business resulting from inappropriate levels of compensation.

As economic power shifts from the West to Asia, Asia will find different solutions to the issues of capitalism, especially now that Anglo-Saxon capitalism has lost its moral authority resulting from the aftermath of the subprime crisis.

Endnotes

1 The title of this chapter is taken from Rajan, R. G. and Zingales, L. 2003, *Saving Capitalism from the Capitalists*, Princeton, NJ: Princeton University Press.

2 From a gala-dinner speech given by Felix Rohatyn at the City University of New York on October 15, 2002 as quoted in Bogle, J. 2009, *Enough: True Measures of Money, Business, and Life*, Hoboken, NJ: John Wiley & Sons: 140.

3 "The bourgeoisie has through its exploitation of the world market given a cosmopolitan character to production and consumption in every country. To the great chagrin of reactionaries, it has drawn from under the feet of industry the national ground on which it stood. All old-fashioned industries have been destroyed. They are dislodged by new industries, whose introduction becomes a life and death question for all civilized nations . . . In place of old wants, we find new wants, requiring for their satisfaction the products of distant lands and climes. In place of the old local and national seclusion and self-sufficiency, we have intercourse in every direction, universal interdependence of nations." Karl Marx, *Selected Works* 1: 112, Moscow, 1969.

4 See Krugman, P. 2009, "The Market Mystique," *International Herald Tribune*, March 28–29, 2009: 7.

5 R. J. Shiller recalled this event in an interesting account in the *International Herald Tribune* ("A crisis created in the mind," March 28–29, 2009: 12). At a conference in October 1989, Lawrence Summers had created a fictional crisis which "would be preceded by an enormous stock market boom . . . [and] euphoria gripped the investors." In this imagined universe, Summers had explained, "'investing without margin was a mistake, since using margin enabled one to double one's return, and the risks were small, given that one could always sell out if it looked like the market would decline.' . . . His fictional account went on to describe the early signs of the crisis: 'In October 1991, problems began to surface,' he said, adding that a 'major Wall Street firm was forced to merge with another after a poorly supervised trader lost US$500 million by failing to properly hedge a complex position in the newly developed foreign-mortgage-backed-securities market.' He went on to describe how this provocation led to a change in psychology and a stock market crash and problems in banks and credit markets. His fiction concluded: 'The result was the worst recession since the Depression.'" It was just the timing that Summers got slightly wrong. "Ultimately," Shiller says, "the record bubbles in the stock market after 1994 and the housing market after 2000 were responsible for the crisis we are in now. And these bubbles were in turn driven by a view of the world born of complacency about crises, driven by a view about the real source of economic wealth, the efficiency of markets and the importance of speculation in our lives. It was these mental processes that pushed the economy beyond its limits, and that had to be understood to see the reasons for the crisis."

6 Franklin D. Roosevelt's Inaugural Address, March 4, 1933.

7 They also represent a disproportionate share of Singapore and Hong Kong's GDP.

8 In his interview with Jay Leno on March 29, 2009, President Obama made the point that for America to prosper, talented young people must

go into manufacturing, medicine, and education rather than financial services.

9   For example, Joseph Stiglitz has pointed out that among "the future leaders of the business community . . . there was a problem—not what had been done, but how the public relations had been handled. Evidently they felt that success in the future would mean not changing ethical standards, but making sure that you had better relations with the press, so they could put the right spin on the story!" See Stiglitz, J. 2003, *The Roaring Nineties: Why We're Paying the Price for the Greediest Decade in History*, London: Penguin Books: xiii.

10 As my friend and colleague Ian Pollard pointed out, swaps are different because each party may have different objectives in mind.

11 "The Quiet Coup," *The Atlantic*, May 2009, at www.theatltantic.com/doc/200905/imf-advice.

12 For a provocative account of the role of the business elites and how they have captured government, regulators and the banks in Indonesia, Hong Kong, Philippines, Singapore and Thailand, read Studwell, J. 2007, *Asian Godfathers: Money and Power in Hong Kong and South-East Asia*, London: Profile Books.

13 Ibid.: 167.

14 Turner, A. 2009, "The Turner Report: A Regulatory Response to the Global Banking Crisis," FSA, March 2009, makes the following ten recommendations:

  1. Understand systemic risks posed by collective action as well as individual actions by firms.
  2. Combine macroeconomic and macroprudential analysis.
  3. Find new ways to deal with "too big to fail" institutions, otherwise moral hazard is the natural consequence.
  4. Insulate the traditional retail banking functions—deposit taking, maturity transformation and credit extension—from irrationality of liquid traded markets created by wholesale banks.
  5. Stop "too big to fail" institutions from using deposits to fund activities of little economic value and high risk (e.g., proprietary trading).
  6. Change the way rating agencies are rewarded.
  7. Review "mark-to-market" as it is pro-cyclical, encouraging asset bubbles in the upswing through increased valuations and accelerating downswings when illiquid markets mean assets cannot be priced.
  8. Review capital-adequacy criteria.
  9. Revisit Value at Risk and allow for Black Swans.
  10. Coordinate approaches globally to prevent regulatory arbitrage.

15 Gomez, P. Y. 2004, "On the Discretionary Power of Top Executives," *International Studies of Management and Organization* 34(2): 37–62.
16 North D.C. 1973, *The Rise of the Western World*, Cambridge: Cambridge University Press; Braudel, F. 1985, *La Dynamique du Capitalisme*, Paris: Arthaud.
17 Alchian, A. 1961, *Some Economics of Property*, Santa Monica: Rand Corporation.
18 Studwell, op. cit.: 191–2.
19 Fukuyama, F. 1995, *Trust: The Social Virtues and the Creation of Prosperity*, New York: Free Press.
20 Bogle, op. cit.: 170.
21 Fukuyama, op. cit.
22 Bogle, op. cit.: 172–3.
23 Keynes, J. M. 1936, *The General Theory of Employment, Interest and Money*, New York: Harcourt, Brace & Company, cited in Bogle, op. cit.: 50.
24 Bogle, op. cit.: 53–4.
25 According to the US Environmental Protection Agency (EPA), "EPA scientists found 82 toxic chemicals in air, water, and soil samples near the dumps . . . The numerous toxic chemicals—a dozen of which are carcinogenic—discarded at Love Canal over the past 30 years have triggered several health problems, including miscarriages, among the area's residents, and have transformed whole sections of this once pleasant community into a ghost town . . . The relief being requested by the government [US$117,580,000 in clean-up costs and reimbursement for more than US$7 million spent by Federal agencies in emergency measures] from these chemical companies represents one of the most significant and costly environmental remedies ever sought in a judicial action." See "US Sues Hooker Chemical at Niagara Falls, New York," EPA press release, December 20, 1979.
26 "Minamata disease came into being as a result of one chemical complex that was, at a certain point in time, positioned at the heart of a new and rapidly growing industry. Because of the company's pride in its own technological prowess, it was blinded to the dangers of the waste effluents that it allowed to enter the human environment. The industry and various governmental organizations understood pollution problems only in terms of economic viability, and these same sectors of society tried to evade and cover up these problems through an initially successful series of oppressive measures. However, the problem reared its ugly head again, and this time the company was forced into a situation in which it could no longer continue operations. The way in which these problems were dealt with is beyond the comprehension of the present age. When industry and government circles were faced with this crisis, instead of attempting to deal in a straightforward manner

with the realities involved, they simply initiated a cover-up in order to maintain traditional social structures and relationships for the sake of profit." http://www.unu.edu/unupress/unupbooks/uu35ie/uu35ie0e .htm, visited on May 3, 2009.

27 "Verdicts in Tainted Milk Cases Upheld," Cui Xiaohuo, *China Daily*, March 27, 2009.

28 See, for example, Stiglitz, op. cit. On page 126, Stiglitz says the following: "Even in the good times, many corporate executives were not content to float upwards with the rising tide [as markets rose taking share prices up with them]. They found ways to boost their earnings— through sham transactions which allowed them to book revenues even if they didn't really have them, or by moving expenses off their books, or by using one-time write-offs (time and again), to try to give the appearance of robust *normal* profits. Their objective was to create the appearance of alluring success—or, at least of alluring promise— and cash out before the world discovered the truth. Thus did one form of deception give rise to many others."

29 "In 1992 . . . CEOs held 2 percent of the equity of US corporations, today [2003], they own 12 percent, which is 'one of the most spectacular acts of appropriation in the history of capitalism.'": Brenner, R. 2003, "Towards the Precipice,", *London Review of Books* 25(3); quoted in Doogan, K. 2009, *"New Capitalism? The Transformation of Work,"* Polity Press: 38.

30 Immelt, J. 2009, "Renewing American Leadership," Speech to the United States Military Academy at West Point, Black and Gold Forum, December 9, 2009.

APPENDIX A:
THE HYNIX CASE[1]

Hynix, the world's third-largest chip maker, became embroiled in an aid and subsidy controversy with the South Korean government, which was seen as exerting pressure on state-controlled banks to provide a bailout package for the troubled corporation.

Hynix incurred net losses of approximately US$7.6 billion in the three years between 2000 and 2003. If the South Korean government had not taken action, the company would have gone bankrupt and more than 13,000 Korean jobs would have been under threat. Micron and Infineon (US and German chip manufacturers and Hynix's main competitors) filed complaints against Hynix, alleging that the corporation was receiving a financial-aid package—consisting of debt-for-equity swaps, loan write-offs, financing on non-commercial terms and export and tax concessions—worth US$11.9 billion. Hynix and the South Korean government denied that any such help was given or that any pressure was applied on state-controlled banks to support Hynix, insisting that all the bailouts were granted for commercial reasons.

Although several of the creditors were partly government-owned, the company pointed out that foreign banks, including Citibank of the US and Commerzbank of Germany, were also involved in the bailout.

The European Union and the US Department of Commerce ruled and ratified decisions in April and May 2003 to impose tariffs on all imported chips of 33 percent and 57 percent (later reduced to 44.7 percent in July 2003), respectively. Although these tariffs were not immediately levied, they are a clear indication that the major trading nations will act against such intervention. It was only following the imposition of the tariffs that the Hynix restructuring started to be undertaken on a commercial basis, with sales of its non-core memory businesses to Chinese and American corporations.

Endnote

1   Sources: Shilov, A., "European Commission Rules Against Hynix Semiconductor: Finally Caught?" March 23, 2003 at: http://www. xbitlabs.com/news/; Chaffin, J. and Ward, A., "Commerce Department Rules Against Hynix," April 1, 2003 at: http://www.ft.com; and Alden, E., "US Keeps Hefty Tariffs on Asian Partners," *Financial Times*, July 24, 2003.

APPENDIX B:
THE SK CASE

SK Group has been involved in a long line of corporate scandals: SK Corp, the group's oil-refinery unit, was investigated for a US$1.2 billion accounting fraud and the Chair, Chey Tae-won, was sentenced to three years imprisonment. While on bail, he faced fresh investigations for fraud. While prosecutors investigated further charges of siphoning funds from stronger affiliates to keep weaker ones going, Chey maintained that it is a common corporate practice and this is what happened between SK Group and SK Global. As major shareholders and other banks looked to undertake another multi-billion-dollar bailout, Kookmin Bank refused to take part and sold off its SK Global loans for 30 cents on the dollar, writing off the 70 percent remainder at a cost of US$264 million. Hana Bank, on the other hand, pleaded with the prosecutors to release Chey from jail to allow them to pursue the healthy affiliates of SK Global. The courts refused.

Business Week[1] quoted JPMorgan Chase & Co. as stating that the "SK case is testimony that things have changed in Korea. But it is also the confirmation that the industry still has a long way to go." It also quoted Hana Bank chair Kim Seung Yu admitting that "banks must work harder to improve their corporate clients' transparency" but that "our immediate priority is to recover loans as much as possible, and I'm not prepared to give that up for the cause of better corporate governance." The article suggested that "Hana could lose about half its estimated 2003 pre-tax profit if it writes off all its SK loans. In a case like that, the temptation to resort to the old remedies is tremendous . . . Most encouraging of all would be if Korea's banks finally learned the lesson of the crisis: Good governance saves money—for creditors and borrowers alike."

Endnote

1 "Commentary: In Korea, Old Banking Habits Die Hard," Moon Ihlwan, *BusinessWeek*, July 14, 2003.

APPENDIX C:
DIRECTOR'S CHECKLIST[1]

In order to take the responsibilities of a director seriously, you must ask yourself these questions:

Before Being Appointed

These questions fall into three parts—what is known about the company and its activities; how the board operates; and how the appointment will affect you personally.

The company

- What do you know about the ownership and control of the company?
- Has the company been involved in any controversy?
- Is the company well regarded?
- Does the company cause any environmental problems through its operations?
- Is the company profitable and is it generating positive cash flow from its operations?
- Are there any problems highlighted in the latest annual report of which you should be aware?
- Does the future of the company look promising—is demand for its products and services rising, stable or declining?
- Who are the competitors and what threats do they pose?

The board

- Is the number of members appropriate given the size and nature of the company?
- Is there anything unusual in the constitution of the company with respect to directors' meetings?
- Is there an appropriate split between executive and non-executive directors (as stipulated by the relevant code)?
- Are the responsibilities of the company divided appropriately between the directors and the management?
- What is the experience, expertise and reputation of the existing directors?
- Does the chair or CEO tend to dominate the board rather than encouraging all directors to participate in important decisions?
- Is there a corporate plan, which defines the long-term objectives for marketing, production, finance, HR and other key aspects of the business, and is it regularly reviewed and updated?
- What papers are presented to the board and do directors receive them on a timely basis to allow adequate preparation?
- Does the chair ensure that matters and documentation brought to the board's attention are sufficient to monitor the company's performance effectively?
- Does the board have a properly constituted audit committee?
- Does the board endorse the relevant codes on CG?

Your position as a director

- Why do you want to join?
- Will you have time to perform your duties properly?
- How often does the board meet?
- If you cannot get to a meeting, can you participate by audio- or video-conference?
- If you are replacing someone who has left, why did he/she leave?
- Is your role a new position and, if so, what agreed authority limits does it have?
- Will you be faced with any potential or actual conflicts of interest?
- Do you feel you can make a valuable contribution and that your opinion will be listened to in the board?
- Will you have unrestricted access to both management and information?

- Does the constitution of the company allow you to be adequately indemnified or insured against liability for action against you by third parties?
- Are there any matters in the company's constitution that could be of concern and what are your rights under them?
- Is the level of remuneration fair in relation to the amount of time required and the risks involved?

After Being Appointed

Once you are appointed as a director the real work begins. The checklist is now much more complicated and covers many more areas, reflecting your involvement as a director in the business and its governance. You need to be able to participate in:

- Evaluating the effectiveness of the board
- Evaluating the effectiveness of management
- Agreeing the long-term strategy and planning
- Short-term budgeting and monitoring performance against short-term plans
- Formulating policy and monitoring implementation
- Agreeing the risk-management policies of the company
- Reviewing the audit function
- Defining the quality of management information
- Ensuring that financial reporting and filing procedures are correct
- Agreeing distributions to shareholders
- Determining the most appropriate methods of funding
- Acquisitions, mergers, divestments and takeovers.

In promoting day-to-day corporate governance, certain areas are more important than others, though all are important. The key areas are:

Evaluating the effectiveness of the board, where a director needs to have answers to the following questions:

- Do all members of the board and any board committees attend all meetings?
- Are the meetings held in a competent and professional manner?
- Do the members take their roles as board members seriously?

- Are members too involved in the day-to-day running of the business to be able to step back and set policy and supervise appropriately?
- Does the company secretary distribute agendas, briefing papers and accompanying notes in sufficient time to allow proper preparation?
- Do audit reports on internal control show that information going to the board is reliable?
- Are there clear, accurate minutes of the meetings that are distributed to all members?
- Are members committed to staying on top of corporate governance issues?

Internal control, where the questions are:

- Are there appropriate policies and guidelines in place regarding control over the accounting system, including setting up a process for identifying and rectifying weaknesses?
- Is there an appropriate system to ensure timely action can be taken as a result of internal-control recommendations made by the internal or external auditors?
- Is an effective strategy in place to control or mitigate the risk of fraud?

Financial reporting and filing procedures, where the following need to be checked:

- Are there procedures or checklists in place to ensure that financial statements comply with the latest standards and that disclosures in the annual report comply with the relevant local codes on CG?
- Are procedures in place to ensure that annual reports or financial statements are distributed to shareholders and filed with the regulatory authorities within the required time?

Review of the audit function—although this should have been performed by the audit committee and reported on by them to the board, as a director you still need to be satisfied that the following questions have been addressed:

- Internal audit
  - Does an internal audit department exist?
  - Does the chief internal auditor report to the right level—that is, the board or audit committee?

- Is the scope and remit granted to the internal audit function appropriate and does it have adequate access to the relevant information?
- Do policies exist to ensure that the effectiveness of the internal audit, including the quality of its reporting, is measured?

- External audit
  - Can you help ensure that the concerns raised by the external auditors are resolved satisfactorily?
  - Where the external auditors have been asked by the board to focus on specific issues/areas, have you reviewed the results and are you satisfied that the appropriate corrective action has been taken as a result?
  - Have you reviewed the draft opinion and are you satisfied with what it says?
  - Have you reviewed the letter of representation?
  - Do you agree with its findings and recommendations?

Policy formulation and monitoring, where the key issues are:
  - Does the company have written policies?
  - Are they reviewed regularly and updated whenever appropriate?
  - Are they properly documented and communicated to the relevant employees?
  - Are random checks made to test that management is enforcing the policies?
  - Does the company have a code of ethics?
  - Is it understood across the company?
  - Is its importance acknowledged by you, the board and, in particular, the CEO?

If you are armed with the answers to all these questions, you will go a long way to ensuring that the standards of corporate governance are met.

Endnote

1   Based on Wallace, P. and Zinkin, J. 2005, *Corporate Governance*, Singapore: John Wiley & Sons: 270–5.

APPENDIX D:
RISK MANAGEMENT
ACCOUNTABILITIES

Boards must recognize that risk is both specialized in the way it arises and general in its impact on the operations of the company as a whole. Directors and senior management must make sure that there are specialists who understand what they are doing when they incur risk while, at the same time, recognizing that the board remains accountable overall for the consequences should the risks materialize. It is not enough for directors to trust their specialists simply because they are specialists, as we have learned with the debacles on Wall Street. Even so, directors cannot do everything and so they must delegate accountability for the various types of risk to different specialist functions, while remembering that they will be held responsible for whatever happens on their watch. This leads to a division of responsibility as follows:

- *The board of directors* provides the highest level of authority and oversight to a company's risk management practices. The board must be proactive and maintain an awareness of any changes in the firm's businesses, processes or organizational structure to respond with appropriate changes to its risk management framework.
- *Senior management* must be involved in the development and approval of policies and procedures and the establishment of risk limits in accordance with the company's risk tolerance and appetite. They must also periodically ensure that the policies are being complied with by instituting internal or external assessments of the risk management framework.
- *Independent risk managers* should work with senior management to establish, review and monitor general operating limits and tolerances for the business lines through the use of measurement

techniques under both normal and exceptional scenarios. Also, independent risk managers should review the theoretical basis of the models used to measure risk. Most important, members of the independent risk management team should be at arm's length from those who create the risks for the company.

• *The finance and control function* should be responsible for analyzing profit and loss (P&L) through a source attribution process. Valuation methodologies and inputs used by line managers in their pricing models should be reviewed by performing reasonableness testing of a business line's P&L. This function should independently review risk reporting information for reasonableness to ensure compliance with the organization's policies and strategies.

The company should be organized in a manner which ensures that all risks are managed throughout the business processes. Each functional area must be aware of its responsibilities with respect to the risks that are inherent in each transaction. Typical functional responsibilities are as follows:

• *Credit* is responsible for establishing credit limits for counterparties based on ongoing reviews of each counterparty's financial condition. It is for Credit to determine collateral, netting agreements, the existence of credit insurance or other credit-enhancement tools. It is Credit's responsibility to monitor current counterparty-exposure amounts against established limits and communicate any excesses to management.

• *Line management* should follow established procedures for entering into transactions with new counterparties and/or products. In doing this, they should be aware of limits for each counterparty and product. Line managers should receive current information about exposures and should use exposure-reduction techniques, where necessary. They should manage risk at the lowest level defined within the business. Furthermore, they should be responsible for ensuring that complete and comprehensive data are provided to an independent risk management function (referred to above).

• *Legal/Compliance* generally is responsible for establishing and monitoring the company's customer relationship, documentation, and regulatory and reporting standards. For example, it should ensure that master agreements are fully enforceable and, where necessary, contain appropriate payment and credit netting provisions. It also should review the company's sales practices to ensure that these have been properly applied by line management in their interactions with customers.

- *Treasury's* primary responsibility is asset and liability management. It is responsible for managing funding and liquidity exposures and should develop appropriate strategies to maintain such exposures within acceptable thresholds. These strategies should be supported by cashflow forecasting, contingency planning, and the proactive monitoring of interest rate and foreign exchange exposures.

- *Operations* is responsible for the capture, confirmation, reconciliation and settlement of a company's transactions and for ensuring that all the necessary documentation is completed, confirmed, reconciled and settled on a timely basis.

- *Information technology* is responsible for the development of analytical tools and systems used throughout the organization to capture, manage and report risk exposures appropriately. This group should be involved in the development and review of valuation models. It should also develop and test disaster-recovery plans to ensure appropriate controls over the company's business processes in the event of a crisis.

- *Internal audit*, if it exists, often takes responsibility for reviewing the company's compliance with its risk management framework. This review should include the validation of the company's risk measurements, a review of the process flows and data integrity and an overall review of the company's compliance with its policies and procedures.

APPENDIX E:
MAKING RISK
MANAGEMENT WORK

A top-down approach is essential for the success of any risk management framework.

The overall business objectives, strategies and related policies of the company must be established at the highest level and be distributed throughout the organization. Consideration must be given to each strategic direction the company intends to take to ensure alignment with its overall objectives, risk appetite and resources.

Customer relationships: The development, establishment and maintenance of customer relationships have both credit and legal implications related to the company's overall risk management framework. These include following established sales practices in the initial dealings with the customer, gathering appropriate legal documentation and actively monitoring exposures with the counterparty.

Transaction initiation: Those responsible for initiating transactions should be aware of the policies and procedures for handling customer relationships and developing new products appropriately. Due consideration must be given to the company's risk appetite for each specific transaction. The transaction initiator must consult with other groups within the company to determine whether the transaction can fit into the institution's infrastructure to ensure proper risk management throughout its life.

Transaction processing: The operational processes of any transaction—from execution through settlement—must be well controlled. Books and records positions should be reconciled to the positions per the transaction initiators. The handling of payments and receipts of cash and securities must be monitored and controlled appropriately. At each step of the transaction process there should be a proper separation of duties.

Evaluation and controls: All risk-related information must be evaluated independently to ensure comprehensiveness and accuracy. Furthermore, business line P&L and the valuation of assets and liabilities should be reviewed and verified on a regular basis as deemed appropriate for the risks taken. Valuation and risk measurement models should be appropriately tested and used within predefined assumptions. There should be appropriate controls in place to ensure this evaluation process is sufficient and effective.

Reporting: Information must flow freely and in a timely way throughout the company. Management should receive regular reports detailing the company's risks and returns. The reporting process must be both comprehensive and focused, providing information that is relevant to the needs of those reviewing these reports.

Information technology: Adequate systems are essential to the success of a risk management framework. The sophistication of a company's IT systems must match the sophistication of its business activities.

APPENDIX F:
RED FLAGS

In assessing whether the company has good risk management procedures in place, there are some useful indicators ("red flags") a director should look out for. The key questions in this regard relate to:

- **Segregation of duties:** Are the reporting lines for business units sufficiently segregated from the operations and control groups? Does each group have a separate compensation program driving its behavior?
- **Independent revaluations:** Who determines the value of what is invested in or borrowed? Is it someone other than the person initiating the transaction?
- **Management reports:** What information is contained in reports provided to management? Who verifies the information? How often are these reports submitted? Who receives them? How is the information acted upon?
- **Profitability of business lines:** Is the profitability of the business unit inconsistent with management expectations? Is it inconsistent with the company's perceived risk/reward appetite? If it has changed, does management know why?
- **Limit-setting and monitoring:** Are risk limits based upon simple notional principal amounts without regard to more sophisticated risk measurement tools, including value-at-risk? How often are risk limits reviewed and updated?
- **People:** Has there been significant personnel turnover, creation of new responsibilities, chronic staff shortages, or compensation issues in relation to the market?

APPENDIX G:
THYMOS AND "THYMOTIC MAN"

"Thymos" means "spiritedness" in Greek. In *The Republic*, Plato famously divided the soul into three parts: reason; desire; and the hunger for recognition (thymos).[1]

Thymos is what motivates the best and worst things men do. Plato described it as the part of the soul comprising pride, indignation, shame, and the need for recognition. It is an aspect of inner life that galvanizes commitment to armed conflict and gives it meaning for many combatants, even for civilians who experience it vicariously. Thymos is the human undercurrent that flows amid the geopolitical externalities of war.

Thymos, however, often causes us to act irrationally, out of pride, and to strive for ends that are unfriendly to our physical well-being. This is the opposite of the Lockean and Benthamite view of the world, which emphasizes man's calculating, acquisitive side by extolling "life, health, liberty, [and] possessions," as in the American Declaration of Independence. Thus, rational, calculating, bourgeois man is a fundamental underpinning of the Anglo-Saxon view of the world and how it should work.

Others do not necessarily agree with this worldview, however.

Hegel argued that man's humanity flourishes most when he transcends survivalist, materialist inclinations and engages his thymotic side by voluntarily risking his life in armed conflict (or other dangerous yet high-minded undertakings). Doing so proves to the courageous person and those who observe him that, while bodily a mere animal, internally he is also a masterful being, free to exercise moral choice, perhaps stake his life, and show himself superior to narrow concern for himself or his goods. According to Hegel, man is thus most truly human when pursuing self-sacrificing, risky, courses of action. Examples of people who live thymotically, as opposed to rationally as utility maximizers, include the person who swims into rough seas to rescue a stranger; the soldier who storms an enemy machine-gun nest to save his mates; or the fireman or policeman who risks his life to help those in peril.

Utilitarians may argue that people are motivated by material things and power. The Platonic and Hegelian view is that these are merely tools for achieving recognition—to make them feel important or part of something important.

Plato argued that thymos drives people to seek glory and to assert themselves aggressively for noble causes; it drives them to rage if others don't recognize their worth; and sometimes it even causes them to kill over a trifle if they feel disrespected.

We only need to think about gang warfare to see that he was right, for Plato went on to argue that people are not only sensitive about their self-worth, but about the dignity of their kind—be it a nation, a clan, or a gang. If a group is denied this sense of dignity and self-worth, it is called "injustice" or, in today's language, a violation of human rights. As a result, thymotic people mobilize to assert their group's significance if they feel they are being rendered invisible by society; or on behalf of those made voiceless by the powerful, even going to the extreme of becoming suicide bombers to make themselves heard.

Endnote

1   *The Republic*, translated by Lee, H. D. P., Penguin Books, 1955.

APPENDIX H:
CUSTOMER VALUE MEASUREMENTS

Information to be shared across the organization so that all can understand the value of retaining a customer and the loss of a customer walking out should include the following customer-based metrics:

- Retention/attrition
  - Gain/Loss ratio
  - Defection analysis
- Customer profitability
- Customer tenure/lifetime
- Acquisition rate
- Referrals
- Complaints
- Leads: Sales by channel

Without customer profitability there is no brand or company profitability. So it is critical to know the importance of customer lifetime value (CLV):

- The discounted lifetime value of customers, calculated by
  - Adding all revenue from a customer or customer segment
  - Subtracting costs
  - Accounting for time value of money

Example of calculation to determine CLV:

- Equation 1: Customer lifetime margin:

$$M = \Sigma tm/(1+i)t$$

where

    t = time
    m = annual margin
    i = interest.

- Equation 2: Retained customer margin:

$$R = \Sigma tmrt/(1+i)t$$

where

    t = time
    m = annual margin
    r = annual retention rate
    i = interest.

- Equation 3: Value of acquired customers:

$$V = n\Sigma tmrt/(1+i)t - a$$

where

    n = number of customers
    t = time
    m = annual margin
    r = annual retention rate
    i = interest
    a = acquisition costs.

- Equation 4: Value of individual acquired customer:

$$V = (n\Sigma tmrt/(1+i)t - a)/n$$

where

    n = number of customers
    t = time
    m = annual margin
    r = annual retention rate
    i = interest
    a = acquisition costs.

Thus the value of 1,000 customers with an average margin (m) of $100 acquired as a cohort at a cost (a) of $8,000 with a 70 percent retention rate (r) and a discount rate of 10 percent (i) over three years is:

$$\text{Year 1} = 1{,}000 \times (100 \times 0.7^1)/1.1^1 = 63{,}636$$
$$\text{Year 2} = 1{,}000 \times (100 \times 0.7^2)/1.1^2 = 40{,}500$$
$$\text{Year 3} = 1{,}000 \times (100 \times 0.7^3)/1.1^3 = \underline{25{,}770}$$

Total =	129,906
Less acquisition cost	8,000

COHORT VALUE = <u>121,906</u> Divided by original number of customers (1,000) to get:

CLV = 121.91.

APPENDIX I:
HONDA'S FUNDAMENTAL BELIEFS[1]

The center of Honda's philosophy is the Company Principle, which was written in 1956. Underlying the Company Principle are two fundamental beliefs:

- Respect for the Individual; and
- The Three Joys.

Respect for the Individual. Respect for the Individual comes from a fundamental belief in the uniqueness of the Human Being. The Human Being is born with the capacity to think, reason and create. We should strive to nurture and promote these unique characteristics in our company.

Honda is comprised of individuals working together for a common purpose. It is the contributions of each associate in our company that create whatever success we have. Every associate is important; every associate should be respected; every associate should be given the opportunity to develop his or her full potential; every associate should be expected to contribute to the company's success; every associate should be honored for his or her efforts and contribution.

Honda's philosophy of Respect for the Individual includes the following three points:

- *Initiative:* Associates at Honda should not be bound by preconceived ideas, but should think creatively and act on their own judgment, while understanding that they must take responsibility for the results of those actions.
- *Equality:* Equality means to recognize and respect individual differences in one another and to treat each other fairly. Our company is committed to this principle and to creating equal opportunities

for each individual. An individual's race, sex, age, religion, national origin, educational background, social or economic status have no bearing on the individual's opportunities.

- *Trust:* The relationship among associates at Honda should be based on mutual trust. Trust is created by recognizing each other as individuals, helping out where others are deficient, accepting help where we are deficient, sharing our knowledge, and making a sincere effort to fulfill our responsibilities.

Respect for the Individual also defines our relationship with those for whom and with whom we do business:

- Our customer—everything we do must exceed their expectations; satisfying the customer is our top priority.
- Our business associates, including shareholders, dealers, suppliers— those who conduct business with our company should get something positive from that experience. The [previous] comments regarding Initiative, Equality and Trust apply to our relationships with our dealers and suppliers as well as to our associates.

The Three Joys. Because of our belief in the value of each individual, we at Honda believe that each person working in, or coming in touch with our company, directly or through our products, should share a sense of joy through that experience. This feeling is expressed in what we call "The Three Joys."

Our goal is to provide Joy: for those who buy our products and produce our products. In that regard, our main concern is for people.

First, there is the "Joy of Buying" for every customer who buys a Honda product. This Joy is a step beyond customer satisfaction. As we define it, there are four steps to successfully creating the Joy of Buying. The customer must first understand the product and its fundamental concept. Second, the customer should accept the product and make the decision to buy the product. Third, the customer must be completely satisfied with the product. Finally, the customer will experience the Joy of Buying if we can provide products and services that exceed our customers' expectations.

Second, there is "The Joy of Selling." To achieve the Joy of Selling, what is important is not just the relationship between the customer and our products. Our products provide the opportunity for a human relationship with the customer. Those who sell and service our products seek to respond sincerely to customers' needs and desires. When the quality and performance of our products are excellent, those who are engaged in selling and servicing our products are proud to represent Honda to the customer. When our sales and service network, especially our dealers and distributors, experience that pride and a positive relationship with our customers, they feel the Joy of Selling.

Third, there is "The Joy of Producing." At Honda, the Joy of Producing includes manufacturing, production engineering and research and development, as well as Honda suppliers. By producing quality products that exceed the expectations of our dealers and customers, we can experience pride in a job well done.

When we realize The Three Joys, we should also be creating joy for society as a whole. Because of the industry we are in, we affect society in many ways. Some are positive—such as personal mobility, the pride in owning a spirited and valued product and the provision of employment opportunities. Some are negative—such as the environmental impact of our product. Social issues, especially safety and environmental concerns, are among the most pressing needs of our society.

In order to create joy for society and gain society's trust, we want to manufacture products and provide services which are needed, while at the same time minimizing any unwanted or negative effects our products, services or other activities may have on society.

Endnote

1   From http://www.unimib.it/upload/hondaphilosophy.pdf: 3–5.

INDEX